THE LITTLE OLD LADY KILLER

ALTERNATIVE CRIMINOLOGY
General Editor: Jeff Ferrell

Pissing on Demand: Workplace Drug Testing and the Rise of the Detox Industry
Ken Tunnell

Empire of Scrounge: Inside the Urban Underground of Dumpster Diving, Trash Picking, and Street Scavenging
Jeff Ferrell

Prison, Inc.: A Convict Exposes Life inside a Private Prison
K. C. Carceral, edited by Thomas J. Bernard

The Terrorist Identity: Explaining the Terrorist Threat
Michael P. Arena and Bruce A. Arrigo

Terrorism as Crime: From Oklahoma City to Al-Qaeda and Beyond
Mark S. Hamm

Our Bodies, Our Crimes: The Policing of Women's Reproduction in America
Jeanne Flavin

Graffiti Lives: Beyond the Tag in New York's Urban Underground
Gregory J. Snyder

Crimes of Dissent: Civil Disobedience, Criminal Justice, and the Politics of Conscience
Jarret S. Lovell

The Culture of Punishment: Prison, Society, and Spectacle
Michelle Brown

Who You Claim: Performing Gang Identity in School and on the Streets
Robert Garot

5 Grams: Crack Cocaine, Rap Music, and the War on Drugs
Dimitri A. Bogazianos

Judging Addicts: Drug Courts and Coercion in the Justice System
Rebecca Tiger

Courting Kids: Inside an Experimental Youth Court
Carla J. Barrett

The Spectacular Few: Prisoner Radicalization and the Evolving Terrorist Threat
Mark S. Hamm

Comic Book Crime: Truth, Justice, and the American Way
Nickie D. Phillips and Staci Strobl

The Securitization of Society: Crime, Risk, and Social Order
Marc Schuilenburg

Covered in Ink: Tattoos, Women, and the Politics of the Body
Beverly Yuen Thompson

Narrative Criminology: Understanding Stories of Crime
Edited by Lois Presser and Sveinung Sandberg

Progressive Punishment: Job Loss, Jail Growth and the Neoliberal Logic of Carceral Expansion
Judah Schept

Meth Wars: Police, Media, Power
Travis Linneman

Hacked: A Radical Approach to Hacker Culture and Crime
Kevin F. Steinmetz

The Gang's All Queer: The Lives of Gay Gang Members
Vanessa R. Panfil

Skateboarding LA: Inside Professional Street Skateboarding
Gregory J. Snyder

America's Jails: The Search for Human Dignity in an Age of Mass Incarceration
Derek S. Jeffreys

The Little Old Lady Killer: The Sensationalized Crimes of Mexico's First Female Serial Killer
Susana Vargas Cervantes

The Little Old Lady Killer

The Sensationalized Crimes of Mexico's First Female Serial Killer

Susana Vargas Cervantes

NEW YORK UNIVERSITY PRESS
New York

NEW YORK UNIVERSITY PRESS
New York
www.nyupress.org
© 2019 by New York University
All rights reserved

References to Internet websites (URLs) were accurate at the time of writing. Neither the author nor New York University Press is responsible for URLs that may have expired or changed since the manuscript was prepared.

Library of Congress Cataloging-in-Publication Data
Names: Vargas Cervantes, Susana, author.
Title: The little old lady killer : the sensationalized crimes of Mexico's first female serial killer / Susana Vargas Cervantes.
Description: New York : New York University Press, [2019] | Series: Alternative criminology | Includes bibliographical references and index.
Identifiers: LCCN 2018045002| ISBN 9781479876488 (cloth : alk. paper) | ISBN 9781479853083 (pbk. : alk. paper)
Subjects: LCSH: Barraza Samperio, Juana Dayanara, 1954– | Women serial murderers—Mexico—Case studies. | Serial murders—Mexico—Case studies.
Classification: LCC HV6535.M4 V37 2019 | DDC 364.152/32092—dc23
LC record available at https://lccn.loc.gov/2018045002

New York University Press books are printed on acid-free paper, and their binding materials are chosen for strength and durability. We strive to use environmentally responsible suppliers and materials to the greatest extent possible in publishing our books.

Manufactured in the United States of America

10 9 8 7 6 5 4 3 2 1

Also available as an ebook

Para Sergio Vargas, con amor, admiración, y agradecimiento.

To Will Straw, with gratitude.

CONTENTS

Introduction ... 1

1. Framing the Serial Killer: El Mataviejitas ... 25
   Serial Killers, Mexican Anomie, and Narcosatánicos ... 35
   El Chalequero, Goyo Cárdenas, and Las Poquianchis ... 48
   The Hunt for El Mataviejitas ... 58

2. The Look of the Serial Killer: El/La Mataviejitas ... 63
   La Cara del Mexicano ... 76
   "Se buscan" "¡Ayúdanos a prevenir!" ... 79
   From El Mataviejitas as "Brilliant" to La Mataviejitas as "Pathological" ... 91
   The "Look" of a Serial Killer ... 106

3. Performing Mexicanidad I: Criminality and Lucha Libre ... 111
   Born Mexican: Born Criminal, Born Wrestler ... 117
   Nicknames, Masks, and Disguises ... 131
   Killing as Performance ... 138

4. Performing Mexicanidad II: Criminality and La Santa Muerte ... 145
   Feminicides in Estado de México and Ciudad Juárez ... 150
   Spiritual Sisters: La Virgen de Guadalupe and La Santa Muerte ... 164
   La Catrina and La Santa Muerte ... 174
   La Santa Muerte and Jesús Malverde: The Saints of Narcos ... 178

Conclusion ... 185

Acknowledgments ... 201
Notes ... 205
Bibliography ... 241
Index ... 259
About the Author ... 271

Introduction

On Friday, February 3, 2017, I traveled to the prison in Santa Martha Acatitla, on the outskirts of Mexico City, to visit Juana Barraza, who is serving a sentence of 759 years for the homicides of sixteen elderly women and twelve robberies. Police officials and news media have declared Barraza to be La Mataviejitas, or the (female) killer of old ladies. To date, she is the only serial killer ever officially identified as such *before* capture to be arrested and tried in Mexico City. From late 2003 to early 2006, as police struggled to find out who had been killing a number of elderly women, they focused their efforts on identifying El Mataviejitas, or the *male* killer of old ladies. This search was the first (and thus far, the only) time in Mexican history that a serial killer was deemed worthy of being hunted down by a dedicated task force. The serial killer was nicknamed, profiled, and tracked—and eventually caught, convicted, and sentenced.

Eleven years before my visit to the prison, on January 26, 2006, Juana Barraza Samperio was arrested as the presumed La Mataviejitas as she was fleeing the scene at which a woman (aged eighty-two or eighty-nine, depending on the source) had been strangled with a stethoscope. A renter had come home in the middle of the afternoon to find his landlady, Ana María Reyes Alfaro, strangled and lying on the floor. Having just encountered another woman exiting the house who had immediately started running away, he cried out for help and started to chase her. Two police officers patrolling the area heard the tenant's calls for help, saw a woman running, and, after a short pursuit, captured Barraza. Newspaper headlines the next day read "Cae Mataviejitas tras consumar otro de sus crímenes; es mujer" (Mataviejitas falls after committing another crime: It is a woman), "Atrapan a la mataviejitas: es mujer y es luchadora" (The [female] Mataviejitas is caught: is a woman and a wrestler), and "Luchadora de 48 años fue detenida luego de estrangular a una mujer. Cae presunta 'mataviejitas'" (48-year-old wrestler was caught after strangling a woman. Alleged Mataviejitas falls).[1]

Figure I.1. Oscar Herrera, Icela Lagunas, and Rubelio Fernández, "Luchadora de 48 años fue detenida luego de estrangular a mujer. Cae presunta 'mataviejitas,'" *El Universal*, January 26, 2006.

Barraza was in fact also a professional *lucha libre* wrestler. Lucha libre is a sport-theater spectacle that has been enormously popular in Mexico since the 1930s. Under the stage name of La Dama del Silencio, Barraza fought as a *ruda*, meaning she employed no proper wrestling technique. As La Dama del Silencio, she wore a bright pink Power Ranger–like suit with silver details along the legs and shoulders and pink-and-silver knee boots. A pink-and-silver butterfly mask covered her face. A photograph of La Dama del Silencio that circulated in newspapers immediately after her identification as La Mataviejitas shows Barraza with what purports to be a World Women's Wrestling Championship belt draped across her shoulder and waist, striking a pose with one hand on a hip, showing off her muscular arm, and the other hand in front of her torso (fig. I.2). Her tall stature (she is 1.75 meters, or five-foot-nine) and athletic phy-

Figure 1.2. Juana Barraza as La Dama del Silencio.

sique have been characterized by criminologists as "masculine," serving as "proof" of her innate criminality. When she was arrested, Barraza was forty-eight years old and had three children: a sixteen-year-old daughter and two sons, one eighteen and the other twenty-one.

Ana Luisa Sánchez, a cultural affairs programmer for the Santa Martha Acatitla correctional facility who escorted me on my visit, told me that when Barraza was arrested, the only thing she asked for was a phone call, so she could let her daughter know she was not going to be able to pick her up from school. Sánchez told me this during the half-hour drive to Santa Martha Acatitla from the subway station where we met. The change of scenery as we moved away from my gentrified neighborhood of Roma was striking, as we passed through areas that were increasingly industrial and poor. The landscape around the four-lane highway was all gray, with large factories seemingly everywhere.

Santa Martha Acatitla is not officially a prison, but rather a "center for social readaptation," with separate facilities for women and men next door to each other. On arrival, I exchanged my official ID for a little piece of photocopied paper with my name, the date, and my signature. This was my pass out of Santa Martha.

A large foyer, all gray cement, with a small registration table at the side welcomes visitors to Santa Martha. Over a built-in cement countertop, I gave my black purse to be checked by security, then went around to pick it up on the other side, having passed through a full-body metal detector like those in airports. This was the only high-tech security device in the correctional facility. On the far side, a female police officer administered a further security check, patting down my whole body. We then went down a long gray hall and up a flight of stairs to arrive at the second floor, where the main offices are, all of them painted a peachy-pink. The secretary to the director of Santa Martha greeted me and made photocopies of my permits. Like all of Sánchez's colleagues, she was very friendly toward me.

I had been able to exchange letters with Barraza with the help of Lucía Nuñez—a researcher working with sexual aggressors, both men and women, at Santa Martha. She had already known Barraza for a long time, and had even bought quesadillas from her in the facility. Barraza supports herself in prison by selling food every Monday and is known to be a good cook. After I'd made many attempts to reach Barraza without success, Nuñez helped me by acting as a go-between. In one letter I wrote to Barraza that Nuñez made sure she received, I explained the purpose of my intended visit—that I wanted to get to know her and to hear her point of view. It is commonly accepted, in criminological accounts and media reports alike, that serial killers want to be "somebody" and that they crave fame and notoriety. Defying this stereotype, though, Barraza had given no media interviews in her ten years of incarceration. A government criminologist and a neuropsychologist had interviewed Barraza immediately after her arrest, but that was all. Neither I nor anyone else knew her perspective on the killings.

I was told that all my permits were in order and that I could go to an adjacent room to meet with Barraza. As I stood up from the couch and left the office to enter that room, I bumped into her as she was coming in. I was immediately struck by her height, especially in comparison to most Mexican women. I had to lift my face to see hers, and my head reached only her chest. I was struck as well by how healthy her skin looked, how bright and luminous it was. Her hair, dyed copper-blonde, was still very short, as it had been in the newspaper photographs that appeared the day she was captured. She was wearing electric-blue eye shadow, blue mascara, and red lipstick. As we bumped into each other, she smiled.

We were directed to the room in which we were to talk. It was small, its peachy-pink paint was chipped and fading, and a plastic bag wrapped around the door handle served as a doorknob. A white, round plastic table occupied most of the room, and we had to edge around it to sit across from each other. There was a gray file cabinet in one corner; in front of it was a small stool, which Sánchez sat on when she joined us for a brief moment. The room had just one small window, high in a corner, which offered no view.

Barraza spoke in a soft voice and smiled the whole time we talked, displaying a perfect set of small white teeth. I had read the description of her by Martin Barrón, one of the main police officers and criminologists responsible for determining Barraza's guilt, who claimed that Barraza's look was cold and calculating, like that of most serial killers. In Barrón's book on the case, the character of Barraza's gaze was further proof that she was indeed La Mataviejitas. Yet to me she did not seem cold and calculating in the least. On the contrary, what struck me was that she smiled even with her eyes.

It was noon, and Barraza, having just come from her scheduled prison activity, had the rest of the afternoon free. Given her alleged status as the serial killer of elderly women, it is astonishing that her "activity" on Friday afternoons involves walking elderly women through the prison courtyard. Barraza has been the "coordinator of the walking activity" since 2010, supervising around fifty elderly women. I was once again taken aback when, smiling and laughing, she began our conversation with a complaint about how the elderly women did not obey her: "You know what they say to me? 'Who do you think you are? You are not the boss of me!'" Between laughs, Juana Barraza, or Juanita as she is called in prison (I addressed her as Juana), told me how the elderly women do not like walking and prefer to sit down. So Barraza gets mad. She cannot work like that!

This casual conversation was meant to break the ice between us, since the meeting had been set up as a preliminary, get-acquainted exchange. I was extremely nervous and stunned by the degree of contrast between everything I'd heard and read about La Mataviejitas and the woman who sat before me. Looking back, I see that this worked to my advantage, as it made me open to just hearing what Barraza had to say, rather than trying to impose my interests and views as a researcher. Since the beginning of this project in 2006, I have been clear that Barraza's culpability is not my focus. Rather, I have been interested in what the circulation of representations and discourses involving a female wrestler and serial killer reveal about international constructions of the serial killer in terms of sex, gender, class, and nationality. In particular, I am concerned with what serial killing (often framed as "killing for the pleasure of killing") represents in Mexican culture—a culture undergoing many social changes that is nonetheless still characterized by conservative, traditional, and moralistic official discourses. I am most deeply interested in what serial killing reveals about which people count as victims and how a criminal is constructed.

Since Barraza and I were having an informal conversation and not a structured interview, I did not ask many questions, but simply followed along as she talked. After her humorous account of her issues with her elderly charges, Barraza told me that, just the day before my visit, her daughter had turned twenty-seven. She had recently finished her undergraduate degree in graphic design. Barraza talked a lot about her kids, and she made a point of letting me know that she was a good mother and had been blessed with wonderful children. I was struck by the importance Barraza seemed to place on convincing me of this. "I can be whatever they want, but not a bad mother," Barraza said. "I have raised very good children." She took evident pride in her daughter having finished university.

We talked for about two hours. When we concluded our conversation and Barraza stood up, I was touched by the fact that while Barraza took elderly women for walks, she herself could hardly walk. She told me she needed surgery but could not afford it. She has a severe spinal injury in her spine, suffered when she was thirty-five years old during a wrestling match. Barrón suggests that Barraza's ruda status and lack of professional training, combined with the fact that her injury forced her to stop wrestling, were what made her seek out other sources of excitement. For many observers, this "need for excitement" led to her "need to kill."

During our chat, I told Barraza that the purpose of my book was to question who counts as a victim and in turn who is considered a criminal in Mexico. She agreed to a formal interview with me, to take place at a later date. I asked why she agreed to be interviewed by me, given that she never grants interviews. She told me that until then she had been scared, though not for herself: "What else could I lose? They destroyed my life, they destroyed my [wrestling] career. I had nothing else to lose. I have been in prison for committing one crime. But I was afraid for my kids, because when you are threatened with the lives of your children, then you do not want to talk." Again, I noticed that Barraza positioned her children, her family, as the most important thing in her life. Every time Barraza talked about her kids her eyes teared up. Of course, the sincerity of this can be questioned, but it is crucial to pay attention to the importance Barraza placed on motherhood.

On the way back, before Sánchez dropped me off at the subway, I asked her if Barraza's sons and grandsons and great-grandsons visited her in prison. Sánchez told me that she had seen them there often. But never Barraza's daughter.

Barraza has been declared the first female serial killer in Mexico. Her "muscular" wrestling body, her "calculating" looks, and her adoration of the banned Catholic saint La Santa Muerte have all been scrutinized in various types of police reports, in periodicals published in Mexico and abroad, and by criminologists, psychologists, psychiatrists, novelists, musicians, and *morbosos* (the morbidly curious) of all kinds. The moment Barraza was declared La Mataviejitas, all of these experts, amateurs, and morbosos rushed to the feast of interpretation.

There were other serial killers in Mexico before El/La Mataviejitas, but again, for none of them was a task force organized and deployed. In all previous cases, it was only after their arrest that they came to be identified as serial killers. Despite the high levels of violence and crime in Mexico, serial killing is a very rare phenomenon. It seemed that after the two "Mexican Jack the Rippers," Mexico had filled its quota of notorious serial killers. There was El Chalequero, an actual contemporary of Jack the Ripper, who between 1880 and 1888 killed a number of female sex workers. Of course, he was labeled a serial killer only in retrospect. Decades later, there was Gregorio (Goyo) Cárdenas, also known as the "Mexican Jack the Ripper," who in 1942 murdered four women—his girlfriend and three sex workers—and buried them in the garden of his house. With these two Mexican Rippers, the country's fascination with this type of criminal appeared to be satisfied. Consequently, I found it worth analyzing why in 2003, for the first time in Mexican history, police announced the possible existence of a serial killer still at large—one who would eventually be alleged responsible for the killing of forty-nine elderly women in Mexico City.

Three aspects of this story deserve closer scrutiny. The first is the type of violence commonly associated with serial murder: "killing for the pleasure of killing" was offically declared to be an "unknown phenomenon" in Mexico.[2] This seems incongruous considering, for example, the cruelty of Mexican drug cartels, such as Los Zetas or the *narcosatánicos*,[3] and the alarming number of feminicides of young brown and marginalized women in Ciudad Juárez and Estado de México. Most of the killings of these young women have been sexual crimes; the women have been tortured, raped, then murdered and dismembered and left in empty lots. The feminicides in Ciudad Juárez happened roughly at the same time that El/La Mataviejitas was allegedly killing elderly women, in the late 1990s.[4] Renato Sales Heredia, deputy prosecutor with the Inquiries Office of the Mexico City Department of Justice said at the time that serial killing is "a terrifying and new phenomenon. . . . [W]hat happens to us today did not happen to us before; it happened in movies, in the United

States."[5] Heredia made this statement while stories of the brutality of Los Zetas—who would torture their victims for hours, decapitate them, or mutilate them—were circulating widely. At the same time, feminist activists were fighting to bring national and international attention to the brutality of the feminicides in Ciudad Juárez. Similarly, the narcosatánicos were known to perform satanic rituals that involved sacrificing humans, dismembering their bodies, pulling out their eyes, and making necklaces out of their bones. Yet "killing for the pleasure of killing" was still considered an unknown phenomenon in Mexico until the revelation of El Mataviejitas's existence shocked the nation in 2003. Why are serial killers more "terrifying" than leaders of drug cartels? What beliefs and assumptions about serial killers make them more fearsome than narcosatánicos? Which cultural clashes are revealed in the contrast between the respective discursive construction of serial killers and narcosatánicos?

The second aspect of the Mataviejitas case that interests me is the extent to which the killing of forty-nine elderly women shocked the nation against the backdrop of the alarming number of feminicides of young mestizo women.[6] Specifically, the search for El/La Mataviejitas started in 2003; between 1993 and 2004, 382 female deaths were registered in Ciudad Juárez.[7] In the same period, "4,379 female deaths" were registered in Estado de México.[8] While the killing of forty-nine elderly women sparked a coordinated search for a serial killer, the killing of young brown women did *not* result in any kind of national crisis or even formal investigation. Two questions arise here: Who registers as a victim? And who then becomes a criminal? Or, in other words, following Judith Butler's work, which bodies are considered grievable and which lives are judged disposable?

When I refer to a shock for the nation, I am questioning the construction of serial killing as a "terrifying" modern category of murder that is commonly narrated as bringing a nation into crisis, although it might well be an age-old problem. In Mexico specifically, I am interested in analyzing which understandings about El/La Mataviejitas and the killing of elderly women brought the nation to a state of shock and crisis. What perceptions and understandings triggered the search for this specific type of murderer? Even if this case happened more than a dozen years ago, and despite the mounting wave of violence that has affected Mexico in the past decade, it continues to be relevant in 2019 for several important reasons. Juana Barraza is serving the longest sentence of any murderer in Mexican history. Despite the increasing number of feminicides all over the country, there has not been a comparable outcry from the media and government to capture those responsible. Examining how a criminal is constructed in this particular case sheds light on the violence currently being experienced in Mexico. My hope is that understanding how notions of *mexicanidad* (Mexicanness) and discourses in criminality have defined who is a criminal and who counts as a victim will help to illuminate the recent violence. I aim specifically to contribute to the already existing feminist scholarship that seeks to understand why feminicides not only continue but have increased with total impunity. How do the ideologies of mexicanidad determine who is an ideal woman and who is not? And how is this linked to which women are deemed grievable by the nation and which are not?

Finally, it became evident to me that the shift in the presumed gender and sexual identity of the killer had to be analyzed more closely in relation to discourses of international criminology and Mexican popular culture. Over the course of the investigation into El/La Mataviejitas, police officials, criminologists, and the media went from casting "him" as "brilliant" to diagnosing "him/her" as "sexually perverted" to finally identifying "her" as "pathological." In accordance with international practices involving serial killing, when it was officially announced in 2003 that elderly women were being targeted, police started looking for a man. Only after witness accounts described El Mataviejitas as wearing a wig and makeup did the police change their focus. Still searching for a man, they came to believe that the serial killer was a *travesti*—a gender-sex identity used for subjects who, having being assigned the male sex at birth, have chosen to identify themselves within a range of versions of femininity.[9] In Mexico and elsewhere in Latin America, travestis are commonly associated with lower-class circumstances, social vulnerability, and sex work.

On October 24, 2005, under political pressure and driven by ignorance, homophobia, transphobia, and international assumptions about serial killers, Mexico City police arrested between thirty-eight and forty-nine (depending on the source) travesti sex workers—"most of them homosexual"—as suspects in the case.[10] After their fingerprints were found not to match those taken from the crime scenes, and their photographs did not resemble the sketches generated from witnesses' accounts, all were released. Even as police concluded that none of the captured travestis was El/La Mataviejitas, chief prosecutor Bernardo Bátiz assured the public that the killer "might not be a travesti but we are certain it is a transgendered person."[11]

The story of El/La Mataviejitas unfolded amid the turmoil of the highly contested Mexican presidential election of 2006. The response to the serial homicides of older women became the center of a battle for political power between the left-leaning party that held power in Mexico City, the Partido de la Revolución Democrática (PRD), and the conservative party in control of the federal government, the Partido de Acción Nacional (PAN). Each had a particular interest in promoting or denying the existence of El/La Mataviejitas.[12]

On one hand, the federal government insisted that violent crime in Mexico City had increased dramatically since Andrés Manuel López Obrador had become mayor of the city and that the serial homicides of older women were symptomatic of this plague. López Obrador was mayor of Mexico City from 2000 to July 2005, when he resigned to become the PRD candidate in the 2006 presidential election. In 2001, he had created a program of public aid entitled Sí Vale, which offered citizens over seventy the equivalent of seventy dollars a month and free public transportation and health care.[13] By contrast, at the same time that this program was being implemented, PAN was shifting away from support for a welfare state toward neoliberal economic policies. The PRD social security program exacerbated the already extant tensions between Mexico City's government and the federal government. In 2006, however, when PAN candidate Felipe Calderón became president, a pension for elderly citizens over sixty-five was put into effect throughout the whole country, providing an equivalent of forty-three dollars a month and free public transportation and health care. In essence, the more conservative PAN co-opted the public program for senior citizens that López Obrador had initiated. In the 2018 election, López Obrador, campaigning for the presidency for the third time, won with an overwhelming majority.

According to news reports in 2005, homicides of older women in Mexico City had been increasing since 1998.[14] By 2003, there were around seventeen registered cases of elderly women murdered under similar circumstances: asphyxiated with various objects such as tights, cables, stethoscopes, and even the belts of their dressing gowns. Police began to trace patterns in these homicides that suggested the possibility that a serial killer—who came to be nicknamed El Mataviejitas (The Old Lady Killer, with the article "el" indicating a male subject)—was responsible. In each case, the victim was a woman around seventy or older, middle or lower middle class, who lived alone near a park or garden.[15]

On November 5, 2003, the police publicly announced that they were on the hunt for a serial killer. They also described a modus operandi: "The serial killer dresses as a nurse from the government program Sí Vale." This modus operandi was politically significant, in that it involved someone pretending to be a nurse from Mexico City's contested social security program.[16] The serial killer had apparently killed only elderly women who were registered in this program. Countering such claims, López Obrador denied the existence of a serial killer and blamed the Mataviejitas phenomenon on a conspiracy by the PAN-led federal government against his administration's social policies.

The pressure exerted by the federal government on Mexico City to find El Mataviejitas increased at the end of 2005 as a consequence of three events. First, the presidential race became a battle between López Obrador (who was ahead of his opponent, according to multiple newspaper and TV polls) and Calderón, whose party engaged in US-style fear mongering against López Obrador and his supporters.[17] Second, news sources were reporting a spike in the number of unresolved murders of elderly women, with the total rising to forty-nine cases.[18] In response, the Mexico City Department of Justice created a special task force called Parques y Jardines (Parks and Gardens), which produced more than sixty-four sketches of the possible serial killer; created seventy thousand information pamphlets and posters, placed in government offices and on the public transportation system; and organized surveillance by federal police (dressed as civilians) (figs. 1.3 and 1.4). Patrols were established close to parks and gardens where police believed El Mataviejitas selected his victims.[19] French police came to Mexico City to give a special course on serial killing. Never in Mexican history had such a task force been deployed; no other victims had ever commanded such a response. The inexplicable killings of elderly women had put the nation into a state of shock.

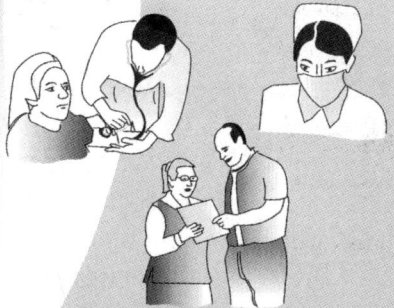

Figures 1.3 and 1.4. Information pamphlets distributed by police in areas of the sort where El Mataviejitas was believed to strike.

The third factor influencing the search for El Mataviejitas was that Bátiz's position as chief of the Mexico City Justice Department was to end with the inauguration of a new administration after the 2006 election. Bátiz had made it a priority to find El Mataviejitas before the end of his term.[20]

On the afternoon of January 25, 2006, Juana Barraza Samperio was caught virtually red-handed and arrested. As noted earlier, she was fleeing the scene where Ana María Reyes Alfaro had been strangled with a stethoscope. Barraza was declared to be the one and only La Mataviejitas—despite the fact that two years before, in March 2004, Araceli Vázquez was arrested and convicted of the killing of one elderly woman, and in September 2004, Mario Tablas was arrested and convicted of the killings of two elderly women. Neither Vázquez nor Tablas was identified as La/El Mataviejitas. In contrast, Barraza, as La Dama del Silencio, gave the media the perfect sensationalizable story.

On March 31, 2008, Barraza was convicted of sixteen homicides and twelve robberies of elderly women. Despite the fact that at least thirty-three cases are still unresolved, the media and police claimed vindication of their earlier conclusion that Barraza was the sole Mataviejitas. If she lives to one hundred years old, she could be released by 2057, as Mexican law establishes a maximum of fifty years for a sentence of life imprisonment.

On the same day that Juana Barraza was arrested, another possible serial killer was also caught: Raúl Osiel Marroquín Reyes, who dismembered four gay men in Mexico City and stuffed their corpses into suitcases. Before the detention of El Sádico (The Sadist) or El Matagays (The Killer of Gays), as Marroquín was subsequently called by the media, "no one knew of multiple homicides of homosexuals."[21] After his arrest, there was no mention of him as a serial killer.

A reporter from the newspaper *La Jornada* noted the "coincidence" that the capture of El Sádico by federal police was reported on the same day as the capture, by "pure luck," of La Mataviejitas by Mexico City police. There was every sign that the feds were in "open competition" with the local police for popular attention—according to *La Jornada*, they were "putting on their own show so that the stage was not occupied solely by city officials."[22] However, the news about El Sádico did not cause the same media uproar as did the identification of Barraza as La Mataviejitas.

If Goyo Cárdenas, the second "Mexican Jack the Ripper," provided the most sensational criminal case of the twentieth century, the arrest of a woman wrestler serial killer became that of the twenty-first century. In the years following her arrest, Barraza has been the subject of intense interest by researchers and the media alike. Criminologist Martin Barrón, for example, has studied her extensively, and neurologist Feggy Ostrosky has performed electroencephalograms (EEGs) on her to prove that her serial killing impulse was innate. Underground pop singer Amandititita composed a *cumbia* song entitled "La Mataviejitas" (2008). Author Victor Ronquillo wrote a novel, *Ruda de corazón: el blues de La Mataviejitas* (Rude at heart: The blues of the old lady killer) (2006). The soap opera–style TV show *Mujeres asesinas* (Women killers) dedicated an episode to Barraza as La Mataviejitas, and the documentary series *Instinto asesino* (Killer instinct), on the Spanish-language version of the Discovery Channel, likewise dedicated an episode to her case (both 2010). Barraza was also featured in the US series *Deadly Women* on the Investigation Discovery channel (2015).

Considering the existence of stories such as those of El Matagays and the narcosatánicos, what was it about Barraza specifically that caused such a media uproar? What compelled experts in multiple fields to study her? What made her story so sensational? I argue that much of the fascination with Barraza lies in the fact that her body, gender, sexuality, and class each transgressed normative ideals for Mexican women, as well as international stereotypes of serial killers. And I explore what Barraza's body, gender, sexuality, and class tell us about notions of serial killing both at the international level and in relation to understandings of mexicanidad that determine which bodies are disposable and which bodies bring the nation to a state of shock and outrage.

Theory, Methodology, and Sources

The term "mexicanidad" has been commonly used to refer to the pervasive ideology of Mexican national identity that is based on an idealized myth of masculinity, embodied in the figures of the *mestizo* and the *macho*. The figure of the macho is understood as the active male figure who compensates for inferiority through the assertion of his virility.[23] The mestizo—the Mexican born of the mix between Spanish colonizers and indigenous women—is idealized and at the same time infantilized. Octavio Paz argued that the idealized representation of the mestizo became entangled with that of the macho in the Mexican imaginary.[24] In contrast, through narratives of mexicanidad, Mexican womanhood has been constructed based on two mythical figures of maternity: La Chingada/La Malinche and La Virgen de Guadalupe. Narratives of the La Chingada/La Malinche figure are bound up with colonization. For Paz, La Chingada is, both metaphorically and literally, the raped mother who gave birth to the Mexican mestizos and mestizas. For Roger Bartra, La Chingada is based on the dark legend of La Malinche, the indigenous woman who betrayed the nation when she sided with the colonizer Hernán Cortés. La Chingada later becomes the mythical figure of La Llorona (The Weeping Woman), the long-suffering Mexican mother, constantly lamenting the loss of her sons.[25] On the other hand, La Virgen de Guadalupe represents the ideal for women, the self-abnegating, self-sacrificing mother, a role that is sacred. The myths of mexicanidad were constructed in close relation to how the idea of the nation was established after Mexico achieved independence in 1810.[26]

From the postrevolutionary era onward, US investment and growing industrial, commercial and cultural presence fueled cultural anxiety in Mexico. North American influence was perceived as an imposition, an invasion and a threat to good Mexican customs and morality giving rise to a new sort of nationalism, faith.[27] New nationalist cultural movements bloomed such as Mexican muralism, the narrative of the Revolution, nationalist music, and the rediscovery of indigenous handicrafts.[28] According to cultural critic Carlos Monsiváis, "each movement and each creator is not specifically nationalist . . . but the whole is perceived and experienced as a nationalism as furious as it is persuasive, with the energy of a compulsive idea: every representation of something Mexican is, without doubt, the exaltation of *the Mexican*."[29] Monsiváis argues that in popular culture, especially between 1930 and 1950, nationalisms translated as "local adorations and praises to machismo."[30] In brief, during Mexico's postrevolutionary era and in the decades that followed, the weight of U.S. culture and industry in Mexico prompted a response in which Mexican nationalism and narrations of mexicanidad translated as machismo. A national discourse was created that "aimed to rescue a true *mexicanidad* (Mexicanness) by emphasizing the 19th century well-to-do families, which were fundamentally the values of Catholicism and machismo."[31] Matthew Gutmann has observed that "[b]eginning especially in the 1940s, the male accent itself came to prominence as a national(ist) symbol. For better or worse, Mexico came to mean machismo and machismo to mean Mexico."[32] There is an important tension here—while Mexico can be defined as a particularly macho country (for example, in relation to violence against women), the terms "macho" and "machismo" do not fully define contemporary Mexico or Mexican culture and society as a whole. While for instance, much of the feminist activist work around feminicides points to a patriarchal and macho culture that allows the killing of women with total impunity and essentializes the macho as a cis-gender man,[33] I want to move away from an understanding of machismo and macho as essentialized in biology, and of masculinity as inherently toxic. I am interested more in a definition of macho and machismo as a position of power that can be inhabited by both men and women and of masculinity as not necessarily toxic.

Understandings of macho and the notion of machismo are porous and permeable, ambiguous and contradictory.[34] Where national postrevolutionary discourses propagated the figure of the ideal Mexican as that of a mestizo/macho, mostly through a heteronormative framework, anthropological research has found that many a Mexican man affirms his manhood through sexual relations with another man, only to prove to himself and others he is not gay or homosexual but rather what is called a *macho probado* or *macho calado* (literally, "proven" or "tested" macho).[35]

The idea of a unified Mexican culture with a mestizo identity that first flowered in the postrevolutionary intellectual environment, crystallized in the murals of Diego Rivera, the prints of José Guadalupe Posada, and folk songs such as "Como México no hay dos" (Like Mexico, there are not two).[36] Discourses of mexicanidad featuring the heterosexual mestizo macho as the ideal Mexican were widely disseminated onscreen during the golden age of Mexican movies in the 1950s. They were further propagated by Samuel Ramos (1952), Octavio Paz (1970), and Santiago Ramírez (1977) in their studies of mexicanidad,[37] and more recently in *telenovelas* (soap operas) and *nota roja* (literally, "red note"—newspapers and other media devoted to the chronicling of real-life violence and crime).

It is important to recognize, however, that the notion of mexicanidad is not a fixed set of norms and discourses. While throughout this book I focus on the constant tensions between the hegemonic depictions of mexicanidad propagated through police and criminal justice narrations and popular culture, I also aim to show how the notion of mexicanidad is malleable and has been continually challenged and remodeled by shifting social practices and cultural transformations.

Similarly, although traditional discourses of mexicanidad propagate virginity for women until marriage and heterosexuality, one must of course not imagine that all Mexican women want to be virgins until marriage and abstain from having sexual relations with other women or other men. It does mean, however, that most Mexicans—men and women alike—must negotiate their genders, desires, sexual practices, and national identities through historically determined cultural categories, through discourses of mexicanidad that traditionally promote female premarital virginity and heterosexuality as virtuous.[38] Although I concentrate on how women are portrayed, on one hand, in media and popular discourses on mexicanidad and, on the other hand, in official criminal-justice discourses, I do not suggest that their various portrayals of the self-abnegating woman are embodied in women's everyday lives without any resistance.[39] My intention, rather, is to analyze how mexicanidad as a hegemonic discourse dictates what is normative femininity and masculinity, and how these notions circulate through popular culture and criminology.

Crucially, feminist criminology informs my methodology. Drawing from the work of Lisa Duggan and Judith Walkowitz, who "refuse the separation of the social life (reality) from representation (myth or stereotype),"[40] I explore cultural representations of serial killers from US films and literature to the nota roja, as well as accounts of female criminals and wrestlers in popular cultural forms such as music videos and pulp fiction. I also understand cultural representations and beliefs concerning Mexican femininity and masculinity as well as representations of serial killer stereotypes as influencing and shaping, as well as interwoven with, media and official accounts.

This book draws, as well, from feminist and cultural theorists who mobilize Michel Foucault's thinking about discourse and discursive analysis to show how cultural beliefs shape, influence, and normalize behavior, attitudes, and knowledges about gender, sexuality, class, race, and ethnicity.[41] These cultural beliefs have an interdependent relationship with criminal justice systems, police, and the media. Like Duggan and Walkowitz, I employ an interdisciplinary approach, drawing on history, feminist criminology, political science, and cultural theory.[42]

I seek, in particular, to illuminate how international discourses of criminality intersected with narratives offered both by the Mexican police and media and within Mexican culture to regulate and perform the parameters of mexicanidad. And how in turn these discourses have defined who counts as a victim and how a criminal is constructed. I use the notion of pigmentocracy to talk about a system of skin color and its relationship with social class to unpack how ideologies surrounding masculinity and femininity are used to determine who is an ideal Mexican. In asking how Mexican masculinity and femininity work in relation to class and skin color, the limits of these gendered and sexed identifications are revealed—and can thus be redefined.

After Mexican independence in 1810, and especially during the "nation-building period" (roughly 1820 to 1825), Mexican elites were deeply concerned with racial mixture, or *mestizaje*. They sought to perpetuate a whiter, more "European" race of people rather than a racially mixed citizenry. The then new science of criminology provided an "objective" language to justify the extension of colonialist values—most pertinently, racism.[43] Mexican criminologists classified lower-class offenders into types of criminals in a manner that dissolved the "boundary between the criminal and the working-class poor."[44] This can be seen as an extension of colonial-era prejudices given that those in Mexico's lower classes were predominantly indigenous and mestizo.

Five hundred years after colonization, the process of mestizaje continues, and therefore, speaking about mestizo/a as a fixed identity in which a specific skin color or certain features are recognizable obscures the persistent racism and classism in Mexico. What used to be *republicas indias*, or indigenous communities, continue to transform and re-form into mestizo communities. The idea of mestizaje as promoted by the hegemonic culture has served to deny, in a systematic way, the existence of a Mesoamerican Mexico.[45] Mestizos and mestizas can be part of the new nation established after the violent process of the Spanish conquest, since this official discourse wanted to assimilate and ultimately disappear indios/as, indigenous people.⁴⁶ In this way, the categories of *indígena* (indigenous) and mestizo/a are problematic.⁴⁷

My reworking of the notion of pigmentocracy as an interlocking skin-color/class system draws on feminist scholar Gayle Rubin's notion of a gender/sex "system," in which sex and gender—although they are not the same thing—may be seen as "a set of arrangements by which the biological raw material of human sex and procreation is shaped by human, social intervention and satisfied in a conventional manner, no matter how bizarre some of the conventions may be."⁴⁸ In a pigmentocratic system, skin tones are perceived based on social and cultural prejudices and linked to particular socioeconomic levels. In this system, class and skin color, though they do not entirely correlate, work as self-reproducing and interdependent power apparatuses and dispositifs. "Dispositif" here follows Michel Foucault's usage: a "heterogeneous ensemble consisting of discourses, institutions, architectural forms, regulatory decisions, laws, administrative measures, scientific statements, philosophical, moral and philanthropic propositions."⁴⁹ I am interested in how class, in combination with the perception of skin tonalities, works as an apparatus from which power is articulated and organized. In the case of Mexico, it is impossible to speak of social class without simultaneously speaking of skin color.⁵⁰ The case of Juana Barraza exemplifies this, as, through the use of scientific language in criminological and popular discourses, her social status and skin color, although not explicitly mentioned, played a determinant role in defining her alleged "inner criminality."

Much of the data for this book was gathered from media reports, publicly available official police documents, and diverse popular cultural sources. I was also given original material used in the search for El/La Mataviejitas by Mexico City police chief Victor Hugo Moneda, including sketches and a photocopy of a manual for the apprehension of serial killers prepared for Mexican police by their French counterparts. After many unsuccessful visits to the headquarters of the municipal Justice Department in search of the original sketches and posters, I was finally directed to the office of Comandante Moneda, chief of operations of the "800-strong police corps responsible for the capture of La Mataviejitas."⁵¹

Finally, much of my research is based on news reports in mass-circulation periodicals representing a variety of perspectives, from the leftist newspaper *La Jornada* to more "traditional" ones like *El Universal* and the avowedly centrist *Reforma*. I also looked at newspapers with more niche audiences, such as *Crónica*, as well as nota roja periodicals like *La Prensa* and *El Gráfico*. I also made use of the Department of Justice's press releases, which were formerly available on its website (such documents are removed after five years). All English translations of Spanish-language news reports, police accounts, and criminological texts are mine.

My research into newspaper and police accounts of El/La Mataviejitas is informed by Stuart Hall's analysis of the "ideological interdependence between the media and the judiciary,"[52] in which the media, in Lisa Duggan's words, "narrativize" material from police authorities. Many news reports, for instance, simply recount assertions made in police press conferences.[53] While some officials in the Department of Justice have accused the media of "sensationalizing" the El Mataviejitas story, I take media and police narrations as intersecting and complementing each other. Both the media and police talked about a male serial killer, and both fixated on Barraza's gender identity once she was arrested.

Chapter Overview

The first chapter, "Framing the Serial Killer: El Mataviejitas," focuses on the difficulty the police, press, and public had in conceptualizing a Mexican serial killer and how this difficulty affected the search for El/La Mataviejitas. I begin with a discussion of women's appropriate social roles as defined by the ideology of mexicanidad, and the ways in which these beliefs about those roles influenced police and media perceptions of elderly women and their classification as victims. I link this discussion to Mexican cultural beliefs concerning serial killing in general, focusing in particular on the idea it is the product of anomie and can happen only in societies that lack moral values. I then explore how, from official discourses to popular culture, Mexicans conceive of their society as strongly grounded in traditional family values, and how this belief structured the search for a serial killer. Finally, I analyze constructions of "infamous" serial killers in relation to the conceptualization of El/La Mataviejitas.

In chapter 2, "The Look of the Serial Killer: El/La Mataviejitas," I shift from criminal stereotyping to the specific visual material police and criminologists used in their quest to identify El Mataviejitas, most especially (1) the sketches police used to identify the male Mataviejitas before the killer's gender was called into question, (2) a three-dimensional sketch, modeled after witnesses' accounts of El/La Mataviejitas, that was photographed and circulated in media reports, and (3) the photographs of Barraza taken by a police criminologist after her arrest.

The analysis of these images is juxtaposed with readings of the captions and other short texts that accompanied them. I focus specifically on the tensions surrounding the sexed, gendered, classed, and skin color–based features of the official sketches used by the police, the media's narrations of El/La Mataviejitas, and the understandings of official criminological discourses as to what a criminal "looks" like. Most of the images I refer to were published in newspapers between 2003 and 2006 and distributed throughout Mexico City.

Chapter 3, "Performing Mexicanidad I: Criminality and Lucha Libre," focuses on the intersections between discourses of Mexican criminology and those of lucha libre. I analyze the merging of personas—on one hand, the serial killer disguised as a nurse and, on the other, La Dama del Silencio, the wrestler persona adopted by Barraza—used in criminological, police, and media narrations, as supposed evidence that Barraza was indeed the serial killer. These discourses, I argue, have served to criminalize La Dama del Silencio, the wrestler, more so than Juana Barraza, the woman. I explore the ways in which criminality narratives and the spectacle of lucha libre intersect within Mexican culture to enforce and regulate the parameters of mexicanidad.

The last chapter, "Performing Mexicanidad II: Criminality and La Santa Muerte," analyzes the notion of mexicanidad in terms of its underlying religious beliefs and their relation to official discourses on criminality. The construction of what constitutes a morally "good" Mexican versus an "evil" one was used in official discourses to pathologize Barraza's religious beliefs as those of a lower-class Mexican who was "evil" by nature. Her religious and cultural beliefs, along with her socioeconomic class, were exploited in media coverage to link her to criminality and "prove" that she was La Mataviejitas. Most importantly, these understandings of what constitutes a criminal have made evident which bodies are grievable and which bodies matter as causes of national concern.

I conclude by trying to answer the questions that prompted this research. I address who counts as a victim and how a criminal is constructed in Mexico in relation to official criminality discourses and their intersections with notions of mexicanidad. I explore the tensions between pivotal figures in the construction of mexicanidad—La Virgen de Guadalupe, La Malinche, and La Llorona—and how they contrast with the actual lives of Malitzin, Juana Barraza, and the victims of feminicide. This discussion challenges how the figure of the macho and the notion of machismo play out in the everyday lives of Mexican men and women.

1

Framing the Serial Killer

El Mataviejitas

Serial killing, like no other type of murder, merges fact and fiction. History and legend have created a cultural figure, who, like no other sort of murderer, has captivated popular imagination. The story commonly starts with Jack the Ripper and the killing of sex workers in London in 1888. Jack the Ripper and America's Ted Bundy, who confessed to murdering at least thirty young women during the 1970s, have become the prototypes of the serial killer: a lonesome and brilliant predator who slays his victims to satisfy an insatiable need. He retreats into the shadows only to strike again with impunity. Serial killing might be a very old phenomenon, but it has been discussed as such only since the term was coined during the 1970s. Over the following decades, the figure of the serial killer has entranced the popular imagination through both factual and fictional cases. All-too-real murderers such as the Zodiac Killer and David Berkowitz, have been popularized no less than fictional serial killers like Leatherface, Hannibal Lecter, and Dexter Morgan.[1]

Serial killers exist in the popular imagination as "media constructs rooted in sociological/criminological/psychological realities."[2] The anxieties, fears, and apprehensions of serial killing refer to a "particular time and place," a cultural flavor that now seems peculiar to the United States.[3] Serial killing has become a quintessentially American experience. What happens when it occurs in a country with high levels of violence and crime but no popular representations of this lonesome predator? Before 2003, when police started the search for El/La Mataviejitas, there had never been a police investigation or prosecution of a serial killer in Mexican history. As of 2019, El/La Mataviejitas remains the only subject whom the police have hunted *as* a serial killer. In this respect, Juana Barraza stands alone.

Although police accounts of Mexican serial killers before El/La Mataviejitas are contradictory, authorities did acknowledge the existence of serial killing in Mexico prior to 2003. But they never launched a targeted search for a specific serial killer until the moral status of the nation was thrown into question by the Mataviejitas case. Serial killing, constructed as a terrifying modern phenomenon, can bring a nation into crisis. There is no certainty about who can be a serial killer or how one may behave. Inhabiting a liminal space of fact and fiction, the figure of the serial killer is particularly terrifying. Many serial killers are believed to be psychopaths, and the causes of psychopathy remain a mystery. A serial killer on the loose could even be your next-door neighbor; since he (the international construct persists that 90 percent of serial killers are men) is "brilliant" and "organized," police have exceptional difficulty tracking him down. A special task force and expert criminologists are needed to have even a hope of catching this super-human slayer.

In 2005, when a serial killer was determined to be responsible for dozens of killings in Mexico City, the nation was brought into a crisis. It was perceived by both authorities and the media as worse than other types of murder cases—not because of the number of victims or the manner in which they were killed, but because of who they were: elderly women.[4]

I am interested in how serial killing, so identified as a peculiarly United States phenomenon, is constructed in a different cultural context. How did the criminological and psychological realities of serial killing particular to the United States affect the conceptualization of a serial killer among the Mexican police, press, and public? And how, in turn, did this affect the search for El/La Mataviejitas? A criminal is constructed in relation to who is believed to be a victim, so to answer these questions, it is important to start the discussion by examining how the ideology of mexicanidad defines appropriate social roles for women— mothers, particularly—since these definitions contributed to police and media perceptions of elderly women as victims.

I proceed to discuss Mexican cultural beliefs concerning serial killing, specifically how it is seen as a product of anomie—that it can happen only in a society that lacks strong moral values. From official discourses to popular culture, Mexicans conceive of their society as strongly grounded in traditional family values. This understanding of Mexican society among its members, informed largely by notions of mexicanidad in popular culture, media, and official discourses, made it particularly difficult for authorities to admit the possibility that serial killing was taking place and to begin an official search for a specific killer. I link this belief—that traditional family values result in a unified society in which serial killers are neither possible nor even imaginable—to the brief history of serial killers in Mexico.

Despite the fact that El/La Mataviejitas is the first serial killer officially investigated as such in the nation's history, it is common knowledge that many others have prowled and killed without having being investigated, or without their crimes attracting comparable attention from the police and media. Indeed, virtually all the captures of other serial killers in Mexico have resulted not from police investigations, but from fortuitous circumstances. How is the Mexican belief in strong family values linked to the brief history of serial killers in Mexico, and to the structure of the search for El/La Mataviejitas?

To understand how Mexican police conceptualized a serial killer—how they fleshed out the killer's profile and how they proceeded in their investigation—I consider the construction of "infamous" serial killers internationally. The international stereotype of the serial killer as male took on a distinctly local flavor after witnesses suggested that it was a "she," prompting police officials to modify their belief that El Mataviejitas was a "he" to include the possibility that he was a travesti—a local gendered identity that refers to individuals assigned the masculine gender at birth who choose to identify with some version of femininity. In Mexico, most travestis are linked to sex work and occupy a marginal place within society, their class status and peripheral sexuality making them easy targets for authorities and others.

For government officials at the time—including Bernardo Bátiz, chief prosecutor for Mexico City's Department of Justice; Pedro Estrada González, special consultant to the secretary of public safety; and Pedro Borda Hartmann, director of the National Institute for the Elderly—the Mataviejitas case represented "a society in decomposition."[5] To these authorities, elderly women who "lived alone" had been "abandoned by their families" and, as a result, lived the rest of their lives "full of nostalgia."[6] Their assumptions negated any possibility that elderly women might choose to live alone. According to Borda, for example, elderly people living alone experience only "solitude," so "they immediately trust" anyone who talks to them.[7] The killing of elderly women spoke to him of a "very dehumanized city."[8] It was this belief—that the victims were living in solitude, yearning to trust someone—that determined for police the modus operandi of the serial killer, more so than the actual investigation or any factual knowledge of serial killing. These unquestioned cultural beliefs about elderly women and what they represent for Mexican culture is what made them count as victims, as worthy of police attention.

When in 2003 the killing of elderly women started to register in increasing numbers, constabulary authorities at both the municipal and national level as well as media outlets all agreed—despite conflicting views on the existence of a serial killer—that the nation was in shock. An investigation was launched, with a psychological profile, a modus operandi, and sketches of the imagined serial killer. All this was done largely because elderly women were perceived as especially vulnerable victims. This vulnerability had less to do with their age than with the fact that they lived alone—their solitude. As Richard Quinney points out, "the conception of a victim is shaped by personal and social values."[9] The social values that shape the conception of a victim in Mexico rest on notions of how the family represents the core of order and progress that date back to the nation's founding. El Mataviejitas was killing the grandmothers of the nation—this is what was most shocking.

Much of the cultural understanding of what the Mexican grandmother represents can be understood through mexicanidad conceptions of women and motherhood, and their intersections with popular culture. Feminist scholars have demonstrated how the notion of motherhood has played a significant role in the social construction of womanhood more generally, not only in the everyday lives of Mexicans and media portrayals of women, but in the "maintenance of political power and economic hegemony," which after the Mexican Revolution in 1910 featured specifically in "debates over citizenship."[10] Nichole Sanders, for example, describes how "doctors, public health experts, criminologists, nurses, teachers, social workers, Catholic women's organizations, feminists, factory owners and factory workers alike saw the symbol of motherhood as something to manipulate in order to create a 'modern' Mexico, to keep a workforce docile, or to agitate for better working conditions and political rights."[11] Even before the Mexican Revolution, since the Porfiriato (1876–1911), "members of social reform movements began targeting mothers as the 'key' to creating a modern Mexico" because they were seen as responsible for raising good citizens.[12]

For William French, this emphasis on women's role in moral reformation brought about a cult of female domesticity in which women were cast as "guardian angels of the home," charged with raising citizens with a "capitalist work ethic."[13] It also served as a means of class differentiation in Porfirian Mexico.[14] In contrast to the prostitute and the tavern, vocational and spatial symbols of the vice-associated classes, "middle-class Mexicans insisted that the women's 'natural' place was in the home," as "motherhood became a civic responsibility that only enlightened women could fulfill."[15]

As French demonstrates, the most important task for women during the Porfiriato was "family formation"; specifically, women were responsible for promoting *hogares blancos* (literally "white homes," signaling whiteness as a position of privilege), that is, "pure houses that radiated cleanliness, punctuality, and usefulness; houses in which mothers exercised skill in preparing schedules and allocating time. Home and work were to adhere to the same capitalist principles."[16] During the Porfiriato, members of every social level were to model themselves after the promoted image of the middle class, especially that of women as "guardian angels of the home," for Mexico to become a prosperous, civilized, and progressive nation under Porfirio Díaz's program of "order and progress."[17] In this period, the ideal model of woman/mother was that of the *mujer abnegada*: "noted for [her] long-suffering, self-sacrificing nature,"[18] who sacrificed herself for her children and husband and served as the "guardian angel of her family."[19] This ideal of the woman as a self-sacrificing mother to whom society and nature had entrusted the most important role of the nation persists today. Scholars agree that motherhood continues to be perceived as "the most important social role" for women—that mothers are believed to be not only the pillars of their families, but the core of Mexican society.[20]

Linked to constructions of mexicanidad that determine who constitutes an ideal woman is the notion that motherhood is sacred. Octavio Paz's *The Labyrinth of Solitude* (1950) defined two archetypes of Mexican motherhood, both based on mythical figures of maternity: La Chingada and La Virgen de Guadalupe. La Chingada is the raped mother—metaphorically and literally—who gave birth to the Mexican mestizos. La Chingada represents La Malinche, one of the twenty *nahua* (indigenous people of Mesoamerica with Náhuatl as their common language) women given in Tabasco in 1519 to the colonizer Hernán Cortés.[21] Born Malinalli, she was also called La Malintzin—the Náhuatl suffix "-tzin" denoting endearment. Over time, this name transformed into the easier-to-pronounce La Malinche. When the Spaniards baptized Malinalli, she was given the Christian name Marina. When she subsequently served as a translator and became Cortés's concubine, she was commonly referred to as Doña Marina or Doña María.[22] La Malinche plays a pivotal role in the conquest of Mexico, as she is said to have betrayed the Aztec Empire. As represented by leading works of history and scholastic texts, official discourses about colonization state that La Malintzin learned of the Aztec plans to destroy the Spanish army and alerted Cortés, thereby becoming the embodiment of disloyalty to her land and the nation (even before the nation existed). According to Roger Bartra, the way in which the legend of La Malinche gets constructed relates directly to how the nation was established.[23] Bartra argues that "the nationalism of the 19th century, as with the current nationalism, needed to invent an original homeland: and this primary nation needed heroes and traitors."[24]

The figure of La Malinche eventually transformed into the icon of La Chingada, the traitor who gave birth in 1523 to the first Mexican, the first mestizo, Martín Cortés, son of the conquistador. Martín was taken to Spain to be educated by a cousin of his father; he stayed all his life in Spain and died there in a battle against the *moriscos* (Moors) in 1569.[25] Martín was narratively recast as the long-yearned-for son of the new Mexican nation, and La Chingada later becomes the mythical figure of La Llorona, the long-suffering Mexican mother, forever lamenting the loss of her sons.[26]

In contrast to La Malinche/La Chingada is La Virgen de Guadalupe, also a key figure in the Spanish colonization of Mexico. The "invention" of La Virgen de Guadalupe helped Spanish settlers and missionaries evangelize the Aztecs and other indigenous peoples. According to legend, in 1531 La Virgen de Guadalupe appeared to an indigenous man, Juan Diego, on the same hill—Tepeyac—where the Aztecs worshiped their goddess Totonatzin. This apparition follows the Christian tradition of apparitions of the Virgin Mary.[27] La Virgen de Guadalupe, however, is brown-skinned and provides refuge to the raped mother. As opposed to La Malintzin, La Virgen de Guadalupe is always loyal, nonsexualized, protective of her sons, and an intermediary with Jesus Christ.

Bartra states that the events of Tabasco in 1519 and Tepeyac in 1531 are the "two powerful symbolic axes that defined the profile of the Mexican woman." After independence in 1810, a "cultural catalysis" takes place and the "complex myth of Mexican women is codified: tender and violated, protective and lubricated, sweet and traitor, maternal virgin and Babylonian female."[28] The love for La Virgen de Guadalupe runs parallel to the cult of the Mexican mother, so much so that the role of mothers in Mexico is at the same time sacred and institutionalized by the state.[29] These constructions of motherhood persist to this day, in part determining who is considered a victim and who is not. I argue that the elderly women killed in Mexico City counted as victims for police authorities because elderly women are perceived as grandmothers, and grandmothers in Mexico continue to hold one of the most important social roles: as guardians of the nation and the ultimate symbols of purity, chastity, and virtue.

The ideal of a mother as sacrificing herself for her family—her sons, primarily—has been further promoted through film. Cultural critic Carlos Monsiváis goes so far as to state that for people in Mexico who are not historians, "reality before film is unknown. There is no knowledge of how families and mothers were before the cameras focused on them."[30] Mexican film studies scholar Julia Tuñón has noted how, from the silent movies to the Época de Oro, the golden age of Mexican cinema (1936–56), the "archetype of mothers" in films was "the figure of mother that is one of a being who gives unlimited love and is capable of absolute sacrifice."[31] In the film industry, "images of mothers were constructed and manipulated to bolster a definition of citizen and citizenship that for women was predicated on motherhood as key to political participation."[32] Actresses such as Mimi Derba, Matilde Palou, and Libertad La Marque were among the most celebrated embodiments of these self-abnegating mothers. Even more than these actresses, the construction of the ideal mother and *abuelita* (an endearing term for a grandmother) was shaped by one of the biggest stars of the time, Sara García (1895–

1980) (fig. 1.1). During the 1940s and 1950s, García "became the most sublime representation of motherhood"; in later years, she became "the grandmother of Mexico."[33] Today, García's grandmotherly visage is the face of the Nestlé chocolate brand Abuelita. After all, chocolate, like a grandmother, is comforting and warm.

García is "the totalizing figure of an idea of a mother and grandmother. . . . The mother is the sentimental blackmail that brings the family together."[34] The melodrama is the key genre for the depiction of Mexican mothers, as established in García's films.[35] In *No basta ser madre* (It is not enough to be a mother) from 1937, García "establishes her very long reign, which has lasted until today."[36] The film's plot centers on the fact that the biological mother always ends up failing because she cannot become the ultimate mother, a spiritual and permanent one. The idea of motherhood is established as an "infinite birth," since "sons never finish being born and mothers never finish giving birth."[37] Even as its ideal form is established as unattainable, motherhood is emphatically presented as the most sacred role for women—a woman without children is thus entrenched as incomplete.

In *Los tres García* (1947), *Vuelven los García* (1947), and *Dicen que soy mujeriego* (1948), García portrays a self-sacrificing grandmother who loves unconditionally, but who is also not afraid to show tough love to her grandsons. She is the matriarch of the family—the mother, the guide, and the protector. As played by García in these films, the love of an abuelita is absolute, and her life is dedicated to mothering everyone around her. She further defined the already established role for the grandmother in Mexico, as a tough but adorable elderly woman who spoils all her grandchildren with love and attention, but knows how to put limits on her grown (mostly male and macho) children. Men can be macho with everyone else, but respect their abuelita. Her grandsons might kill each other and disobey the law, but as long as they show respect to their sacred abuelita, they continue to demonstrate decency in the eyes of society.

When police were looking for El Mataviejitas in 2005, chief prosecutor Bátiz described the women who were killed as belonging to "a helpless, very vulnerable sector of society, which before was respected, even among delinquents."[38] This statement evokes a scene from *Los tres García*, in which the police pay a visit to a grandmother, Laura García

Figure 1.1. Sara García.

(played by, yes, Sara García), to ask for help in controlling her delinquent, misbehaving grandchildren. In the movie, the police have tried everything but the three young García cousins—*rancheros* played by Pedro Infante, Abel Salazar, and Victor Manuel Mendoza—do not obey or respect them. (Infante, a matinee idol, himself played a crucial role in defining the ideal of Mexican men and masculinity during this Época de Oro.[39]) The three Garcías respect and fear no official authority—not the mayor of the town, not the police. In a typical scene, they enter a cantina and start shooting their guns for sport. The only person they respect, and therefore who has any authority over them, is their abuelita, Laura (Sara) García. As if the Mataviejitas case had interrupted a classic movie of the Época de Oro, Bátiz could not believe that abuelitas were being killed—in the popular imagination, they were always respected by everybody, even delinquents.

Monsiváis states that Sara García represented not a "real mother" or even an "ideal mother" but the "institution of motherhood itself."[40] There are no other recognizable roles for a grandmother in Mexico but those she portrayed. Grandmothers hold the family together, as matriarchs. There might be disputes among family members, but when it comes to Sunday dinners with the abuelita, all must be forgotten in her presence. In the films in which García plays an abuelita, we infer that she must have had a husband because she has grandchildren, yet his presence onscreen is not always required. García as a grandmother is always desexualized—"her body itself is an institution, representing the rotundity of housewives."[41] This desexualization renders her akin to La Virgen de Guadalupe, the ultimate sacred mother.

It is important to note that the grandmothers played by García do not live alone. In *Los tres García*, for example, her residence is shared with domestic servants, whom she virtually abuses with endearment; her grandsons may come and go, but it is always implied that they exist to take care of her and in different phases of their lives have lived or will live with her. These living arrangements are typical of Mexican families. Among both mestizo and indigenous populations, domestic arrangements typically follow a "Mesoamerican familiar system."[42] According to David Robichaux, this develops as follows: after a couple decides to initiate their union, their life as a couple starts in the home of the man's parents; depending on their financial resources, after a while the couple might move out. This happens with all the men in the family, except the last one, "who with his wife stays in the paternal house, takes care of the elder parents and inherits the house."[43] This common dynamic is implicit in many Mexican films, including, for example, *Los tres García*.

As embodied by García, the grandmother further corresponds to an ideal in terms of skin color and class. García was the daughter of Spanish parents who came to Mexico in 1895 for work. Soon orphaned, she was raised in a Catholic school for girls of Spanish descent.[44] Considering the pigmentocratic system in Mexico, it is almost impossible to imagine an ideal grandmother embodied by an indigenous woman or a dark-skinned mestiza. García's whiteness and Spanish background, I argue, were key to establishing her image as the ideal mother/grandmother.

In the eyes of the public, there was little if any distinction between Sara García the person and her cinematic embodiment of the ideal Mexican grandmother. In *Mecánica nacional* (1972), García tried to break the stereotype of the self-abnegating, self-sacrificing grandmother by appearing as she was "in real life": as a "gluttonous" elderly woman, who spoke with "double entendre and humor."[45] The film was rejected by both critics and audiences. García retreated, returning to the screen as a sweet, kind, ideal grandmother in the telenovela *Mundo de juguete* (1974). Significantly, this ideal grandmother existed only in the fantasy world of the main character, a little girl, always appeared in a house of chocolate. I argue that García played a similar role in the Mexican imaginary—as an idealized grandmother who exists only in a fantasy world. This image was far more acceptable to audiences than that of the real García—and even the ambitious *Mecánica nacional*, which tried to present an alternative, more realistic image of an older Mexican woman, did not hint that García had lived for sixty years with Rosarito, her female "companion."[46]

Serial Killers, Mexican Anomie, and Narcosatánicos

It was noon when a worker for Sí Vale, a government social program providing assistance to Mexico City citizens over seventy, entered the house of Benitez Lugo to replace her identification card. Lugo lived alone, close to a park. Like many of the elderly women allegedly robbed or killed by El Mataviejitas, Lugo spent her days at home. The modus operandi of El Mataviejitas, according to police, was to gain the trust of elderly women, enter their homes, and then strangle them. Media reports spoke of the elderly women as if they were all grandmothers who would trust anyone who talked to them or knocked on their door. The assumption was that they so desired company they would invite virtually anyone who asked into their homes and offer a glass of water or an entire meal. The killer was preying on their solitude, on their need for company, on their need to mother. For police, grandmothers living alone were an easy target for El Mataviejitas because, abandoned by their families, they were just waiting at home, hoping for visitors. All these victims wanted was to mother—there was no other conceivable social role for them.

The stereotypical figure of the grandmother is at the heart of the persistent belief that family values are strong in Mexico, in contrast to the United States and European countries, which are cast as more individualistic and morally deficient. Nora Jiménez argues that "Mexican identity underlines in a notable fashion family cohesion, and the fulfillment of the obligations that the family imposes."[47] This aspect of Mexican identity is only heightened by the migrant experience: "the omnipresence of family links in the solidarity networks that emigrants build contrasts with the imperative individualism in the society of the United States."[48] Most Mexicans believe that it is this individualism, the lack of solidarity networks, of strong family bonds, that drives individuals to the cold brutality of killing strangers. For example, the Columbine High School massacre of 1999, in which two students in Colorado murdered twelve students and a teacher before killing themselves, was seen in Mexico as the product of a society lacking in moral values. By extension, kids killing kids represents the lack of a mother who knows how to raise good children, and the absence of grandmothers who keep families together. As exemplified by the statement of deputy prosecutor Renato Sales Heredia quoted in the introduction,[49] Mexicans tend to believe that the sorts of crimes and violence considered typical of the United States result from a modern anomie. Serial killing, or "stranger killing" as it was called until the 1970s, is the most extreme instance of this criminality attributed to social isolation.

In Mexico City, the killing of elderly women caught the attention of government officials largely because it was perceived as such a sign of anomie. That elderly women would (supposedly) allow anyone into their homes for a cup of tea was interpreted by authorities and the media as an outcome of their "abandonment by their families."[50] Larissa Lomnitz and Marisol Pérez Lizaur analyze the concept of *gran familia* (great family)— "composed of a couple, their children, and their grandchildren"—and suggest that, in Mexico, it is "the basic unity of solidarity between all the social classes."[51] The possibility that an elderly woman might *choose* to live alone is at odds with the values of a traditional, conservative, Catholic society and, most importantly, at odds with constructions of mexicanidad. Heredia even stated that the killing of elderly women does not happen in municipalities where elderly women live within the "nuclear family."[52] It is important to note here that the concept of the "nuclear family" in Mexico encompasses not only parents and children, but can readily be extended to grandmothers.

Grandmothers living alone was thus for the media and police a sign of a society in "decomposition"—the lowest level of violence in which not even a grandmother is respected. Since authorities consider that older women living alone "only have solitude, which is why when someone talks to them they trust them immediately," the homicides of elderly women were widely interpreted by news media as indicating that something was "wrong with society."[53]

These views on elderly women contrast with an awful, and still unresolved, series of crimes of gender violence known as Las Muertas de Juárez. Police state that since 1994, at least 460 women have been murdered in Ciudad Juárez, in northern Mexico. According to a November 2003 National Human Rights Commission report, another 4,587 women have disappeared.[54] Most of the women killed in this wave of violence were young, poor, mestiza, brown, and living in precarious conditions— many were raped, tortured, and dismembered.[55] And nongovernmental and civic organizations believe the number of young, marginalized female victims is in fact much higher than the official figures.

Even the reported statistics of 460 young women murdered and 4,587 disappeared in Ciudad Juárez present a stark numerical contrast with the 49 elderly victims in the Mataviejitas case.[56] In spite of public outrage and international pressure, officials continue to deny gender violence has been a factor in Las Muertas de Juárez. For the most part, local and national authorities have failed to even investigate these crimes.[57] Again, by way of contrast, a full-scale search for El Mataviejitas was launched in Mexico City once it was determined that a serial killer was on the loose. Given the backdrop of the mass killings in Ciudad Juárez and horrific number of feminicides in other factory towns, it is striking that the killing of elderly women in Mexico City is what officials cited as evidence of something "wrong with society."[58]

The Mataviejitas case illustrates which bodies count as victims, which bodies are grievable, which bodies are a matter of national concern. It is not the bodies of young mestizo women brought Mexico into crisis. It is definitely not the bodies of homosexual men dismembered and stuffed into suitcases. Rather, it is the bodies of elderly women—representatives of one of the most important values of mexicanidad, of what constitutes being an ideal Mexican, which is adherence to strong family values, values that translate quite literally as elderly women living in the same house as their children.

Richard Quinney argues that a "victim is a conception of reality as well as an object of events. All parties involved in any sequence of actions construct the reality of the situation."[59] Quinney suggests that the conceptions of victims are socially constructed across multiple segments of a given society. I would add that they are also imposed upon a given culture by others.

The loneliness of elderly women, of grandmothers who reside alone and have thus presumably been abandoned by society, eerily echoes the loneliness of the serial killer—the anomie that drives him/her to kill strangers. The abandonment of individuals on a pervasive, societal scale, is precisely what is seen as creating the serial killer. The loneliness of the serial killer is what drives the commission of what Mark Seltzer calls "senseless" crimes, and the loneliness of the grandmothers is what makes them count as victims to the degree that their deaths bring a society into crisis.

The bodies of elderly women contrast sharply with the bodies of Las Muertas de Juárez, the young mestizo women, whose cruel, horrific murders do not count in a patriarchal society where "local and state authorities continually stigmatize the victims as prostitutes and drug addicts."[60] Moreover, their particular brand of loneliness does not fit into the strong family values that the ideology of mexicanidad promotes. To provide for their families, many worked for *maquiladoras* (foreign-owned factories), which hire exclusively women for most jobs. Instead of fulfilling their maternal roles by staying home, providing a *hogar blanco*, and caring for their parents or husband and kids, they are forced to work outside of the home—which leaves them figuratively alone within the context of Mexican culture. Indeed, as the repeated stigmatization of the victims as "prostitutes and drug addicts" indicates, it is widely perceived as a moral transgression when a woman does not perform her "honorable" and "respectable"—her sacred—role of homebound mother.

In her research on the history of prostitution in Mexico, Katherine Bliss argues that the regulation of women's sexuality was inseparable from the regulation of appropriate motherhood. Prostitutes were identified as dangerous partly because of the possibility of their spreading sexually transmitted diseases like syphilis, but most importantly for what they represented.[61] Even today, sex workers continue to represent deviance and degeneracy in contrast to the ideal woman/mother, whose sexuality is controlled through marriage.

The social values that shape the conception of a victim in Mexico, which have been in place since the Porfiriato, dictate that women's most important task is that of family formation, education, and protection. A woman who is seen as not fulfilling this role to the established standard—that is, providing a *hogar blanco* for her husband and children—is outside the parameters of mexicanidad, and her body does not count as that of a victim.

It was in 2005, a year before the arrest of Barraza, at a symposium on serial killing held at the private University La Salle in Mexico City, that Heredia announced "a terrifying and new phenomenon: the presence, now indisputable, of a serial killer. That which happens to us today did not happen to us before; it happened in movies, in the United States. However, violence and crime have also become globalized—the serial killer of elderly women, El Mataviejitas, is an example of this."[62]

The "now indisputable" presence of a serial killer in Mexico City seemed almost "unimaginable," as though it were the last straw. Why is a lonely serial killer worse than, say, a collective of drug dealers who kill innocent people to acquire their bones for satanic rituals? What is it about a serial killer that seems so exceptionally evil and monstrous in a country where homosexual men are dismembered, women are *entambaladas* (their bodies entombed in large containers with cement), and students are disappeared with the acquiescence of the state?

In 1989, a decade before the Mataviejitas case, the crime story of the decade was that of the "narcosatánicos," as they were dubbed by the news media. The story of these murderous, devil-worshipping drug traffickers made international headlines and inspired a novel by Barry Gifford, later adapted as *Perdita Durango* (1997) by Spanish film director Álex de la Iglesia. The narcosatánicos were led by Adolfo de Jesús "El Padrino" (The Good Father) Constanzo and his romantic partner, Sara Aldrete. Constanzo, Aldrete and other members of their cult were hiding in a Mexico City apartment in Mexico City when they heard approaching police sirens. Constanzo immediately killed himself. Aldrete was arrested. [63] Both were found guilty of the homicide of fourteen people "sacrificed during a satanic ritual," illegal possession of weapons, narcotrafficking, and drug possession. Aldrete is still in prison—the same prison as Barraza, Santa Martha Acatitla—where she has found a new passion: literature. Aldrete has written a book, *Me dicen La Narcosatánica* (They call me The Narcosatanic), and an essay, "El amor mata lo que ama" (Love kills what it loves), relating her experiences of love and crime. Her writing has been well received, winning her the José Revueltas literary award, as well as recognition from the National Institute of Fine Arts.[64] And she is allegedly responsible for teaching Barraza how to read and write. Barraza, illiterate before going to prison, is now finishing high school.

The capture of Aldrete and Constanzo was fortuitous. Police were not looking for serial killers or even narcosatánicos. The disappearance of thirteen Mexican victims did not generate any government attention. Under pressure from the United States, police were in fact looking for an American student who had disappeared in northern Mexico, Mark Kilroy. At the US-Mexico border, police conducting a routine inspection found a truck containing marijuana, which led them to the nearby ranch of Santa Elena, where more drugs and arms were found. Police also discovered fourteen bodies at the site, including that of Kilroy, dismembered and butchered, along with knives, machetes, animal parts, skulls, candles, blood, bones, and incense—a hoard of items associated with the Afro-Cuban religion *santería*. The signs were clear: the bodies had been used in satanic rituals. The owners of the ranch did not hesitate to identify their godfather, El Padrino, as they felt protected—not only in a black-magic spiritual way, but because Constanzo also "satanically" protected high-level government officials, who in turn protected his network of narcotraffickers and drug dealers.[65]

In northern Mexico, it was known that Constanzo loved cruelty and saw it as necessary for the "consolidation of his tyranny."[66] He freely killed and mutilated his victims in extreme "gore"-movie style, leaving "bodies cut to pieces and bones made into necklaces."[67] But what ended Constanzo's impunity was not the killing of travestis, drug addicts, or even police officers, not the dismembering of bodies and the pulling out of eyes. No, the line Constanzo crossed was the kidnapping, torture, and murder of a foreigner, the Texan Mark Kilroy.[68] Mexican bodies did not count as victims to the Mexican police, but that of Kilroy, the American, did.

Considering murders of almost unimaginable violence like those committed by the narcosatánicos, why is it that serial killing is considered so much more "terrifying"? Despite the fact that the killings by the narcosatánicos made international headlines, the type of violence commonly associated with serial killing—"killing for the pleasure of killing"—was still considered an unknown phenomenon in Mexico until El Mataviejitas shocked the nation in 2003. What beliefs about serial killers make them more fearsome than even narcosatánicos?

Seltzer discusses the emergence of serial killing as part of what he calls the US "wound culture . . . [the] public fascination with torn and open bodies and torn and open persons, a collective gathering around shock, trauma, and the wound."[69] This "addiction to violence" is represented in popular cultural forms such as films and TV shows. Whereas there are not many accounts of the narcosatánicos in US popular culture, the figure of the serial killer occupies a prominent place. According to Seltzer, serial murder constitutes the "most popular genre-fiction of the body and the bodily violence" in US culture.[70] The representation of serial murder in popular culture has contributed to a gendered, classed, sexed, and geographically located serial killer construct.

In representations of serial killing, "it is apparent that criminological fact and literary fiction have become irretrievably intertwined."[71] Films based, however tenuously, on real-life cases such as *Henry: Portrait of a Serial Killer* (1986), *The Silence of the Lambs* (1991), *Ed Gein* (2000), and *Hannibal* (2001) blur the line between fiction and actuality, implying a treatment of "facts" and thus contributing to the construction of the figure of the (invariably) male serial killer.[72] As Caroline Picart and Cecil Greek have observed, these films have "specifically chosen" main characters who are "all white young males—a rare area in which fact and fiction converge in so far as most serial killers who have been caught fit this raced and sexed demographic."[73] These cinematic killers are typically presented as smart and calculating. Their motivation—killing for pleasure—is depicted as arising from a combination of biology and social maladaptation.

In each of the movies noted above, the young white male serial killer transforms into the terrifying yet compelling embodiment of evil. As Seltzer describes, serial killing is "represented as at once a horrific departure from normalcy and as abnormally normal."[74] That is, a seemingly normal person who has a family, job, and friends harbors an obscure trauma or pathology that is suddenly triggered, transforming him into a recognizable monster. In the most common narrative scenario, the serial killer is, for the most part, a person just like you, me, or a neighbor—as long as he is a white male who lives in the United States, of course.

Indeed, virtually every cinematic representation of serial killing in the US based on a "true" case excludes the possible identification of serial killers with different raced and sexed populations, like Latino Americans, African Americans, or Asians, reinforcing the perception that serial killing is a predominantly white phenomenon.[75] The near-impossibility of identifying serial killers with any demographic other than young, white American men is further seen in TV crime shows. For example, the Las Vegas–set *CSI: Crime Scene Investigation*—a show popular both in the United States and in Mexico—along with its spinoffs set in Miami and New York, perpetuates the same construct of serial killers that American films do: as, overwhelmingly, white males. Of the fifty-two serial killers depicted on *CSI* at the time of this writing, almost 90 percent are white men (almost all of whom are portrayed as brilliant and "organized"); only six are (white) women. One serial-killer episode is dedicated to Los Zetas.

Intertwining fact and fiction, popular films and TV programs of this sort lead audiences to believe that what they portray on the screen reflects, at least to some extent, what happens in actuality. For viewers outside the United States, these cultural texts also suggest that serial killing is a particularly US phenomenon. After watching these films and shows, I have no fear of running into a serial killer on the streets of Mexico. Serial killers live in the United States and speak English. As Heredia stated, serial killing "happens in movies, in the United States," where the line between fact and fiction is blurred, and where the killing of strangers occurs as the result of an overindividualistic society.

By contrast, the representation of crime in literature and films that involve Mexico City hardly deals with themes of serial killing. Rather, they support the perception that violence and criminality in Mexico are primarily the result of a corrupt government and the traffic in drugs. Mexico City is a frequent setting for films in which the theme of violence is predominant and clearly socially stratified. Such films contribute to the construction of mexicanidad, as violence and crimes are typically committed out of necessity, in order for characters to survive and to provide for their families. Mexican films about crime and violence thus set the society's own "wound culture" apart from that of the United States.

Take, for example, a genre of popular films set in Mexico City that includes *Lolo* (1992), *De la calle* (2000), *Perfume de violetas, nadie te oye* (2000), and *Ciudades oscuras* (2002). Each portrays lower-class crime as the result of poverty and marginalization.[76] The protagonists are young, mestizo, poor, and male (except for *Perfume de violetas*, where the lead characters are two girls), who live in marginalized urban spaces and who turn to criminal activity out of desperation. Crucially, these films contribute to the construction of mexicanidad, as the protagonists' criminal acts are also the result of strongly held family values. In *Lolo*, Dolores Chimal (aka "Lolo"), leads an ordinary family life until he is violently robbed by policemen, leaving him in the hospital. This sets off a series of misfortunes that end with Lolo killing an elderly woman by accident, while desperately trying to take care of his mother. It is his necessity, his bad luck, and mostly his love for his mother that leads to his crime.

The 2013 film *Sobre ella* shares many characteristics with these earlier films, but the central characters are not young, mestizo, and poor. On the contrary, it portrays how the bourgeoisie of Mexico City are affected by violence—one such character, for instance, is murdered during a mugging because he has only two hundred pesos (about ten dollars) on him. This film continues to portray crime as the result of poverty and marginalization of the lower classes.

The criminal characters in all of these films do not necessarily want to rob or to kill; they are compelled to commit criminal acts by their dire economic circumstances—an implicitly national condition. It is their desperation to help their families, their mother, or simply to survive, that drives them, not any desire for some kind of thrill. They are shown as filled with shame and remorse after they cross over into the criminal world.

In popular films that show crimes committed by middle-class individuals, such as *Amores perros* (2000) and *Un mundo raro* (2001), they tend to be nonviolent: blackmail, corruption.[77] But again, the criminal acts are not depicted as the product of an organized, brilliant mind cold-bloodedly pursuing thrills.

In sum, Mexican films of both sorts represent criminals and crimes according to socioeconomic status, wherein the lower classes commit violence and often kill, while the upper and middle classes commit primarily white-collar felonies.[78] But what is consistent at all social levels is that killing for the pleasure of killing is not what is represented. Additionally, in all the aforementioned films, Mexico City is named as the location where the crimes take place. Using the specific name of a city in a fictional text calls for a recognition that goes further than responding to what appears onscreen—"a proper name remits us to reality."[79] Naming Mexico City obliges the viewer to associate the story with real-world news reports, relating the fictional crimes and criminals to a familiar reality, and creating imaginaries of crimes and criminals very different from those promoted by American popular culture.

Another prevalent cultural form that constructs public notions about crime and criminals is the nota roja, "a term used for the chronicling of violence and crime in Mexico"[80]—not precisely synonymous with either "tabloid" or "true crime magazine," "nota roja" refers more broadly to periodicals with gruesome textual and photographic content. The nota roja tradition arguably defines Mexico's own wound culture and its particular fascination with torn and open bodies. Analysis of this mode of violent chronicle reveals further constructions of mexicanidad, propping up Mexicans' persistent belief that their country is defined by a culture of strong family values.

The nota roja is characterized more by the morbidity of body parts frozen in the photographs it presents than by the writing itself. The front page normally features a close-up photograph of a dead victim at the scene of the crime, full of bloody details, disfigured or burned, welcoming the reader "into a world of death and scandal."[81] The origins of the nota roja can be traced back to the police reports that have featured in Mexican periodicals since the nineteenth century, providing a space for "censorship and proscription of a new morality towards the formation of a certain social norms."[82] During the Porfiriato, the nota roja established itself as a way to construct public opinion, in which the sensational news of the day expressed the governing elite's anxieties about the working classes. The focus was on "robberies, the circulation of fake currencies, fights, crime, suicide and prostitution," the last of which was invariably portrayed as stemming from the precarious "working conditions endured by rural women, who were believed to be more inclined to delinquency and vice."[83] The nota roja did report on what are now recognized as the first serial killings in Mexican history—the murders committed by El Chalequero, responsible for killing as many as twenty female prostitutes in Mexico City between 1880 and 1888.[84] The identity of "serial killer" had yet to be coined, making him one—in a discursive sense—only in retrospect. At the time, the crimes of El Chalequero served mainly to demonstrate the occupational hazards faced by prostitutes.[85]

To this day, the nota roja continues to influence public opinion about what a crime is and how crime should be emotionally processed. Carlos Monsiváis explains that nota roja "constitutes one of Mexico's greatest novels, from which everyone may retain the fragmentary memory that typifies for them an idea of crime, corruption and plain bad luck."[86] The nota roja contributes to the perceptions that crime in Mexico is largely a result of corruption and drug trafficking, that violence is committed out of desperation that stems from economic necessity, or, alternatively, that it is frequently prompted by passion. Most importantly, in a county with high levels of violence and crime, one of the main functions of the nota roja has been to "exorcise urban violence" by transforming horrific events "into a spectacle."[87]

The nota roja has long defined for its own audience and for other popular cultural forms like cinema and literature which crimes are deemed shocking to the nation. Serial killing is not one of these crimes.

Considering mexicanidad is based on traditional, conventional family structures, it is not surprising that the crimes that nota roja has deemed the most horrific tend to center on the destabilizing of strong family structures.

Another set of serial killings covered by the nota roja took place in the 1940s, when Goyo Cárdenas, a chemistry student, strangled four women—his girlfriend and three sex workers. "Goyomanía," as Monsiváis calls it, erupted as Cárdenas was portrayed as the Mexican equivalent of Jack the Ripper. Stories about El Estrangulador de Tacuba, the strangler of Tacuba (the Mexico City neighborhood where the murders occurred) featured in the nota roja every day for months. An illegal pornographic movie circulated for many years allegedly featuring his orgies.[88]

The nota roja followed the news of the Cárdenas case obsessively in part because its emphasis on female sexuality catered to a prurient interest among those who consumed crime periodicals. The story later allowed the nota roja to serve a mediating role between the police and the people when, in 1976, Cárdenas became a poster child for the Mexican prison system's rehabilitation policies. Cárdenas was released with a law degree that he obtained while incarcerated at Lecumberri and went on to practice law, defending other prisoners. Upon his release, Cárdenas was praised by the government for his transformation, acclaim echoed by the nota roja.[89]

Other sensational crimes widely covered and reimagined within Mexican popular culture show a recurrent emphasis on disruptions to the family structure and the violation of normative ideas about femininity. A famous example occurred in the 1970s, when Trinidad Ruiz Mares killed her lover, Pablo Díaz Ramírez, a hairdresser, with a baseball bat because he had abused her children. Ruiz mangled her dead lover's body, made tamales with his separate body parts, and then sold them—thus acquiring the nickname La Tamalera Descuartizadora (The Tamale-Making Mangler).[90]

The most notorious crimes in Mexico, like those summarized here, are regularly narrated as if they were fictional stories. Indeed, there is often only a fine line between what actually happened and the ways in which these crimes are re-created in films, novels, or popular songs. Even as these crimes are the focus of sensationalistic coverage in nota roja periodicals, they provide the basis for films and novels by prestigious artists such as Arturo Ripstein, José Revueltas, and Jorge Ibargüengoitia.

In both the cinema and nota roja, the majority of crimes portrayed result from passions letting loose, jealousy, adultery (with domestic violence as the stereotypical crime) or greed, money laundering, corruption (stereotypically involving the drug trade), almost inevitably among people who know each other. The crime stories that have been taken up most intensely by both the mainstream press and nota roja, and that have circulated through films and novels, centered on the rupture of families, like the mother killing her abusive husband to protect her children from him. As rates of criminality and violence have increased dramatically in Mexico since 2006, this has been linked by the mainstream press and nota roja alike to drug trafficking and organized crime. Murder, even brutal murder, thus continues to be depicted as the result of passion, resentment, lechery, bribery, fraud, being caught with the wrong person at the wrong time, misfortune in drug dealings, or engaging with organized crime—but not someone's congenital desire to kill strangers. These cultural forms fix the limits of comprehensible criminal violence, separated their audiences from the unexpected threat of "a mentally deranged person [who] may suddenly cross the path of someone like you; one day a young couple opens the door confidently, letting in the evil that will be their downfall—a crime which, on exhibiting their intimacy, will blow it up to enormous sinful proportions."[91] Crime and violence are distinguished very clearly through different popular cultural forms in the United States and Mexico. While each country has a "wound culture" involving public fascination with torn-open bodies, their representations of crimes and violence come from different traditions, distinguishing the "types" of criminals and the "types" of crimes that are narrativized in each country, and so establishing and reaffirming their different national identities.

It is not only Hollywood movies and popular TV shows that have cast serial killing as a peculiarly US phenomenon. Criminological texts have also contributed to this notion. As Seltzer puts it, serial killing "wounds an idealized American culture that is at the same time seen as a wound culture."[92] He observes, as well, how international accounts of serial killing demonstrate that "as the influence of American culture spreads to less developed countries . . . the fear is that, unless checked somehow, the disease of serial murder will spread as well."[93] The Mexican public's fascination with open, bloody bodies, as photographed in the nota roja tradition, echoes the US wound culture and its representation in popular culture. However, I argue, the Mexican tradition functions most importantly as a way to set Mexico apart from the United States and its wound culture, which is believed to be worse. To acknowledge the existence of a serial killer in Mexico is thus to question Mexican identity itself.

Again, Mexicans think of themselves as having strong moral and religious values, rooted in what constitutes the core of society: family. In the logic of mexicanidad, devotion to family values prevents stranger killing, or killing for the pleasure of killing, which characterizes a desensitized society. The pivotal concern is not the relative brutality of a murder; it is about who the victim is. It is, for instance, not nearly as horrific to kill out of jealousy, out of passionate, melodramatic emotion of the sort that characterizes mexicanidad, or even the killing of narco dealers, as it is to kill a stranger out of an urge to kill.

The idea that there are no serial killers in Mexico is based on the prejudicial belief that serial killing is an alien phenomenon, performed by white males in the United States. A serial killer is worse than a narcosatánico because serial killing happens "up there," in a society defined by excessive individualism, deficient morality, pervasive anomie. Serial killers are worse than narcosatánicos because they speak of a society in decay.

El Chalequero, Goyo Cárdenas, and Las Poquianchis

The Mexican conceptualization of serial killing as an alien—specifically US— phenomenon, embroils the conceptualization of a Mexican serial killer in all the complications of a cultural clash. Analyzing this clash—between Mexican culture and the unquestioned adoption of US and European narratives of serial killers—reveals how international assumptions about serial killing affected the search for El Mataviejitas. I will start with a brief account of who has been considered a serial killer in Mexico.

As noted, the history of serial killers in Mexico can be traced back to the 1880s and Francisco Guerrero. The Spanish expression "a chaleco," which can be translated as "by force," led to his nickname of El Chalequero.[94] Like Jack the Ripper, to whom he was compared by the Mexican press,[95] Guerrero "forced himself" on women, soliciting the services of sex workers, often raping them and then slitting their throats. It was in 1880 that disappearances of sex workers started to be noticed (prostitution was legal at the time and controlled by the government). It was not until 1886, however, that the case attracted substantial attention. Female corpses started to appear near a river, Río Consulado. Around twenty bodies were found, many of them butchered, and still police had no clue as to the killer's identity. Guerrero was finally arrested in 1888, and not as the result of any search for him; instead, one of his intended victims was able to escape and reported him to police.

According to Pablo Piccato, Francisco Guerrero "operated with full knowledge that women knew and feared him, and that nobody dare to accuse him."[96] Piccato argues that "women did not accuse Guerrero of rape because they all thought that he would be acquitted by a jury, and that policemen and judges [would] only add to their humiliation, mainly because they were prostitutes, domestic workers or peddlers."[97] For Carlos Rougmanac, a leading criminologist who was in charge of Guerrero's case, "rape did not amount to perverse behavior"; he concluded that Guerrero's sexual life was "normal" since he did not "masturbate" or engage in "acts against nature," (i.e., homosexuality), despite the fact that he had confessed, among other things, to liking sex "with minors who were virgins" and to biting.[98] Guerrero provided an explanation for his crimes that satisfied Rougmanac: they were a result of the victims wounding his "macho self-esteem."[99]

Guerrero was tried and sentenced to twenty years in prison. However, in 1904, he was released along with many other prisoners following a presidential amnesty for political prisoners. He lived with his daughters, also sex workers, for four years before he killed again. In 1908, El Chalequero was found, hands still covered with blood, at the shore of Río Consulado after having killed an eighty-year-old sex worker. He was arrested again and given a life sentence; just two years later, in 1910, he died.

Rougmanac regarded the comparison between El Chalequero and Jack the Ripper with "a certain pride" since it "conveyed the progress of the capital," which came not only with European technology, architecture, and fashion, but also their "new forms of crime."[100] It was as if having a notorious sexual predator, and reading his (violent sexual) crimes as those of a "European" criminal, meant Mexico City had achieved world-class status. However, unlike the crimes of Jack the Ripper, which constitute a story of "mystery," as Piccato argues, those of El Chalequero tell a story of "impunity."[101] As determined by criminologists and psychiatrists, El Chalequero was not considered a "pathological case, but rather a normal example of sexual conduct among the poor."[102] Piccato's analysis of his trial, its reporting in the penny press, and the official discourses of criminologists and psychiatrists sheds light on how sexual crimes have been treated far more as a "criminal phenomenon, than a social problem" in Mexico.[103]

Despite the case of El Chalequero, most accounts—including that of the Procuraduría General de Justicia del Distrito Federal (Mexico City's Department of Justice)—claim there was only one serial killer in the country before El/La Mataviejitas: Gregorio "Goyo" Cárdenas (Goyo is a diminutive of Gregorio), El Estrangulador de Tacuba. In 1942, Cárdenas killed at least four women and buried them in the garden of his home in the Tacuba neighborhood over the span of fifteen days.[104] Twenty-seven years old, he was pursing an undergraduate degree in chemistry, with a scholarship from the government-owned national oil company PEMEX (Petroleos Mexicanos). In August, Cárdenas solicited the services of a sixteen-year-old sex worker, María de Los Ángeles González. He took her to his house and, after engaging in sexual relations, when the girl went to the bathroom Cárdenas strangled her with a cord. He then buried her in his lawn. Eight days later, he repeated the pattern, this time hiring a young sex worker whose identity is still unknown. Six days later, Cárdenas hired yet another minor, Rosa Reyes Quiroz. According to police reports, Reyes did not engage in sexual relations with Cárdenas and in fact resisted. However, she suffered the same fate as the two previous sex workers; she was strangled with a cord and buried in Cárdenas's back garden. Four days later, Cárdenas killed Graciela Arias Ávalos, also a chemistry student, whom he had been dating and whose father was a well-known lawyer, Miguel Arias Córdoba. Cárdenas picked up Arias after school and drove her home; according to his account, after she refused to kiss him, beat her to death in his car, right in front of her house. He then brought Arias to his own home and left the body under his bed. It is known that Cárdenas raped her many times after she was dead.[105] The next day, he buried her body next to the corpses of the other three girls in his garden.

Four days later, Cárdenas was hospitalized by his mother, apparently at his own insistence. In the hospital, he was interviewed by a private detective in connection with the search for Arias. Cárdenas confessed to having killed her and buried her body in his garden. Hours later, police came to the hospital and Cárdenas himself took them to his house and showed them the buried bodies. He also showed police his journal, in which he had recorded his crimes. Cárdenas then prepared his own declaration using a typewriter.[106] The headlines in nota roja periodicals the next day read "Gregorio Cárdenas relates his confessions" (*Alarma!*), "Monster makes brutal confession," and "Monster pretends he is crazy" (both *La Prensa*).

In 1942, Cárdenas was sent to the ward for the mentally ill at the Palacio de Lecumberri prison. His lawyers were able to transfer him, briefly, to an actual mental institution, Manicomio General de la Castañeda, where he was treated with electroshocks and injected with sodium pentothal to determine if he was actually mentally ill or just "pretending."[107] Inexplicably, during his stay in the mental hospital, Cárdenas enjoyed privileges that other patients did not, such as free entry to the library, visits, occasional outings to the movies with female friends, and even a day trip to Oaxaca.

In the years after Cárdenas returned to the Palacio de Lecumberri, he acquired a law degree, became a painter, played musical instruments, and wrote five books, including *Celda 16* (1970), *Pabellón de locos* (1973), and *Adios Lecumberri* (1979). Cárdenas was considered a testament to the effectiveness of the reformatory system. After he had spent thirty-four years in prison, his lawyer, Salvador Salamerón Solano, argued for the "unconstitutionality of the case," on the basis that the maximum sentence for a convicted killer was thirty years.[108] A judge ordered Cárdenas's release in September 1976, citing "lack of proof"—never mind that the police had found the bodies buried in his garden and that he had confessed.[109] Upon his release, he was feted by national legislators at the Chamber of Deputies. Cárdenas reportedly dedicated the rest of his life to helping low-income prisoners.[110]

Prior to the case of El/La Mataviejitas, Cárdenas occupied the most prominent place in the history of crime in Mexico; his was called "the case of the century."[111] The figure of Mexico's "first" serial killer—though, paradoxically, the second "Mexican Jack the Ripper"—has circulated in any number of popular cultural forms what Monsiváis called "goyomanía": from jokes on his name to the sale of thousands of ropes supposedly identical to the "authentic" one he used to kill his first three victims.[112] For years, in nota roja journals, an "exclusive" interview with or feature on Cárdenas would appear in a nota roja journal almost every week.

Reading Cárdenas's confessions, one can well imagine how he became the serial killer celebrity of the century: "[T]hey were women of the street. . . . I offered them money. I took them to my home, where they sated me. After having them, I do not know what I became, what I felt; it was something horrible, a horrific hatred towards those women, all women, an inexplicable frenzy . . . the invincible impulse to destroy, to tear, to kill . . . and I killed them!"[113]

Although these confessions are undoubtedly misogynistic, they are talked about only rarely in terms of gender violence and much more in relation to the debate over Cárdenas's alleged insanity or as confirmation of stereotypical narratives of serial killing: the killer possessing "superior intelligence," for example, or having sexual relations with the victims before killing them. Meanwhile, the fact that his first three victims were sex workers led to their stigmatization in police and other official accounts, while the press effectively excused his crimes.

Cárdenas got all the press attention as Mexico's first "authentic" serial killer and is even talked about by journalist Ricardo Ham as having a "place of honor"—a place that, for example, El Chalequero never had.[114] Cárdenas died in 1999 as still a public figure, both the Mexican Jack the Ripper and a poster child for the success of prison reform. The stories of Cárdenas would seem to give Mexico a place in the history of serial killers. Indeed, media and popular crime narratives often refer to Cárdenas as "our serial killer"—he put Mexico on the global stage, on the list of the world's bloodiest cases. Renditions of the Cárdenas story continue to focus more on his alleged pathology and what his case reveals about the penitentiary system than on the actual murders. The deaths of his victims seem to inspire very little indignation, let alone fury; their families have garnered little public sympathy. In neither his story nor that of El Chalequero were the women who were killed a cause for much concern; indeed, some of them are still anonymous.

In 2007, the Police Cultural Center in downtown Mexico City mounted an exhibition about serial killers, complete with a catalogue. In the section on Mexican serial killers in Mexico, along with El Chalequero and El Goyo, there is mention of Las Poquianchis—the González sisters, who for more than twenty years hired young women supposedly to work as maids only to exploit them sexually to the clients of their *cantina* (bar) before killing them.[115]

In 1964, the story of Las Poquianchis (the derivation of the nickname is uncertain) became a defining case in the history of female criminality in Mexico. Delfina González, María de Jesús González, and María Luisa González were sentenced for murder, kidnapping, criminal association, pimping, sexual assault, injuries, corruption of minors, threats, obstruction of justice, and violation of laws against inhumane treatment.[116] The three sisters had lured young, mostly lower-class girls between thirteen and fifteen years old, promising to place them in good homes as maids. Instead, they pimped the girls in their bar, tortured and abused them, and then killed and later buried them either in their own backyard or in the bar in which they had been pimped. The González sisters—with the protection of government officials—killed hundreds of young women and children, although the killings of only eight are recognized legally.[117] Historian Fabiola Bailón has analyzed the story of the Poquianchis in relation to narratives of the 1962 abolition of prostitution houses in Mexico that appeared in the nota roja magazine *Alarma!* and in a 1976 movie of the same name directed by Felipe Cazals. Bailón notes how in these texts the three sisters are clearly "demonized" as "exploiters" and "killers" of other women, while the "repentance of the young girls is exalted."[118] This is a very different treatment than that accorded to Cárdenas, a distinction that mirrors the one between the discourses surrounding male versus female serial killers around the world.

Although the case of Las Poquianchis is very well known, they have not officially been recognized as serial killers. In his book *México y sus asesinos seriales* (2007), Ricardo Ham—curator of the Police Cultural Center exhibition—writes that he does not consider the González sisters serial killers "since their motive was economic"; he underscores the point with the statement that "serial killers' motive is specifically a variety of psychological needs, power and sexual compulsion."[119] Likewise, neither the Department of Justice nor criminologist Martín Barrón consider Las Poquianchis to be serial killers. The debate over nomenclature aside, this particular case of woman-on-woman violence garnered nothing like the police response provoked by the case of El/La Mataviejitas.

The arrests of Las Poquianchis, according to accounts in *Alarma!*, were put in motion when a couple of survivors reported them at a police station in Guanajuato. The young girls showed clear signs of abuse and malnutrition. The case became widely known after the González sisters were arrested, but as not a result of actual police investigation or an official search for the victims. Instead, the nota roja press, popular-culture discourses, and narrations of the abolition of brothels focused on the "pupils" as victims of Las Poquianchis and corrupt authorities, as well as a "product of the social conditions and poverty of peasant families."[120] The young girls in the case were said to be "repentant" of prostitution.

The CCP exhibition also included, as a "ramification" of serial killing, the case of "El Padrino" Constanzo and Sara Aldrete, the nacosatánicos. As noted earlier, the victims of the narcosatánicos counted only when a foreigner, Mark Kilroy, disappeared. A search for the killers was finally launched then; however, no search was ever made for the travestis they had killed.

Finally, some accounts of Mexican serial killers include those who committed their crimes in the United States, like Juan Corona, who was found guilty of the 1971 killings of twenty-five illegal workers in California, and Rafael Reséndiz, who was sentenced to death for killing at least four people in Texas, where he was executed in June 2006.

Despite the contradictory perspectives on who qualifies as a Mexican serial killer, it must again be emphasized that—with the sole exception of the Mataviejitas case—Mexico City's Justice Department had never undertaken an investigation of a designated serial killer. Aside from that same, sole exception, no Mexican news outlet has ever published a story about a serial killer's modus operandi or psychological profile or number of victims prior to a suspect's capture. All of these subjects have been determined to be serial killers (or not) after their capture. As of this writing in 2019, this continues to be true.

Since Juana Barraza, the alleged La Mataviejitas, Mexico has seen a couple of other serial killers—again, identified as such only after their arrests. One of these, as noted in the introduction, is Raúl Osiel Marroquín Reyes, who was captured by federal police in Mexico City the same day as Barraza'a arrest.

According to the Department of Justice, Marroquín is responsible for six kidnappings and the homicides of four homosexual men. He had an accomplice who was not caught, Juan Enrique Madrid Manuel. Marroquín, a military veteran, would contact young homosexual men in cafés or bars in Mexico City's gay enclave, Zona Rosa. Once he gained their trust, he took them to a hotel or to his own apartment. Marroquín extorted them, tortured them for five to seven days, and finally strangled them to death. Afterward, he dismembered the bodies and stuffed them into black suitcases, which then he left in different public venues around Mexico City.[121]

Before Marroquín's detention, Mexico City police were not looking for a serial killer of homosexual men. It was only once Marroquín was found, and had confessed to many of his crimes, that he was labeled a serial killer and nicknamed El Matagays and El Sádico—because he liked torturing and killing by asphyxiation, little by little. Though his homicides would seem to be a clear example of killing for the pleasure of killing, police authorities never suggested that they were a result of societal anomie. Marroquín talked about his crimes as actually bringing "good to society," on the basis that his young homosexual victims were "bad for society" because, he claimed, they "perverted children." One of his victims was HIV positive; Marroquín stated that killing him was a particular service to society, preventing "propagation of the virus."[122] While the more progressive fraction of society recognized that his killings were a result of homophobia, again, his victims hardly counted as such to the police.

It is uncertain why the official title of serial killer was granted to but not to, for example, El Poeta Canibal, El Coqueto, or more recently, El Matanovias.[123] In 2007, a year after Barraza and Marroquín were captured, José Luis Calva Zepeda was arrested after police found him in his apartment cooking and eating the dismembered remains of his girlfriend, Alejandra Galeana Garavito, who had been reported missing. Police found "the upper body cut in pieces and stored in the refrigerator while her forearm was being cooked in a pan on the stove."[124] Police also believed Calva Zepeda was responsible for the killing of Olga Livia, a teacher, and another woman, a sex worker whose name is unknown.

In December 2007, Calva Zepeda allegedly committed suicide, although his family believes he was raped and brutally killed in prison.[125] Calva Zepeda was nicknamed El Poeta Canibal when it was revealed that he sent poems and roses to lure his victims; he was also dubbed El Canibal de la Guerrero for the neighborhood where he lived. According to news reports, after his capture, police investigated the possible connection between Calva Zepeda and the killings of "at least five women that appeared dismembered in different neighborhoods in Mexico City, in Chimalhuacán and Bordo de Xochiaca."[126] These are poor areas on the outskirts of the city—technically parts of Estado de México, a state known for its high number of feminicides.[127]

In December 2012, twenty-nine-year-old César Armando Librado Legorreta, aka El Coqueto, was sentenced to 240 years in prison for the murders of seven women and rapes of eight.[128] El Coqueto worked as a public bus driver on a route that goes from Valle Dorado, in Estado de México, to Chapultepec, in central Mexico City. Working the night shift, Librado Legoreta took the opportunity to rape and kill women who were alone and then throw their bodies into the Tlalnepantla canal.[129] His nickname is especially disturbing: El Coqueto means, literally, "the flirt." His nickname is a testament to how little regard there is for young, poor mestiza women in Mexico, and speaks to the state's complacency in the face of rampant feminicides. His killings—yet another example of the country's systematic violence against women—are rendered comic.

In 2017, there is the case of El Matanovias (The Girlfriend Killer). Jorge Humberto Martínez Cortés is allegedly responsible for the deaths of two of his ex-girlfriends, each of whom was found dead after moving in with him. Yang Kung died in September 2014 and Campira Camorlinga in December 2016.[130] It is uncertain in each case if the cause of death was suicide or strangulation by Cortés. The families of the victims have sought to focus public attention on them as potential homicides.[131] The press has been following a narrative similar to the one it applied to El Poeta Canibal; since the victims are ex-girlfriends of the alleged killer, it has been treated like a case of domestic violence and not "killing for the pleasure of killing." In some accounts, El Poeta Canibal, El Coqueto, and El Matanovias are considered to be serial killers, but none of the three has officially been labeled as such by the Mexico City police.

Even more recently, a pair of serial killers has been identified in Ecatepec, Estado de México, not far from where Juana Barraza lived. For six years, Juan Carlos Hernández and Patricia Martínez, a married couple, lured young women to their house to kill and dismember them. Their bones were sold to an unidentified person and their flesh fed to the couple's dogs. The couple was categorized as serial killers only after their capture, which did not result from any investigation into the disappearance of their victims. In October 2018, the couple were walking on the street, ferrying several large plastic garbage bags in a baby stroller, when police stopped and searched them, serendipitously discovering that they were carrying human remains. The number of women killed by Los Monstruos de Ecatepec (The Monsters of Ecatepec), as they were dubbed by the media, is unknown, but Juan Carlos has confessed to twenty feminicides. As of this writing, they still await trial.

In general, the stories of these serial killers are presented as if serial killing were an isolated phenomenon, one that has much more to do with the "monster" within the individual criminal subject than with any reflection of a misogynistic, homophobic, and *machista* society. Most of the serial killers discussed above killed young, poor women. El Chalequero, Goyo Cárdenas, and Las Poquianchis killed female sex workers, many of them underage. These victims are barely mentioned in police reports or media narratives. The capture, sentencing, and imprisonment of these serial killers have not resulted from police investigations involving either serial killers identified as on the loose or the whereabouts of young lower-class women, sex workers, or homosexual men who have disappeared.

The criminalization of these serial killers fits a narrative based on the "monstrosity" within a serial killer; that is, the murders committed by these serial killers are talked about in the press as the result of a pathology. Both Cárdenas's misogynistic confessions and Marroquín's homophobic remarks, for instance, were discussed more in relation to debates over their "insanity" than in terms of gender violence. The killers are criminalized for who they are, and less so for what they have done: raped, killed, and butchered young mestizo and indigenous women and homosexuals. In turn, those who have been killed have not counted as victims in any culturally significant way—their stories have not shocked the nation.

The Hunt for El Mataviejitas

In November 2003, as soon as the existence of a serial killer was declared in Mexico City, police had recourse to a certain set of characteristics and personality attributes thought to apply to any such criminal. This set of traits was constrained by gender, sex, class, and skin color—the starting point, as always, was the assumption that the serial killer would turn out to be a white heterosexual man. On this basis, police started to search for *El* Mataviejitas.

Richard Collier has examined "the ways in which the (sexed) bodies of men" are constituted "as an 'absent presence' within contemporary discourses around crime and criminality."[132] As stated earlier, it could well be the case that most serial killers caught in the United States to date do fit the conventional profile, but that hardly means that all young white men are potential serial killers or that all serial killers have to be young, white American males. What is problematic is not only the unquestioned "absent presence" of whiteness, maleness, and Americanness in serial killing, both in scholarly accounts and in popular culture, but, most importantly, the impact of this belief structure on the Mataviejitas investigation.

When the Mexican Justice Department formally announced that a serial killer was at large, deputy prosecutor Renato Sales Heredia stated that "more than 90% [of serial killers] are men; with average or superior intelligence, who have suffered physical, psychological, or sexual abuse; who come from unstable or disintegrated families; and who, since childhood, have shown tendencies toward fetishism or sadomasochism."[133] The description that authorities gave of El Mataviejitas corresponds to every other international serial killer account, largely based on traits of notorious examples such as Ted Bundy and Jack the Ripper. These two world-renowned figures—both adult white males who killed an unknown number of young women—have defined much of the masculinized construction of serial killing. As Mark Seltzer has argued, "the absence of any knowledge of the identity of the killer has made Jack the Ripper the prototype of the serial killer"[134]—but it is important to add that, like Bundy, it *is* known that Jack the Ripper was a white male.

El Mataviejitas was believed by authorities to share the characteristics of serial killers in the United States. Mirroring popular and professional descriptions of Bundy, chief prosecutor Bernardo Bátiz described El Mataviejitas as a person with a "brilliant mind, very astute, and cautious."[135] While assisting in the manhunt—which was not launched in earnest until mid-2005—criminologist Martín Barrón declared that the majority of serial killers are "maniacs of order, fetishists, with perfect control of themselves, high IQ, stable job, childhood emotional disorders, married and with kids."[136] These assumptions all appear to be based on the stereotype of serial killers in the United States, whose "actions are naturalized as male."[137] None of this stereotyping of El Mataviejitas corresponded to any actual evidence gathered at the crime scenes where elderly women had been killed or with any knowledge of prior serial killings in Mexico.

Descriptions by police and Barrón of El Mataviejitas reveal more about their beliefs about serial killers' characteristics—beliefs imported from United States—than about any fact-based understanding of their manhunt's focus. As Seltzer points out, there is nothing more visible in the proliferating "official literature on serial killing than its relentless banality."[138] To which one might add that literature's endless contradictions, which render it virtually useless. For example, on the one hand, Alan Fox and Jack Levin have stated that serial killers act methodically and kill people who are known to them.[139] On the other hand, some criminological studies suggest that the brutality of serial violence is linked to its impersonality, that is, the targeting of strangers, in which "there need be no motives of hatred, rage, jealousy, or greed at work; the victim need not have taunted, threatened, or abused the killer."[140] These contradictory accounts of serial killing in the foreign literature seem to have simply been adopted wholesale by Mexican prosecutors. Heredia stated that the crimes of El Mataviejitas were "distinguishable because there was no personal relation between the victim and the criminal. The homicide is not moved by jealousy, revenge or money."[141] At the very same time, authorities were claiming that El Mataviejitas was driven to kill elderly women because of a "deep resentment" toward a feminine figure, probably because of childhood abuse.[142]

In the United States, serial killing is viewed by the criminal justice system, in criminological research, and by the media as essentially an exclusively male crime.[143] Again, this view was adopted without question by the Mexican justice system. Both countries, like many others in the Western world, share the belief that female offenders are "exceptional cases." When women kill their husbands or kids, their crimes are due to passionate impulses or social marginalization. Candice Skrapec points out "the amazement at the revelation that women have long been, and continue to be, multiple murderers," as this "violates the idea of femaleness," which is "tied to [women's] traditional nurturing role."[144] In fact, as Skrapec has noted, there have been many female serial killers in the United States and throughout the world, and their attributes overlap greatly with those of their male counterparts. Female serial murderers are from diverse backgrounds (including poverty, privilege, and nobility) and they kill for economic gain, personal satisfaction, or sexual motives. The impossibility of thinking of a female serial killer and the idea that sexual failure correlates with serial killing is explored in the next chapter.

In response to the supposed novelty of the serial killer phenomenon in Mexico, Heredia stated that Mexico City's investigative apparatus "must have enough bravery to recognize that it needs help." This help, he said, must come "from the United States, who have suffered [the serial killer phenomenon] for a long time and have developed the criminal profiling technique," which, according to Heredia, is "based in the meticulous analysis of the crime scenes."[145]

The profiling of El Mataviejitas defined the places where police searched for the serial killer, but most importantly, it defined the sex, gender, and class of the unknown assailant. From criminologists to police officials to feminist academics, there was a consensus that Mexico lacked a "scientific" system to track down serial killers and that Mexican police should therefore rely on US expertise. Although it is not clear if the United States ever actually assisted the investigation, as we will see, help did come from France.

Profilers in the United States are widely believed to be effective—even necessary—since they "have studied the cases and elaborated a profile of the killer, put their finger on it with impressive frequency."[146] However, as Seltzer has pointed out, "profilers have all in all been generally ineffectual in tracking down the killers." He quotes a former FBI serial homicide investigator who, in a *Vanity Fair* interview, stated, "I mean, how many serial killer cases has the FBI solved—*if any?*"[147] Similarly, in Mexico City, the profile of El Mataviejitas seems not to have contributed to the arrest of the killer, but rather only to expose the banality and futility of profiling.

Ignoring eyewitness accounts—one saw a "tall, 1.70m, robust woman with black hair"; another said, "I believe it was a woman, I am not sure because [she] was very tall. But she was blond and shorthaired. [She] used glasses and had a bag"—authorities based their profile of El Mataviejitas on international accounts of serial killing in which the criminals are unvaryingly male.[148] As noted at the beginning of this chapter, cultural beliefs that have defined, through the pervasive ideology of mexicanidad, who constitutes an ideal Mexican in terms of gender, sex, class, and skin color have blinded the search for and conceptualization of serial killers. The ideal Mexican woman is a self-sacrificing and self-abnegating mother, in contrast to her deviant counterpart who, if not a sex worker, is definitely a woman whose sexuality is not controlled through marriage. The idea that women can be serial killers transgresses the notion of femininity and femaleness—and hence the idea of family and moral values—in which the Mexican identity itself is so deeply rooted.

Despite multiple eyewitness accounts, police still could not imagine a female serial killer; instead, they eventually revised the profile of El Mataviejitas—now he was a travesti. According to a police statement, El Mataviejitas "was a man with homosexual tendencies who dresses like a woman"—building on a cultural trope that equates homosexuality with sexual failure, which in turn correlates with serial killing. Numerous travesti sex workers were arrested and taken into police custody, only to be released after no evidence was found to connect them with the crime scenes. Bátiz assured the public that the killer "might not be a travesti but we are certain it is a transgendered person."[149]

This chapter has explored how the intertwining of fact and fiction in both police investigations and media narrations regarding serial killers in Mexico affected the hunt for El Mataviejitas. The unidentified serial killer was seen as more "terrifying" than La Tamalera Descuartizadora, than even the narcosatánicos or the perpetrators of any number of horrific crimes because "killing for the pleasure of killing" is associated, in Mexico, with a "dehumanized" society in which strong family values are absent. In the Mataviejitas case in particular, this cherished notion of family values upon which Mexico is constructed is what determined the worthiness of the elderly women as victims, alarming the nation. These women's bodies matter to the nation because they represent beliefs at the very core of the society.

The cultural beliefs of mexicanidad reinforce which bodies matter to the nation and which do not. The serial killer is understood to be a young, white American male; Mexican criminals are mostly from the lower classes and have darker skin, or they are deviant others, travestis. A victim is a grandmother, a sweet, kind, and loving woman, not a working young mestiza or a lower-middle-class homosexual man. Under this logic, rather than understanding the violence of serial killing, we come to understand how the discourses of mexicanidad are constructed.

2

The Look of the Serial Killer

El/La Mataviejitas

Sketches of the killer were among the tools considered most essential by police in the search for the figure universally assumed for over two years to be *El* Mataviejitas. More than sixty-four sketches were created and distributed in the areas of Mexico City where El Mataviejitas was believed to have attacked, most of which were close to gardens and parks. Indeed, the search operation was called Parques y Jardines, since it was believed that El Mataviejitas preyed on elderly women as they were walking or sitting alone in parks near their homes. Most of these areas were located in typically middle- to lower-middle-class neighborhoods. The sketches were displayed in the windows of almost every patrol car, made into posters and put up in government offices, and displayed in subway stations and on buses throughout the city.

In search of these sketches, I visited the office of the Mexico City Justice Department in Delegación Cuauhtémoc, trying to get copies of the original sketches and posters of El Mataviejitas, which I had seen only in newspapers. After many fruitless visits, I was finally directed to the office of Comandante Victor Hugo Moneda, operations chief of the "800-strong police corps responsible for the capture of La Mataviejitas," as he told me more than once, evidently to emphasize that it was the hard work of the police that led to Barraza's arrest and not total happenstance.

I arrived for my appointment with Comandante Moneda on time at 7 p.m. (after two hours on public transportation); however, the person responsible for photocopying had already left for the day, making it "impossible" for me to get any documents and requiring that I return the following morning at 10 a.m. The next day, Comandante Moneda made time in his busy schedule to talk to me amid calls about homicides, a constant stream of "Roger"s and "Copy"s over his walkie-talkie, and the clamor of a TV (on which a talk show guest was assuring the public that female orgasm was possible). His office featured a shrine to La Virgen de Guadalupe and, most importantly, in and around it were four buff men with guns at his photocopying disposition. Comandante Moneda's gun was on his desk. I was given various photocopies of one of the most important documents used by police in their Mataviejitas search, the report drawn up by French police on the serial killer for a course they gave to police officers in Mexico City. Comandante Moneda explained to me the three different prototypes of serial killers outlined in the French report and their modus operandi. He was proud of the Mataviejitas arrest, which he saw as the result of the hard work and unbeatable scientific approach used by the police under his command, and not a fortuitous event. Though reluctant to offer much detail about his personal experience of the case, as he was in the process of writing his own manuscript, he confided that he had shared more with me than with the movie producer who had previously approached him.

I believe that a sketch can serve as reassurance to victims, survivors, and witnesses—and, in this case, to the public—that authorities have the knowledge and experience necessary to find the person responsible for a crime. The use of police sketches, however, has been challenged as perpetuating the long tradition of marginalization of the lower classes—in Mexico correlated heavily with darker skin and indigenous features—building on the use of photography for criminal identification established in the nineteenth century. In addition, the use of sketches in the Mataviejitas case is problematic because of the way they perpetuated the masculinization of criminality, especially with regard to serial killing.

Analysis of the use of sketches in the search for El Mataviejitas reveals how national imaginaries of masculinity and femininity and their relationship to class and skin color have been reinforced through discourses of criminal description and depictions. These national imaginaries of who constitutes a criminal in turn determine notions of who constitutes an ideal Mexican versus a criminal Mexican in terms of class, skin color, gender, and sex.

I find that the images that police and criminologists used to identify El/La Mataviejitas, as well as the texts that accompanied them in police press releases and their media "narrativization,"[1] tell a story not only of how a serial killer is constructed but also about understandings of criminality and its relationship to class, gender, and skin color. The images I refer to include those published in newspapers and distributed throughout Mexico City, as well as two additional sketches made available to me by Comandante Moneda during our August 2007 interview, when I was beginning this project. While journalists and criminologists asserted similarities between Barraza and the sketches, I argue that the widespread confidence in the sketches is based more on international discourses of serial killing than on relevant investigation and evidence.

Equally important as analyzing the details of the sketches themselves is understanding the software used to produce them, as their technological basis contributed to the perception that they were precise and informatively based on the various "types" that constitute representative Mexican faces as "objectively" determined by physical anthropologists and forensic specialists. This software, called La Cara del Mexicano (The Face of the Mexican), or CaraMex, was designed to facilitate the identification and arrest of criminals through image creation. Police did not find La Mataviejitas as a result of these sketches, yet they and the software behind them were considered a success by journalists, criminologists, and police officers like Comandante Moneda—not to mention one of CaraMex's own developers, Carlos Serrano, with whom I had a chance to talk at his office at the National Autonomous University of Mexico in April 2017.

After this analysis, I question whether the sketches actually depict a "prototype" of a criminal more than a portrait of El/La Mataviejitas. Historically tracing discourses of criminality, I challenge the assumption prevalent in Mexico (although long challenged internationally) that criminality is innate and thus visible in the physical traits revealed in photographs and sketches. And I look closely at the chronology of narratives relating to the sketches after the arrests of travestis as the possible Mataviejitas. I pay particular attention to the shift in gendered and sexed constructions around the Mataviejitas case among criminologists, police officials, and the news media when a woman was arrested, and how the sketches were then reinterpreted and re-presented. I focus mainly on a three-dimensional bust of El Mataviejitas that was created by a Justice Department artist; photographs of it were posted in police stations and, years later, it was featured in the Police Cultural Center serial killer exhibition. Publicized in the media mostly after the arrest of Juana

Barraza, the bust—repeatedly referred to by police as a "sketch"— was used as "evidence" that Barraza was indeed La Mataviejitas because of her alleged similarities to it—for example, the bust was adorned with a red sweater and Barraza was wearing a red sweater when she was apprehended.

Once Barraza was criminalized and determined to be La Mataviejitas, within a couple of hours of her arrest, she was photographed by criminologist Martín Barrón. In his 2006 book *El nudo del silencio: tras la pista de una asesina en serie, La Mataviejitas* (The knot of silence: Following the tracks of a female serial killer, La Mataviejitas), he presented a set of photographs to support the assertion that Barraza's "looks" prove that she is indeed La Mataviejitas. More than Barraza's culpability, I am interested in the circulation of representations and approaches by media and authorities to conceptualize a female serial killer. More than determining whether Barraza is La Mataviejitas, I am concerned with how the narrativization of her story reveals how a criminal, specifically a serial killer, is constructed.

The first official sketch, based on eyewitness accounts of the last person seen with the victims,[2] was made available to the public in December 2003, a month after police first declared the existence of a serial killer with a specific modus operandi: "a [male] homicidal dressed as a [female] nurse," pretending to be a worker from Sí Vale, Mexico City's economic assistance program for elderly citizens.[3] However, it was not until more than a year and a half later, on August 25, 2005, that police started a rigorous hunt for the killer, creating two new sketches and distributing them all over the city (fig. 2.1).[4]

The black-and-white sketches of El Mataviejitas follow the photographic tradition of criminal representation. Since its origins in the nineteenth century, photography has been used as a forensic aid and scientific tool to present as "objective" and "neutral" the "facts" of crime scenes and criminals:[5] "the image is intended to function as a kind of evidence, an irrefutable testimony to the existence of facts."[6] These "scientific" interpretations, however, do not consider what has been consistently demonstrated by scholars of criminology—that "facts are not neutral" and they come embedded with the "cultural burden of meaning."[7] For instance, in looking at a sketch of a criminal, and even when in the presence of an alleged criminal, we are predisposed—not only

THE LOOK OF THE SERIAL KILLER | 67

Figure 2.1. Sketches of El Mataviejitas distributed around Mexico City.

because of certain sexed and gendered characteristics of the subject, but also because of certain emotions, like fear—to think of that face as evil. In the case of Mexico's pigmentocratic system, this predisposition is especially problematic because it serves to marginalize mostly mestizo, lower-class citizens, a population that correlates strongly with darker skin color.

The sketches of El Mataviejitas expose the nineteenth-century criminological assumption that photography helped to "identify criminals because, it was believed, he or she looked like one."[8] Although this assumption has long been challenged internationally, in Mexico it continues to inform how criminals are constructed. The sciences of physiognomy and phrenology shared the belief that "the surface of the body, especially the face and head, bore the outward signs of inner character."[9] Based on this notion, a team drawn from the Universidad Nacional Autónoma de México (UNAM—the National Autonomous University of Mexico) and the Mexico City Justice Department collaborated in 1996 to create the CaraMex application, now used throughout Mexico as a tool to identify criminals.

Bernardo Bátiz declared in a 2004 press conference that "the phenotypes [of CaraMex] correspond to indigenous and lower-class Mexicans, most of them men."[10] Through the use of CaraMex to design the sketches of El Mataviejitas, Bátiz continued the nineteenth-century tradition of positive criminology, in criminalizing phenotypically a certain type of Mexican. Moreover, this Mexican criminal type—"indigenous and lower-class," implicitly dark-skinned mestizo—contrasts with the ideal post-independence Mexican, who is white, with a more Spanish phenotype (a further association with economic affluence). Before analyzing how CaraMex was developed to identify what the "face of a Mexican" looks like, a brief history of mestizaje and its relation to criminality in Mexico is necessary.

According to Carlos Serrano, CaraMex's co-creator, the software takes as a point of departure the understanding of Mexico as a country that is in "biological terms mestizo" and in which there is "ostensibly the numeric predominance of these phenotypes," although there are also "different regions and sectors of Mexican society" in which there are "physical features characteristic of the components of the population" that arrived after the sixteenth century.[11] According to Serrano, the success of CaraMex lies in its providing a system of identification that takes into account all the variabilities of the face of Mexicans. Rather than based on an "average" Mexican face, which according to him, is an "abstraction," CaraMex provides a "random sample of the most frequent traits found throughout Mexico and therefore can be chosen more easily when wanting to identify a person."[12]

This approach, however, ignores that the "racial divisions" of the early colony were soon blurred and have been ever since. The developers of CaraMex evidently considered mestizaje to be a plain, biological, neutral fact, in which the physical features of the Indian people identified them as "Indian" solely by their "darker" skin, without considering, as Alan Knight puts it, that "the identity of Indian was invented by Europeans"[13] and that it is largely determined by cultural and social attributes such as "language, dress, religion, social organization, culture and consciousness."[14]

Traditionally, the notion of mestizaje was used throughout Latin America to describe the mixing of races and cultures, specifically between the Spanish and the Indian people as a result of sixteenth-century Spanish colonization.[15] However, mestizaje, rooted in biological discourse, also represented inferiority inasmuch as during the colonial period (1510–1810), within the structure of a race-based caste system, the notion of the mestizo as a "bastard" prevailed.[16] Since colonization, the *sistema colonial de castas* (colonial caste system), a hierarchical system of race classification in New Spain, established a social stratification based on three major demographic groups: "white" or "Spanish," "Indian," and "black." Taxation and legal classification were different for each group—although within the judiciary and in matters of administration, the population was divided into just two entities, Spanish and Indians, while the African slaves were categorized as "merchandise."[17]

The casta system permeated every aspect of life in New Spain, not least the arts. A new subgenre of painting emerged, in oils on canvas or copper plates, which portrayed the new racial mixes as well as the clear social differences to which colonial society had given rise. Casta paintings represented heterosexual couples from different racial groups as well as the outcome of their unions, conventionally a young son. In the best-known works, those of Miguel Cabrera (1695–1768), each image was accompanied by the term that described these subjects within the casta classification system, for educational purposes. For example, within the new casta classification, the following principles were established: of a Spanish man and an Indian woman is born a mestizo; of a Spanish man and a mestiza woman is born a *castizo*; of a *castizo* man and a Spanish woman is born a Spaniard; of a Spanish man and a Negro woman is born a mulatto; of a Spanish man and a mulatto woman is born a *morisco*; of a Spanish man and a *morisco* woman is born an *albino*; of a Spanish man and an *albino* woman is born a *torna-atrás* (roughly, a "turn-back"), and so on. In total, there were sixteen possible combinations.

These classifications were taken as a neutral and objective background for the phenotypes of mestizo Mexicans in the development of CaraMex, without considering that the perception of Indian and part-Indian populations is inscribed within a structure of power in which the persistent racism and classism in Mexico toward those with darker skin is justified. The notion of mestizo, a race in which all Mexicans are the same, has worked only to justify and mask the racism that is rooted in biology. Clearly, "in the obsessive concern with color and status which characterized this *sociedad de castas*, only one thing was certain: to be black or indian was bad, to be white was good."[18] These beliefs, established in the sixteenth century, continued into the twenty-first with the development of CaraMex for criminal-identification purposes. And although the casta system and slavery were officially abolished in 1821, this did not translate into an erasure of these divisions in the everyday life of Mexicans, the state, or of the elites in power, who were the "whiter" *criollos* (Spanish descendants). The casta system was not truly eliminated, but only transformed—both into a rigid class structure and as scientific, biological, and phenotypical knowledge, available to serve as a fundamental component of the "face of the Mexican" for the creators of CaraMex. The main objective of the software, they say, is to show the variability in phenotypes in a mestizo and mestiza presented as objective and neutral; in this way, their "objective" biological standpoint continues to obscure the persistent racism and classism in Mexico.

Historically, mestizos and mestizas have commonly been understood as the mixed descendants of the Spanish and Indians through the literal and metaphorical rape of colonization. However, many scholars have shown the complexity of this construction in which mestizos are not simple, "empirical hybrids," a straightforward result of the biological or cultural mixing of two entities, and that "hybridity is not so much the natural product of an 'us' meeting a 'them' but rather the recognition—or creation—of an 'us' and a 'them.'"[19] In this way, the notion of mestizo suggests "a complex conceptual hybridity" that "has been a product of long-term, unequal dialogues in social fields of domination, exploitation, and subjectification."[20] The CaraMex developers, in accepting the notion of mestizo as a point of departure from which to understand "the face of the Mexican," failed to recognize that the identity of Mestizo and Indian is not biological, not racially determined, but socially, and that the "inherited somatic features of 'Indian' and 'mestizo' people may be indistinguishable, individually or collectively."[21] Approaching mestizos as a solely biological and racial category also fails to consider the cultural connotation of mestizo as inferior that has long informed Mexican discourses on criminality.

Criminology in Mexico emerged as a science during the late nineteenth and early twentieth centuries, representing the "order and progress" necessary for the modernization of society during the Porfiriato (1876–1911). After independence in the early nineteenth century, the process of political stabilization during the Porfiriato made possible material advances while increasing social inequalities in the country as a whole, but especially in Mexico City.[22] Elites saw lower classes, who had been migrating to the city, as "potentially delinquents," and this perception led to a politics of control.[23]

Mexican criminology thus emerged as a reflection of "elites' anxieties about lower-class criminality."[24] These anxieties, "an unacknowledged subtext in officially sanctioned classic criminology, would become a recognized element of mainstream criminological discourse."[25] This criminological discourse left a legacy of a classist, racist, and sexist approach to criminality that is evident both in the creation of CaraMex and the police use of sketches in the search for El Mataviejitas.

In 1892, two Mexican criminologists, Francisco Martínez Baca and Manuel Vergara, published *Estudios de antropología criminal* (Studies of criminal anthropology), an account of research they had been commissioned to perform by the state of Puebla, to be presented at the international exposition in Chicago. Martínez and Vergara developed a "scientific methodology" to determine the characteristics of the Mexican criminal. In addition to biographical data (name, age, religion, sex, trade, and the latitude and climate in which the subject developed), this methodology included craniology (the measurement of the skulls of deceased criminals), anthropometrics, physiognomy, and a psychological study.[26] Martínez and Vergara took photographic images of at least three hundred indigenous inmates and prepared the data set, which was then compared with European data to establish the physiology of criminals.[27] Just like Mexico's first "scientific" criminologist, Rafael de Zayas, Martínez and Vergara concluded that the "ferocious and shocking aspect that most criminals exhibit, whose evil passions are reflected in their visages, . . . is what distinguishes the delinquent man from the honorable man."[28] It was believed that offenders' criminality was innate and reflected in their faces. Photographs of criminals were classified according to type of crime—it was believed, for example, that the "lips of rapists were 'thick and arched' while the lips of robbers were 'plegados' [puckered] and those of murderers, 'thin.'"[29] The look and gaze of the various criminal types were also identified. Martínez and Vergara concluded that murderers had a "glossy, cold, and haughty look," thieves had a "piercing, penetrating, and fixed stare" and "avert their eyes when spoken to," and rapists had "large, protruding eyes, and a clear and bright look."[30]

All the criminals studied by Martínez and Vergara were of the "indigenous race," as they referred to the subjects they analyzed. In none of their classifications of criminals were there upper-class or "whiter"-looking Mexicans. In fact, keeping in mind that "European anthropologists" had established a "general rule that robbery predominated in colder climates, and crimes against people, in hotter climates," Martínez and Vergara stated that, as a "principle," they knew that "Indians were robbers in whichever climate they lived."[31] In their "scientific" study of the brains and skulls of the prisoners held in the Puebla penitentiary, Martínez and Vergara concluded that although Cesare Lombroso's theories of the "born criminal" had been criticized, they should nonetheless be integrated with their studies to find out "which anatomo-pathological characters of each criminal type are so persistent that they resist all kinds of influences and then it is impossible to doubt the truth of those laws."[32] As Robert Buffington points out, this classification served to delimit the characteristics of the criminal Mexican and the ideal Mexican. The criminal Mexican was indigenous or darker-skinned mestizo, while the ideal looked more "Spanish"—that is, white.

Martínez and Vergara followed Francis Galton, who in 1883 introduced the term "eugenics" "to define the study of the hereditary differences of mental, moral, and physical traits amongst individuals, classes and races, and the measurements of social control which could be taken to ensure the general improvement of the species."[33] Galton used eugenics in conjunction with the "methods of analysis and techniques" of composite photography to predict the "incidence of physiological and psychological characteristics between successive generations."[34] Galton believed that "it was possible to predict the occurrence of hereditary character which was the prerequisite for the planned improvement of the race."[35]

Mexican criminologists classified only lower-class offenders, dissolving the "boundary between the criminal and the working-class poor," in accordance with existing racist and colonialist prejudices in Mexico, where the poor classes were commonly indigenous.[36] After independence, elites, in their efforts to make Mexicans modern and European, were concerned with racial mixture, and criminology provided an "objective" language that justified colonialism and racism.[37]

One of the most prominent Mexican criminologists of the twentieth century was Carlos Roumagnac, who wrote *Los criminales en México* (Criminals in Mexico) in 1904. Roumagnac similarly developed a typology of the Mexican criminal through photographs and extensive interviews of both incarcerated men and women, basing his "scientific" methodology on the work of Lombroso and praising Martínez and Vergara's study. Roumagnac's typology system was based on heredity, environment, and circumstance.[38] His typologies classified criminal faces as "ugly" or "attractive," "sad" or "happy," "good" or "bad."[39] Physical attributes like the size of the head (length and width), ears, feet, fingers, forehead, and nose, among other parts of the body, were considered alongside personal background (class) and skin color, defined loosely as a large or small amount of pigment. Rougmanac's "scientific interviews" with the prisoners included asking them whether or not they regretted their crimes, if they knew what regret meant, and if they believed in God, as well as determining their level of education. Rougmanac then decided whether the answers were true—although, of course, he claimed not to *interpret* but to scientifically measure their level of criminality. These "scientific" interpretations in which criminality was believed to be visible, and the result of lack of education and one's environment and economic needs, marginalized mostly lower-class mestizos and mestizas.

Racism and classism toward those with darker skin and a preference for "white features" persists to this day.[40] In contrast, during the post-revolutionary period, a shift to the idealized Mexican as the figure of a bronze mestizo was promoted visually through the muralist movement led by Diego Rivera, Alfaro Siqueiros, and José Clemente Orozco, in which this figure and revolutionary imagery were intertwined. Around the same time, in his 1925 book *La raza cósmica* (The cosmic race), José Vasconcelos, chancellor of the National Autonomous University of Mexico and responsible for commissioning many of the works of the muralist movement, idealized the mestizo as a "superior" race that would "save" all Latino Americans from the "white" dominance of United States.[41] Vasconcelos's "mythohistory" of mestizaje relocated the "beginnings of Mexican history even more firmly in the Aztec past, rather than the Spanish Conquest." His influential writings on the "cosmic race" permeated all aspects of Mexican sociocultural, political, and economic policies. The mestizo was the "cosmic race" as it had blood from Europeans, Asian-descended Native Americans, and Africans, in this way transcending each and embodying a "superior race." Mestizos were idealized as possessing a new "consciousness of their mission as builders of entirely new concepts of life."[42] Although mestizaje was revised in positive terms, becoming the "cornerstone of a new nationalist project, a state-led 'cultural revolution' that was explicitly anti-imperialist and anti-colonialist," racism toward darker-skinned Mexicans has persisted.[43]

In recent years, the notion of mestizaje has been challenged so as to open up a discussion about "skin color differences" and "skin tones," and their relationship to socioeconomic opportunities, economic affluence, and social stratification. Andrés Villarreal, for example, states that in Mexico "skin color is becoming even more important in the allocation of social status."[44] Academic studies on social stratification and skin color have noted their correlation since the early 1960s. For instance, Pierre L. Van den Berghe's research on "comparative race relations" concludes that "the correlation between phenotype and class status also remains; European-looking Mexicans are disproportionately represented in the upper and middle classes; however dark mestizos and Indians are found in significant numbers at all class levels."[45] It would be very difficult to find a system of categorization for skin color differences, since these vary enormously; nonetheless, as Van den Berghe observes, "wealthier Mexicans" consistently tend to prefer "European features" that are "whiter," since these are seen as "positive traits."[46] As such, "whiter" Mexicans tend to "occupy higher socioeconomic positions."[47] Mónica Moreno Figueroa argues that the "*darker* skin tones of the mestiza/o, which nevertheless can vary enormously, do not ultimately have the last word in determining if this group can or cannot (consistently) occupy the space of racial privilege, of whiteness."[48]

Moreno defines the position of "whiteness" as that of "legitimacy and privilege" that is not necessarily associated with "white bodies," drawing from the "framework of recent critical studies on whiteness."[49] That is, not all "white" bodies occupy sites of legitimacy and privilege, because of the specific historical junctions of "social categories such as labor, class, gender, education and taste."[50] Borrowing from Moreno's work, in the case of Mexico, this project takes the notion of "whiteness" as "a social norm that is relational and contextual, normalized and ambiguous."[51] To attain "whiteness" in Mexico means more than just possessing a determined skin color; it depends on "where, when and with whom you are" and requires a "daily exercise of comparison and self-assessment."[52] In this way, "privilege is available to those that inhabit whiteness, but it can easily be taken away because such inhabiting is precarious."[53]

Mexicans with darker skin "have significantly lower levels of educational attainment and occupational status, and they are more likely to live in poverty and less likely to be affluent, even after controlling for other individual characteristics."[54] Further, they are the objects of "racism" and "may in fact face discrimination in the labor market."[55] In this way, skin color in Mexico determines privilege, legitimacy, affluence, education level, and labor opportunities. As obvious and unsurprising at it sounds, all insults in Spanish refer to lower-class individuals, *nacos*, to *indios*, and to those who do not have a mother (and therefore are imagined capable of anything). *Indio* is an insult because it denies part of our identity, a self-hate—not recognizing myself in myself or the other.

CaraMex considers mestizaje as a "biological" prime, an objective and scientific fact of the many variabilities that the face of the Mexican can have, but ignores that the phenotypes of the Mexicans in its archive are those of the lower-class mestizos, mostly male, revealing assumptions about class, gender, sex, and skin color that have characterized Mexican criminology since the nineteenth century. The pigmentocratic social system of Mexico that was evident in photographs that served the Porfirian elite in criminalizing, through phenotypes, the indigenous, mestizos and mestizas, the rural, and the poor is perpetuated with CaraMex.

La Cara del Mexicano

CaraMex was created between 1993 and 1996 primarily by Carlos Serrano Sánchez and María Villanueva Sagrado, physical anthropology researchers from the Institute of Anthropological Research (IIA) at UNAM. Jesús Luy and Arturo Romano, representatives of the Mexico City Department of Justice, were also involved, and engineer Karl F. Link was responsible for the programming.

The objective was to create a system of identification based on facial features. For the creators of CaraMex, "features express in their whole a singularity, an identity, that works to recognize the individual," that is, to identify criminals.[56] The promise of CaraMex was that its images would be more "objective," "scientific," and "precise" than a *portrait parlé*, or hand-drawn sketch, which has the "natural propensity to establish a personal artistic style."[57] CaraMex would also be more cost effective, because less time is required to produce a computer sketch than a *portrait parlé* and the process can be done by anyone with a minimal amount of training as opposed to requiring a skilled artist.

The software tried to compile the variability of the phenotype of the mestizo Mexican population through the creation of an archive of different facial features and accessories. The final archive was made using photographs of "2,890 individuals, of which 1,285 are female and 1,605 are male."[58]

In the information provided to the public about CaraMex, the software is introduced by way of Alphonse Bertillon's system of criminal identification. Bertillon, a Paris police official, invented the first modern system of criminal identification by codifying social statistics in the 1830s and 1840s into anthropometrics, using the optical precision of the camera and a refined physiognomic vocabulary. Under the premise that the software shows only the phenotypes as they present themselves in a given instance through a photograph, CaraMex's creators (like Bertillon) did not take into account what Allan Sekula pointed out: that "the camera is integrated into a larger ensemble: a bureaucratic-clerical statistical system of 'intelligence.'"[59] Similarly, Serrano and Villanueva used the precision of the camera to create "objective" phenotypes of the Mexican face for the purpose of criminal identification, ignoring that the selection of these phenotypes and the use of the camera are invested in ideol-

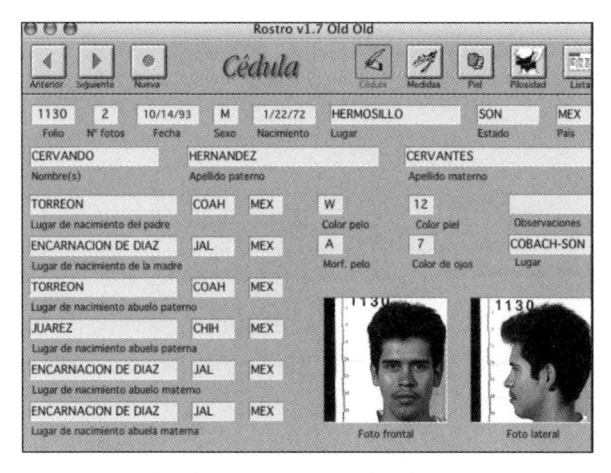

Figure 2.2. Screenshot of CaraMex software.

ogies of mestizaje and their relation to presumptions about criminality. In their presentation, the CaraMex developers show that in creating a "complete" archive they took samples of phenotypes from certain "Mexican families," from all the regions of Mexico where indigenous communities live, such as Otomí, Mixteca, Tzotzil, Maya—and, it also states, "Chinese"—as well as to regions like the coast of the Gulf of Mexico, and from the North and Mexico City. In their attempt to represent all of Mexico's mestizo population, researchers included photographs from individuals from all over the country, both rural and urban, indigenous and mestizo. But the resulting software fails to show the subtext: that indigenous and poor mestizo populations are more likely to be criminalized than Mexicans with more European features.

In its collection of digital photographs, CaraMex followed Bertillon's system. The photographs were taken following the standard he established—frontal and left profile of each individual—with the same distance and lighting used in each. While constructing the archive, aside from the photographs, the creators collected personal data that focused on the origin of each subject's parents and (just like Rougmanac and Martínez and Vergara) noted the "shape and color of the hair, the eye color and the skin color" of the individuals photographed.[60] To complete the bank of information, a cephalometric (head measurement) analysis and "morphoscope and morphometric measurements" were also included.

What CaraMex hides under its language of "objectivity" and "neutrality" is that physiognomy necessitates an "interpretative process." The isolation of the profile of the head and its various anatomic features, in order to assign a characterological significance to each (e.g., forehead, eyes, ears, nose, chin), further hides that physiognomy requires interpretation by the culture in which it develops.[61] It hides that the skin color, the color of the eyes, the expression lines that have to be recorded on the identification card are all characteristics interpreted by the subject doing the analysis, not simple or neutral facts that are impartial.

The final archive of CaraMex contains 466 files. Of these, 405 are distributed in twenty-six different directories of facial features, from the general form of the head to the particular characteristics of a face, including "wrinkles, or warts and moles."[62] The rest of the files are contained in three directories under the rubric of "accessories": "earrings, lenses and various types of hats."[63] As with Bertillon's system, "the assignation of interpretative process required that distinctive individual features be read in conformity to a type."[64]

The anthropologists behind CaraMex ignore what Sekula pointed out about Bertillon's "criminal archive": that it "came to existence on the basis of mutual comparison, on the basis of the tentative construction of a larger 'universal' archive, that zones of deviance and respectability could be clearly demarcated." In "The Body and the Archive," Sekula talks about an inclusive archive and a shadow archive. The broad archive "necessarily contains both the traces of the visible bodies of heroes, leaders, moral exemplars, and celebrities and those of the poor, the diseased, the insane, the criminal, the nonwhite, the female, and all other embodiments of the unworthy."[65] Left out of the CaraMex archive are those mestizos who can occupy spaces of privilege within the pigmentocratic system of Mexico, that is, the mestizos whose other social attributes like class, gender, and labor occupy the space of privilege that "whiteness" offers.

Offering an "automated *portrait parlé* backed up scientifically, which requires little time and produces facial images very close to reality,"[66] CaraMex has been praised as a success and adopted by justice departments throughout Mexico. The reality that CaraMex gets close to, though, is the reality of a pigmentocratic system in which "the criminal body has already been defined as criminal by means that subordinate the image"[67]—that is, a criminalized body in terms of gender, class, and skin color.

CaraMex's anthropologist co-creator Carlos Serrano—while believing personally that criminality is not innate but a result of environmental circumstances, and thus not visible in physical traits—acknowledges the contribution of Benjamín A. Martínez, who created the *Manual para el operario* (operation manual) (1930) for the identification of inmates based on qualitative facial characters. Indeed, Serrano considers Martínez a "valuable forerunner of forensic anthropology in our country."[68] Serrano walks a delicate line; despite his own understanding of criminality as a result of economic needs and environmental causes, he and his software treat phenotypes and photographic images as objective and neutral—as showing a scientific truth without acknowledging the underlying subtext of racism and classism in Mexico.

The forensic and physical anthropologists who created CaraMex consider photographs as "scientific truth," even in the face of the Bertillon system's failures. Yet CaraMex's photographs, like those in the archive compiled by Bertillon, are "deployed not only against the body of the representative criminal, but also against that body as a bearer and producer of its own inferior representations."[69]

"Se buscan" "¡Ayúdanos a prevenir!"

The two composites of El/La Mataviejitas created using CaraMex based on eyewitness accounts were presented publicly in August 2005. The composite sketches appeared side by side under the banner "Se buscan" (Wanted). Underneath, text reads "¡Ayúdanos a prevenir!" (Help us to prevent!), "Si lo has visto, llámanos" (If you have seen them [masculine plural], call us), and "Están relacionados con los homocidios de las adultas mayores" (They are related to the homicides of elderly women)[70] (fig. 2.3). The poster also lists emergency police phone numbers. Although the poster does not specify whether the sketches represent a man or a woman, the police declarations and media narrations accompanying the sketches implied that El Mataviejitas was a man and always referred to the serial killer as "he."

The news reports covering the release of the sketches referred to a male serial killer who was believed to be responsible for the homicides of at least four elderly women, quoting chief prosecutor Bernardo Bátiz, who stated that the sketches were based on the testimony of eyewitnesses who had "directly seen the [male] serial killer."[71] Paying close attention to the sketches—which appear to depict either a woman or a feminized man—and to the news and media narration about them—which referred to a male serial killer—reveals an important contradiction concerning the sex and gender of the figure they portray. This raises questions about their usefulness, their "neutral" and "objective" portrayal of the serial killer, and both the actual knowledge of and the biases held by police in their search. The sketches, rather a scientific tool to help detain the serial killer, seem to be based more on assumptions of what the serial killer should look like—that is, a man.

The two sketches presented side by side in 2005 do not seem to resemble each other. The sketch on the right resembles a woman, with shorter hair and some bangs, while the sketch on the left could be a man; their features are very different, as well. It is not clear if they are portraying one potential El Mataviejitas or two. In contrast, the sketches provided to me by Comandante Moneda are from a manual that was produced by French police for use by their Mexican counterparts (fig. 2.4). At the beginning of January 2006, one hundred Mexican agents were educated about serial killing by three French police officers in a week-long, thirty-hour course. It was believed the course would be useful because the Mataviejitas case was determined to be like that of Paulin Thierry, the Monster of Montmartre.

In 1987, Thierry was arrested and convicted in Paris for the killings of over twenty elderly women. He was a young, gay, HIV-positive, unemployed transvestite from Martinique whose otherness in France was inextricably linked to his crimes.[72] As Thierry had cross-dressed and killed elderly women, police in Mexico believed El Mataviejitas was also a male serial killer who enjoyed dressing in women's clothing, as a nurse specifically, to kill similar victims. Mexican police therefore modeled sketches after Thierry, believing the serial killer they sought was a "feminized" man.

Composite sketches, in this case created with CaraMex, allowed the witnesses to select from among a repertoire of eyes, ears, mouths, chins, hair, and so on, to create an image that ideally encompassed all of the features of the perpetrator. As several US studies have concluded, however, "facial composite systems produce a poor likeness of the intended target face."[73] In large part, this is because witnesses see the person's face

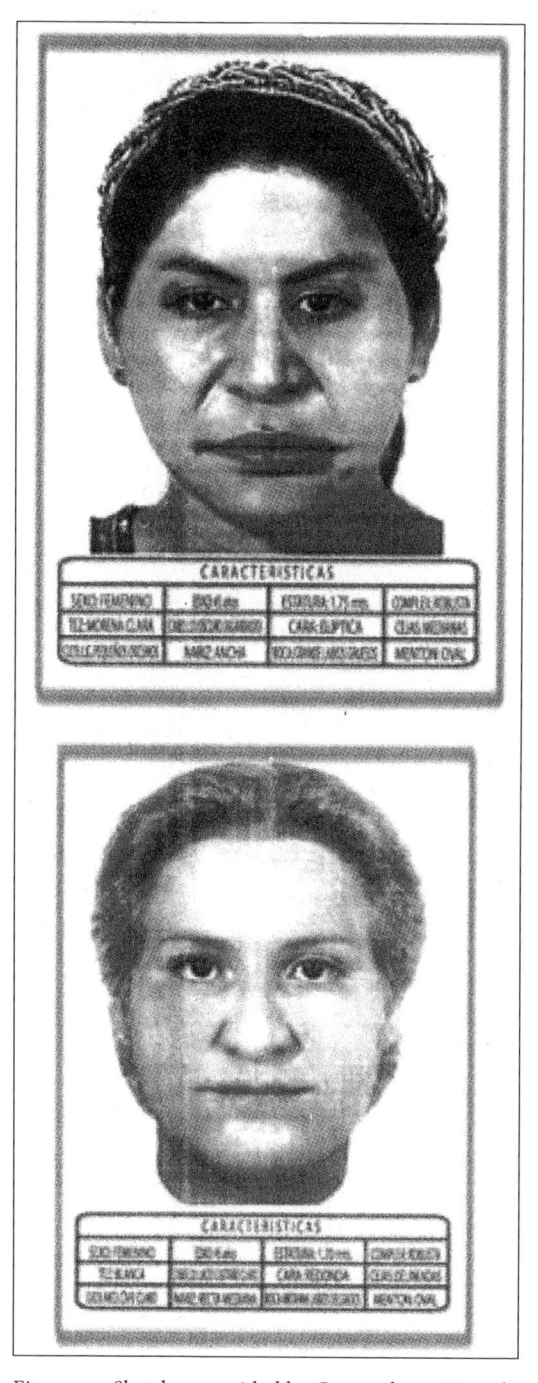

Figure 2.3. Sketches provided by Comandante Moneda.

as a whole instead of as an assemblage of specific features. Even if computer software allowed witnesses to describe the face as a whole instead of focusing on details, research suggests this approach would equally fail to produce a likeness of a specific face.[74] Many factors influence the accuracy of a composite sketch, for example, the capacity of a witness to communicate the appearance of the suspect. Composite photographs could produce an approximation of a suspect but not the "objective" and absolute features of the actual serial killer. What is important to highlight here is that regardless of whether composite software works, the images it produces are not "objective" and, further, composite faces result in an image more similar to an "average" individual than to the specific features of a particular one.[75]

By early October, two months after the citywide distribution of the sketches, a total of forty-six people had been taken to police stations, fingerprinted, and photographed based on their resemblance to the images of El Mataviejitas.[76] In addition, more than three hundred people were interviewed by police after witnesses had reported "their resemblance to the sketches."[77] Some media reports claimed that more than five hundred people were detained as possible suspects.[78] The resemblance of the sketches to so many people calls into question the "neutrality" and "objectivity" of the sketches precisely because they resemble a sort of "average." Although narratives on serial killing commonly refer to serial killers as ordinary citizens—that is, people who look "just like you or me"—police use sketches they claim portray the specific features of one individual.

Furthermore, considering the assumption by police and news reports that El Mataviejitas was a man, contradicting eyewitness accounts, it is significant that most newspaper reports and police statements did not specify the sex and gender of the detainees and invariably referred to them with the masculine plural. They could still have been considering the possibility that the killer was female, because in the Spanish language the plural is always masculine and presumably includes both men and women, but when referring specifically to the serial killer, the police and media always spoke about *El* Mataviejitas. Only one report at the time, in the newspaper *Crónica*, stated that both men and women had been detained and interrogated because of their resemblance to the sketches.[79] From the other reports, readers are left to assume that most of (if not all of) the subjects interrogated and photographed were men.

Photography and composite sketches have made the body readable as a text. The readable content in this case is the associations made between the composite of El Mataviejitas and the codified characteristics of the serial killer, who, despite witness accounts of an individual resembling and dressing like a woman, is constantly talked about as a middle-aged man, following the sexed and gendered stereotyping of serial killers. Not only was the killer believed to be a man, but the narration that accompanied the sketches characterized him as "astute," of "brilliant intelligence," and "cautious," who acted alone and was "smart enough to know not to leave fingerprints," further aligning El Mataviejitas with the international profiling of serial killers.[80]

As noted, the "average" individual in Mexico is mestizo, commonly codified as a lower-class individual with relatively dark skin. While the black-and-white sketches did not directly suggest skin tone, the features represented correspond to those of a racialized Mexican. The features depicted in the composite sketches are based on those of indigenous, mestizo, lower-class Mexicans, as stated by chief prosecutor Bátiz. The sketches do not portray faces with more "European" features, that is to say, those that normally correspond to upper-middle-class Mexicans. The sketches clearly do not portray an upper- or middle-class individual; on the contrary, they reinforce the nineteenth-century idea that criminality is associated with indigenous and darker mestizo individuals, without acknowledging that this very notion is permeated by cultural understandings and historical fears of who a criminal is and what he or she looks like. The sketches in this case make visible a racist, classist, and sexist "scientific" approach to criminality prevalent in Mexico since the nineteenth century.

And while the sketches of El Mataviejitas seem to portray a woman and/or a feminized man (fig. 2.4), they are also steeped in assumptions based on international accounts of serial killing, in which the criminal is consistently male. A week after the release of the sketches, the newspaper *Reforma* reported that the Mexico City Justice Department had given a detailed account of the psychological profile of El Mataviejitas: a middle-aged homosexual male who was abused during childhood and grew up surrounded by women. According to police, "other serial killers of elderly women have been sexually abused during childhood and hated geriatric women."[81] Police also made specific reference to Thierry,

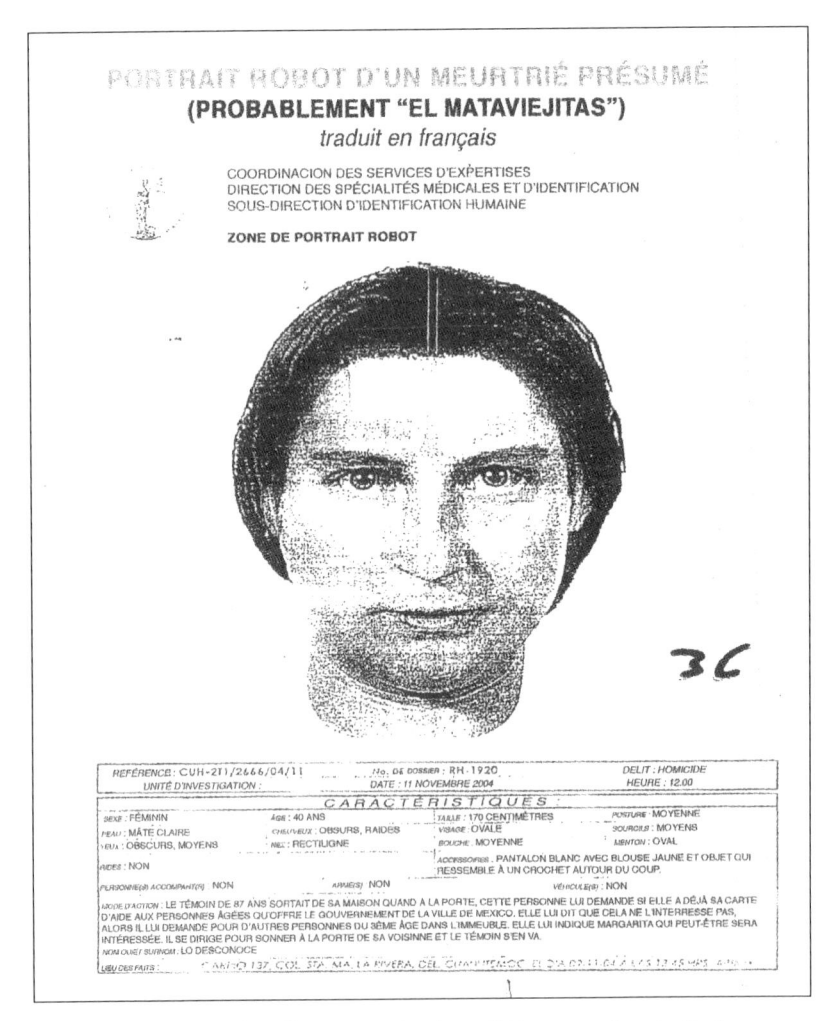

Figure 2.4. "Portrait robot d'un meurtrié présumé" (Automated portrait of a suspected murderer)—sketch provided by Comandante Moneda.

the Monster of Montmartre.[82] So again, that psychological profile had more in common with a "prototype" of a serial killer than with information gathered by the police in their own investigation.

Two years into the investigation, police presented both a physical and a psychological profile of El/La Mataviejitas. According to the physical profile, the killer was "a man, dressed as a woman, or a robust woman, dressed in white, height between 1.70 and 1.75 meters, robust complexion, light brown, oval face, wide cheeks, blonde hair, delineated eyebrows, approximately 45 years old."[83] As for the psychological profile, police stated that they were looking for "a man with homosexual preferences, victim of childhood physical abuse, lived surrounded by women, he could have had a grandmother or lived with an elderly person, has resentment toward that feminine figure, and possesses great intelligence."[84] This profile of El/La Mataviejitas resembles that of Thierry, who "dressed as a woman" to kill elderly women, had "homosexual preferences," and in his childhood had lived with his grandmother, who was physically abusive to him.[85] According to Mexican police, Thierry also gained the trust of his elderly victims before killing them and, as in the case of El/La Mataviejitas, "robbed small amounts of money from their homes."[86] Philippe Dussaix, an inspector from the criminal unit of the Regional Directorate of the Judicial Police of Paris who conducted the week-long police training course in Mexico City, stated that Thierry had not been arrested as a result of "chance or luck, because that does not exist." According to Dussaix, Thierry was arrested due to the work done by police, "especially a sketch made after witness accounts."[87] This statement further suggests the extent to which Mexican police based their profile of El/La Mataviejitas on international assumptions about serial killing—and specifically on the case of the Monster of Montmartre—including their belief that sketches are key to the arrest of a serial killer. What is astonishing is that the police in Mexico ignored eyewitness accounts (of a woman) and instead based their assumptions about El/La Mataviejitas on the case of the Monster of Montmartre, despite explicit instructions from the French police that sketches of serial killers should be based on witnesses' accounts.

The physical profile given of El/La Mataviejitas clashes significantly with the psychological one. According to the physical profile, police were looking for a man dressed as a woman or a robust woman, while according to the psychological profile, they sought a man with homosexual tendencies. This may be because, as Bátiz stated, "there is no certainty" of the sex of the serial killer, but police were certain of "many elements" of the killer's "behavioral traits" in determining the psychological profile.[88] The fact that police had more certainty of the psychological profile than of the physical one—despite numerous descriptions by witnesses—again leads to the conclusion that the authorities aligned the profile of

El/La Mataviejitas primarily with that of Thierry, the alleged Monster of Montmartre.

Cultural prejudice, ignorance, discrimination, and homophobia consequently led to the detention of travesti sex workers in late October 2005. While the Spanish term "travesti" is commonly translated in English as "transvestite" or "cross-dresser," I subscribe to Cabral and Viturro's view that the term is used in Latin America to designate "those persons that having been assigned the masculine gender at birth have chosen to identify themselves in different versions of femininity and who may or may not surgically or hormonally modify their bodies."[89] Travestis are organized in "a struggle, which is conceived as the articulation and the process by which modes of control and reproduction of political systems of hegemonic relations are questioned."[90] Most importantly, more than just choosing to dress in clothing traditionally assigned to the opposite gender/sex, as transvestites and cross-dressers do, travestis are organized in a political and social struggle for the "state and society [to] accept *travestismo* as an identity of its own."[91] Travesti thus not only defines a gender identity, it is a political and activist category, whose members seek to become legal subjects: "being travesti is not the same as being transgender and without SRS [sex reassignment surgery]; it is another space and another identity outside the structures of sex and gender normativity that is specific to Latin American sites."[92]

As such, the gender-sex identity of travesti cannot be translated into English accurately without political, social, and cultural contextualization. The term in Spanish brings together a generalized condition of social vulnerability, an association with sex work, exclusion from basic civil rights, and the acknowledgment of a unique political identity. Many travestis use the term *vestida* to refer to one another. "Vestida" literally translates as "dressed," feminized by the terminal "a." Travestis in Mexico use the term to stand against the historical marginalization of their communities.

Since investigators had established that El Mataviejitas's pattern involved the use of "great physical force," and witnesses had described a "man or robust woman with very manly characteristics that possibly used a wig"[93] as well as "a thick layer of makeup,"[94] police concluded that El Mataviejitas must be a travesti. Only a travesti, authorities decided, could possess the physical strength necessary to kill an elderly woman and at the same time wear makeup and women's clothing. The possibility of a female serial killer escaped their imaginations.

At the end of October, two weeks after chief prosecutor Bátiz had stated that "the [male] serial killer is 1.70 meters, robust and dresses as a woman, although the sex of the offender has not been determined," between thirty-eight and fifty[95] travesti sex workers were arrested, taken into custody, and photographed, their fingerprints taken and compared with those left by the serial killer. I believe that when Bátiz referred to the profile of El Mataviejitas as that of a "male serial killer whose sex has not been determined," he confused sex and gender, and what he was trying to say was that the "sexual orientation" of the serial killer had not been determined. Determining the killer's sexuality was crucial to the police, who were searching for a homosexual subject, based on the case of Thierry.

Social and cultural changes, however unevenly, have been taking place in Mexico regarding the acceptance of homosexuality, suggesting that homosexual communities are now accepted as part of the national identity. While in 1996, Claudia Schaefer called the recognition of homosexuality a national "illusion,"[96] there have been significant shifts. For instance, in 2006 same-sex civil unions were recognized under state legislation, and in 2010 same-sex marriage and same-sex adoptions became legal in Mexico City. In 2015, Mexico City was declared by its then mayor, Miguel Ángel Mancera, a "gay-friendly city"—in Spanish, more precisely, "una ciudad amigable LGBTTTI" (lesbian, gay, bisexual, transgender, transsexual, travesti, and intersexual). Though these advances have been important, openly gay writers like Luis Zapata, for instance, believe that the victories of same-sex communities have benefited only those in Mexico City, with few exceptions.[97] Gays and trans subjects, especially from the working class, continue to suffer discrimination, hate crimes, and homophobic acts. Much of Mexico's social and political changes are centralized in Mexico City and largely benefit those with wealth, mobility, and social capital—in this case, those homosexual communities that already occupy the spaces of privilege that whiteness offers in Mexico. While Mexico has joined the international LGBTTTI struggle in recognizing the importance of, for example, gay marriage and the reputation of being a gay-friendly city, this has not translated into progress for all gay, homosexual, trans, and queer communities.

Indeed, it can be argued that the recognition of gay marriage in Mexico is the result of the emergence of homonationalism in a neoliberal context.[98]

According to Dean Spade, there is considerable evidence of how the laws of inclusion and anti-discrimination, like gay marriage, do not work (when they do not seek results that radically modify the distribution of privileges, but remain as merely legal measures) because (1) they are not effective as dissuasive measures (for example, a person does not stop committing a homophobic act because there is a law that punishes them); (2) they create a false impression that the excluded community, thanks to the law, is finally being treated like any other (politicians, for example, can say that they have already done their work and that we are all equal before the law, when in practice there are still dismissals due to discrimination or inequality in access to opportunities); and, above all, (3) they do not modify the economic and power structures from which they arise.[99]

A 2016 press release from the Comisión de Derechos Humanos del Distrito Federal (Human Rights Commission of Mexico City) seemed to recognize these truths: while it hailed the forthcoming "celebrations in June, the month of gay pride, featuring the LGBTTTI pride march XXXVIII 'All the Families, All the Rights'" as representing "an opportunity to strengthen, endorse, and advance the respect and promotion of the human rights of LGBTTTI people," it made a point of condemning the recent "killing of seven people as a result of the shootings in the LGBTTI bar 'Madam,'" in Veracruz, plus the "1,310 homophobic hate crimes that have happened in Mexico between 1995 and 2015, that is, an average of 5.4 people a month."[100] And these are the official numbers; the Citizens Commission against Homophobic Hate Crimes argues that many more cases have gone unreported.

This data is backed up by a report from the gay rights group Letra S, which states that Mexico is second on the list of countries with the most hate crimes against homosexuals.[101] The report includes an analysis of the killing of gay men between 1995 to 2010 as reported in *La Prensa*, a nota roja periodical in Mexico City.[102] Although the report does not specify the social class of those murdered as a result of homophobia, it would not be a stretch to suggest that many of them are of lower social status.

Although gay marriage might be considered a huge accomplishment for the LGBTTTI movement in Mexico (in only twelve of the country's thirty-one states, plus Mexico City, is gay marriage completely legal; in the rest, local laws require that a same-sex couple seeking to get married first acquire a writ of amparo, or protection of their constitutional rights), it has not translated into fewer hate crimes, or even less discrimination. The legalization of gay marriage has sparked more hate and discrimination among some Catholic groups. More than 80 percent of the country is Catholic, for whom gay marriage and adoption go against the "basic family structure."[103] After the Supreme Court ruling that legalized gay marriage throughout Mexico, the Frente Nacional por la Familia (National Front for the Family) organized at least 120 different protests all over the country. On September 17, 2016, thousands of religious people, including Catholics, evangelicals, and Mormons, protested in different states against gay marriage and adoption.[104]

An ultra-right Catholic organization known as El Yunque (The Anvil), which had operated secretly in Mexico since the 1950s, recently came forward as the "hand behind" the Frente Nacional por la Familia. Leaders of El Yunque, many of whom also hold prominent positions in the right-wing party PAN, wield considerable political power in Mexico; during the 2018 presidential campaign, the group argued for the PAN candidate, Ricardo Anaya, as promising a "presidency of the family."[105]

In the hunt for El Mataviejitas, police raided the (mostly) lower-class areas of Mexico City where travesti sex workers are known to work. Why didn't police look for the potential travesti serial killer or male homosexual serial killer in the gay bars in the upper- and upper-middle-class neighborhoods of Condesa and Polanco? In my opinion, based on a few observations of gay bars in Mexico City, class defines gender transgression in the capital. Among the middle and upper classes, gay and lesbian bars rarely transgress their respective genders. That is, in middle- and upper-class gay bars in Mexico City, the clientele are either "masculine" gay men or "feminine" lesbians. On the other hand, gender is more often transgressed in working-class bars. These spaces are occupied much more by "effeminate" and "feminine" gay men and by "masculine" and "butch" lesbians.

Because economic survival occupies a central role in Mexico and Latin America in general—much more so than in the United States—labor becomes a main point of contention in a socially stratified society. Middle-class and working-class subjects have a very different range of employment possibilities; there is a lot of discrimination in Mexico City based on how the privilege of whiteness is perceived to be inhabited. Vestidas and travestis, who frequently work in beauty salons or are sex workers, commonly have a lower-class status. Subjects who mainly identify as gays tend to have more middle- or upper-class status and are much less effeminate than travestis or vestidas. Much of the time, gender transgressions correspond to the spectrum of labor available to working classes, which is very different from that for middle classes. In Mexico, these class differences are part of an economic system that is embedded in a pigmentocratic society endemic to colonization. In a conventional and Catholic culture, any sexed and gendered transgression by the working and lower classes further contributes to an already perceived deviance.

To return to the detention of dozens of travestis in October 2005, police determined that none of the fingerprints collected matched those found at the crime scenes. Declaring there had been no discriminatory intent in the travesti roundup, Bátiz stated that "the serial killer might not be a travesti but we are sure he is *transgénero* [transgender]."[106] The continuing impossibility of conceiving of a female serial killer exposed the gendered construction of criminality that framed the manhunt. Bátiz's persistent belief that El Mataviejitas must be someone who fell outside the norms of mexicanidad—a transgendered person, for example—exposes a dominant homophobic and transphobic ideology in which nonnormatively gendered and sexed bodies are already read as criminal.

According to Sekula, photography "came to establish and delimit the terrain of the *other*, to define both the *generalized look*—the typology—and the *contingent insistence* of deviance and social pathology."[107] The "other" Sekula talks about is the criminal who has traditionally been photographed for identification and classification and whose otherness separates the normal from the "abnormally normal." In Mexico, the other and the abnormally normal are the serial killer and the nonnormative genders and peripheral sexualities, the travestis, those who occupy the liminal space between genders. Travesti working-class subjects are consistently othered and criminalized because their gender, sexuality, and class are perceived as deviant. The sketches used by police in this case in fact depicted a "prototype" of a criminal instead of El

Mataviejitas. Police were searching for an archetype—who, in Mexico, is clearly not a middle- or upper-middle-class (homosexual) individual but a lower- or working-class nonnormative-gendered subject. Further, police equated homosexuality with sexual failure, which in turn is commonly correlated with serial killing. Sexual failure or sexual compulsion (cannibalism, for instance) is linked to serial killers in many popular-culture narratives, such as the internationally successful film *The Silence of the Lambs* (1991).[108] The serial killer is portrayed as both an attractive and repulsive figure, a brilliant and calculating mind whose desire to kill is a result of pathological sexual desires. Caroline Picart and Cecil Greek, in "The Compulsion of Real/Reel Serial Killers and Vampires: Toward a Gothic Criminology," explore the striking similarities between the figure of the serial killer and the mythic figure of the vampire, the way both are represented as superhuman charismatic predators who kill out of compulsion, mostly sexual.[109] Similarly, Seltzer has signaled that the identity of the serial killer is commonly intertwined with that of the sex criminal.[110]

There is no evidence of sexual violence in either police or media narratives of El/La Mataviejitas—even if one can argue for a Foucauldian power relation with the victims that is potentially sexual. In other words, if one were to argue that El/La Mataviejitas killed for the pleasure of killing, because of having the "power" to do it (being a robust, strong person murdering weak, defenseless, and vulnerable elderly women), the power in itself could be read as pleasure, and all power could potentially be sexual. I would rather argue that the profiling of El Mataviejitas as a homosexual, and thus a sexual failure, follows the international assumption that the acts of a serial killer (as a sex criminal) represent those of a particular "species of person."[111]

From El Mataviejitas as "Brilliant" to La Mataviejitas as "Pathological"

On the afternoon of January 25, 2006, in a working-class Mexico City neighborhood, a renter was coming home when he noticed that his elderly landlady's door was open. Stepping into the doorway to say hello, he saw his landlady, Ana María Reyes Alfaro, strangled on the floor. He also saw a woman fleeing the crime scene. He exited the house and started shouting, "¡Policía! ¡Policía!"[112] Two police officers on patrol heard him. After a brief chase—the woman was running against the traffic—the officers captured her. The woman running from the victim's house—who was carrying two plastic bags that, according to news reports, contained a stethoscope and a list of beneficiaries of the government program Sí Vale—was Juana Barraza Samperio.

The two police officers immediately called their boss and said, "We captured La Mataviejitas," to which he replied, "Really?"[113] Within minutes, the media, Bátiz, and a host of officials were on the scene. As one headline the next day put it, "Mataviejitas Falls after Committing Another Crime: It Is a Woman."[114] Police officers stated that when they detained Barraza they "knew right away" that she was the killer they were hunting for—despite the fact they had been searching for a man. According to the officers who arrested Barraza, "the sketches were very similar [to Barraza] and when more police officers showed up at the crime scene they stated the same."[115] Never mind that more than five hundred people had been brought to police stations as potential suspects because of their resemblance to the sketches.[116]

More than determining whether and to what extent the sketches resemble Barraza, I argue that they simply did not assist in her arrest. In fact, before she was finally apprehended in January 2006, Barraza had gone "at least three times to the Mexico City Justice Department." Reportedly she went to "surrender" but then changed her mind and went back home.[117] According to one news report, she once lingered outside a police station where Bátiz was on site. She observed the officers coming and going, but then thought of her children; not wanting to abandon them, she left, said her lawyer Juan Mendoza.[118] Yet before she was identified as La Mataviejitas, nobody recognized her supposed similarity to the sketches—not even the officers at a police station when she was (allegedly) the most-wanted criminal in the land. But as soon as Barraza was called La Mataviejitas, news reports and criminologists focused on her resemblance to the sketches, though they almost never specified what the "similarities" were. More than one news report on the day of her capture, for example, showed a photograph of Barraza right next to one of the sketches.

What's more, Barraza had been interviewed during a wrestling event at the Arena Coliseo by TV Azteca only a week before she was arrested and declared La Mataviejitas. In the nationally televised interview, Barraza talked with enthusiasm about how much she enjoyed lucha libre and how she identified as a ruda.[119] Although the program was broadcast on national TV, no one—not the police or news media, or members of the public—identified Barraza as appearing "very similar" to the sketches. In addition, the subject of a sculptural bust depicting the serial killer created for the police (which I analyze below) wears a red sweater; in her televised interview, Barraza was actually wearing a red sweater and *still* nobody identified her as La Mataviejitas. Barraza also wore a red sweater on the day of her arrest—and this time, the "resemblance" was treated as evidence that Barraza was indeed La Mataviejitas. But on national TV, Barraza in her red sweater had been perceived as just another very enthusiastic lucha libre participant.

Among all of the images created and distributed by the police, one three-dimensional bust in particular has been used to demonstrate that Barraza was indeed La Mataviejitas; it is now on permanent display in the Police Cultural Center (fig. 2.5). The bust—routinely referred to as a "sketch"—was created in November 2005 by Patricia Payán of the Mexico City Justice Department following the same principles as the CaraMex sketches: based on the information from all the sketches, Payán manually constructed a three-dimensional composite of *plastilina* (plasticine or modeling clay). Before Barraza's arrest, no media report attributed a specific sex or gender to the bust. After her arrest, though, the bust's supposed resemblance to Barraza was praised by the media. As with the sketches previously analyzed, this three-dimensional work served primarily as a reassurance to the public that police had a detailed understanding of who they were looking for. Press and police accounts repeatedly refered to the similarities between the three-dimensional bust and Barraza herself, especially pointing to the fact that "both the sketch and Juana Barraza were wearing a red-colored sweater,"[120] but, as just mentioned, neither police nor media identified these similarities when Barraza appeared in a red sweater on national TV. When she was arrested and called La Mataviejitas, the color of her sweater was read as a "sign of aggressiveness." In addition, one report noted that "the corpulent build, the dyed hair, and the height of Barraza coincide totally with the three-dimensional sketch of La Mataviejitas."[121] Since the three-dimensional composite is just a bust, I wonder how Barraza's "corpulent build" and "height" could be detected in it.

94 | THE LOOK OF THE SERIAL KILLER

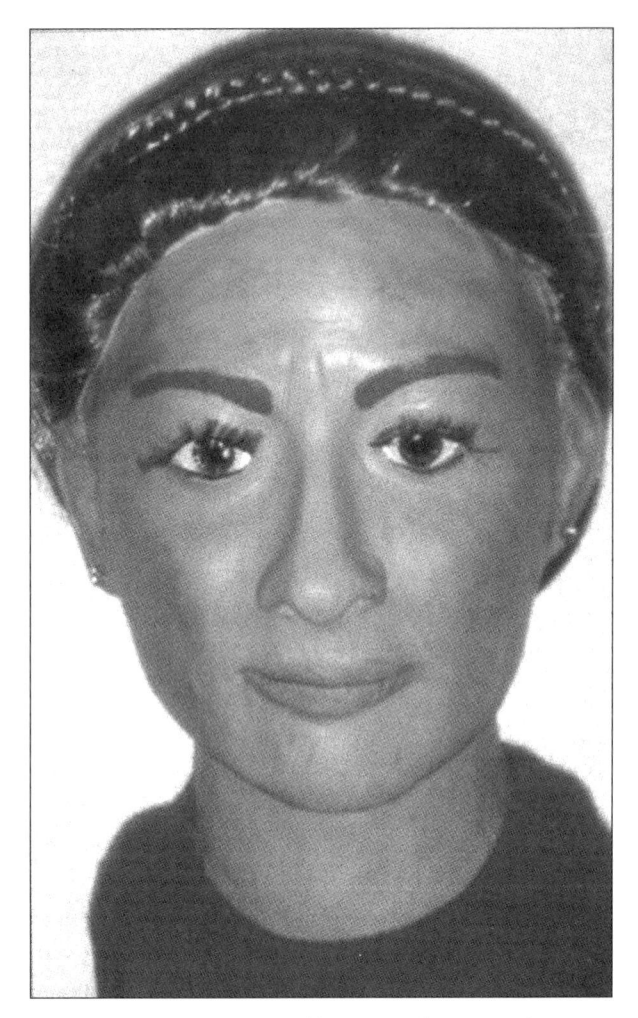

Figure 2.5. Three-dimensional bust created in November 2005 by Patricia Payán of the Mexico City Department of Justice.

Barraza does not wear glasses and there are no known accounts or images of her wearing a bandana. The bust as it now appears in the Police Cultural Center, and in a photo published in *El nudo del silencio*, by Martín Barrón, has no glasses but features a hair bandana, while photos printed in Mexican newspapers after Barraza's arrest portray the bust with both glasses and a bandana. Whether the bust resembles Barraza or not is important only because, as mentioned earlier, composite sketches could potentially resemble many different people, but they were nonetheless used as evidence to criminalize Barraza as the one and only Mataviejitas. It is also important to note that police and criminologists would repeatedly claim that the bust does resemble Barraza, presenting this as proof that the sketches were key in the capture of La Mataviejitas, even though Barraza was detained by chance. Two police officers ran after a woman without knowing what she had done and without having seen her face. The officers who captured Barraza were not following any clues provided by the sketches, but simply answering an individual's cries for help. The arrest of La Mataviejitas was similar to that of the Monster of Montmarte: a result of luck, not sketches.

Police and media narrations aimed to persuade the public that Barraza's arrest was due to knowledge about who the serial killer was and the scientific evidence shown in the sketches. In doing so, they chose to focus on the apparent "similarities," although the only specific similarity most mention is the red sweater worn by both the bust and Barraza. Since police and anthropologists believed so much in the isolation of the specific features of the face, one imagines they would focus more on those allegedly similar features than on the color of a piece of clothing. Plus the glasses and bandana that evidently adorned the bust when it was originally publicized by the media are never mentioned.

This three-dimensional bust is praised for its similarities with Barraza even though the police were never looking for a woman. As opposed to the two widely publicized police sketches, the bust was not publicized until after Barraza's arrest, when it was held up as a confirmation that she was La Mataviejitas without any mention that police and media had actually been looking for a man and then a travesti. The "knowledge" of El Mataviejitas was based on stereotypes of who a serial killer should be—a middle-aged man, a homosexual—rather than the results of the police investigation or any other actual information. The sketches alone, contrary to what police have claimed, are not compelling evidence that Barraza is actually La Mataviejitas.

As soon as Barraza was declared La Mataviejitas (with the feminine "la" suddenly replacing the masculine "el"), the serial killer narrative changed dramatically. Police descriptions of the character of the killer shifted from "brilliant and astute" to "pathological," replicating international constructions around female serial killing. Contrary to the stereotype of male serial killers as brilliant men who "possess traits that are desirable even if these skills are used for evil, ... incarcerated violent women are seen as strange, alien creatures, and often, as being beyond redemption."[122] Feminist approaches to criminology have pointed out the difficulty of imagining violent women, who can be represented only as "bad or mad." According to Helen Birch, "The idea that women are capable of extreme violence is anathema to most of us. Meanwhile, in courtrooms and newspapers throughout the Western world, women who kill are divided into two camps: bad—wicked or inhuman; or mad—not like 'ordinary' women. The extreme defines the norm."[123] Many feminist criminologists have pointed out, as Paula Ruth Gilbert puts it, that "our reluctance to criminalize women betrays our fears of the falling apart of our social fabric."[124] In constructions of mexicanidad, the idea of a woman being a serial killer or a murderer puts a crack in the foundation on which the idea of nation was established. It is unimaginable within constructions of mexicanidad that the guardian angels of the home and of the nation are capable of killing—and even more astonishing that women could kill women, which is tantamount to killing the nation. In reality, it is the state that is responsible for their deaths, the state that is allowing an average of "7 women a day [to be] killed in Mexico."[125]

As Gilbert describes, feminist criminologists have argued that "violent women are seen neither as sane nor as women."[126] Culturally, violent women are seen as pathological, different not only from other women, but, mostly, from men. Violent women's aggression is different from men's aggression. They are different because of their pathology. These women are then punished more harshly, with longer sentences and more intense social stigmatization. Not only do these punishments affect the women who have committed the crimes, they also function as warnings to other women. This can be seen in the case of Barraza's prison sentence of 759 years—the longest sentence ever given to a murderer in Mexico, longer than those given to the narcosatánicos, much longer than those given to other convicted serial killers. As Susan Edwards has written, "women who face criminal charges and are outside the judiciary's idea of normal womanhood are punished for this deviancy as well as for the actual crime, and that the severity of the sentences is dependent on the extent that their offence and behavior deviate from dominant gender expectations."[127] Barraza's extraordinary sentence in particular appears to serve as a punishment not so much for what she did but for what she is.

Since the nineteenth century, violent women have conventionally been linked with aggression, which is seen as a masculine trait, and thus a sign of criminality. Numerous feminist criminologists have challenged such discourses. For instance, Dana Crowley Jack describes aggression, in relation to Darwinian theory, as "still the bedrock upon which gender dualisms are erected: active/passive, warlike/peaceful, competitive/cooperative, separate/connected, and more. The thought of women's aggression arouses inchoate fears of an unnatural blurring of gender lines that have been drawn by evolution. If women are overly aggressive, then gender, as our society has defined it, will no longer exist."[128] Men can be aggressive, but aggressive women fall outside the norms of femininity. Jack also points to the ethnic, racial, and class stereotypes that intersect with the "myth that women are not aggressive." Socially marginalized, poor, working-class women are often caricatured and punished for their more overt antisocial behavior.[129]

Representations of Barraza aligned her with international discourses of female criminality, that is, in Caroline Picart's words "as being a woman who did not know how to be a real woman (as defined by the patriarchy). This dimension is very much in line with the gendered (and raced and classed) dimensions of being a female criminal."[130] Female murderers defy the standards of womanliness, and thus the perdominant way they are talked about is in terms of their maleness or masculine appearance.[131] Media reports and official accounts in Mexico have been no exception, with their portrayal of Barraza as "robust, strong, and of abrupt ways and decisive voice," "corpulent," and with "manly features."[132] Although her sexual orientation has not been the object of media and police scrutiny, her nonnormative female body has served as justification for their aligning her with representations of violent women as mannish, which in international narrations of female serial killing correlates heavily with "lesbian."

Media representations of Barraza as a violent woman make common reference to a "psychological profile" that defines her as "aggressive." This aggression, according to police, is what drove her to commit the multiple murders: "Juana kills out of *coraje* [rage],"[133] or "Barraza killed because she held resentment toward her mother."[134] In this way, police were able to align her with the previous psychological profile of El Mataviejitas. As soon as Barraza became La Mataviejitas, police, criminologists, and media found much "evidence" of her "aggressiveness" and the "rage" that must have driven her to kill elderly women.

In both Mexico and the United States, "male aggression" is both a simple, even biological male trait and a characteristic of machismo. Campbell points out that male aggression is viewed as "*imposing* control over others," while "women's aggression" is equated with the "*failure* of self-control," producing a "double standard."[135] This double standard is prevalent in official discourses of female violence. Most importantly, "traditionally women who kill are seen as insane, unnatural or aberrant."[136] They are routinely described as "monstrous"[137] and therefore pathological, while men who kill are often depicted as intelligent, even brilliant. "[A]ggression is a primary marker of masculine/feminine difference, and constructing women's aggression as unnatural helps mask the political character of gender inequality (indeed, of gender itself)."[138] In short, aggression is a natural trait in men but a pathology in women.

Furthermore, the creator of the three-dimensional bust took on the task of tracking previous homicides of elderly women and finding out if these homicides had occurred during a full moon. For Payán, the full moon "produces behavioral changes... in humans."[139] She then tracked Barraza's menstrual cycle alongside the full moon and these other killings of elderly women. On the day of her arrest, Barraza was menstruating and thus influenced by the concurrent full moon, said Payán, which led her to strangle Alfaro Reyes; the red sweater she was wearing was additional "proof" of her pathological "aggressiveness."[140]

This association of menstrual cycles and the full moon with aggressiveness that leads to serial killing has roots in the nineteenth century, when women were seen "as predators and vampires who could destroy both men and civilization."[141] It is easy to demonstrate that this association is more subjective than scientific; after all, not all women who menstruate under the influence of the full moon become so aggressive that they kill elderly women—or anyone at all. This "scientific" notion serves to further blur the line between fact and fiction that characterizes serial killer narratives.

After Barraza's arrest, police found an amulet of La Santa Muerte (The Holy Death) in her bag, and officers searching her house discovered "an altar to La Santa Muerte, with a snake and an apple as offerings"[142] and another altar to "Jesus Malverde, the saint of drug dealers."[143] Cultural assumptions around the adoration of La Santa Muerte were represented in media discourses as a testament to Barraza's perverse personality (as only *dangerous* people worship La Santa Muerte), situating her as a dangerous working-class individual. I analyze Barraza's connection to La Santa Muerte and Jesús Malverde in relation to the notion of mexicanidad and official discourses of criminality in chapter 4.

Media depictions of Barraza as existing outside of traditional constructions of femininity are further characterized and "scientifically" validated as pathological by criminologists and neuropsychologists. Feggy Ostrosky, a renowned neuropsychologist at the UNAM Department of Psychology, conducted several different psychophysiological tests on Barraza. The tests consisted of showing Barraza different images while measuring her cerebral activity. Ostrosky concluded that Barraza "showed very little sensorial reaction to violent, loving, calm or neutral images. . . . [T]he measure of her cerebral activity reflected very little sensitivity before the seriousness of the images she was confronted with. We showed her a chair, which for most people does not represent any sensation; however, she told us she felt something agreeable when she saw the chair, because she could rest in that chair, and when she observed an image of a woman, she said she felt nothing."[144] The tests results were presented as scientific evidence of Barraza's "psychopathy," reinforcing her alignment with international "serial killers." Ostrosky does not specify which serial killers, but rather presents serial killing in general as a result of biological predispositions that are visible in the brain. This "scientific" evidence is presented as "objective" and "neutral," ignoring Ostrosky's subjective interpretation of the test results. Presenting two images and deducing from an EEG that Barraza is pathological because she derives more of a feeling of comfort from the image of a chair than from that of a woman requires subjective interpretation of cerebral activity. I am not a scientist, but then I am not pretending that my view of the test results is objective and neutral. I can deduce that Barraza probably associates more comfort with a chair than with a woman because she suffered great abuse at her mother's hands—she has likely had more agreeable experiences with chairs. In contrast, Ostrosky identifies herself as an expert in analyzing and studying the brain (a claim backed up by her credentials) and as such she presents her results as objective when they are *also* an interpretation. The problem is that her analysis is presented not as an explanation but as an objective, impartial, detached analysis that has served to criminalize Barraza not for her crimes but for being a species of person, a dangerous individual, a "killer" whose brain is different than a "normal" one and whose criminality is innate.

In addition to the EEGs, Ostrosky performed a neuropsychological test from which she concluded that Barraza "presents an alteration, not very severe, in the levels of her frontal lobes," which explains why it is hard for her to "inhibit and sequence stimulus."[145] Again, the "stimulus" Ostrosky is referring to is subjectively interpreted, though presented as neutral evidence of Barraza's innate criminality (figs. 2.6 and 2.7). I am frankly not sure exactly what Ostrosky means by an "alteration" of the frontal lobe and by "stimulus," and she offers little elaboration. In his book, Barrón "corroborated" Ostrosky's findings by reference to "the reflexions of Adrian Raine," a British psychologist specializing in neurobiological and biosocial causes of violent behavior, who states that "poorer functioning of the prefrontal cortex predisposes to violence [sic] for a number of reasons."[146] According to Raine, those range from the "neurophysiological level," which "can result in a loss of inhibition or control on phylogenetically older subcortical structures such as the amygdala, which are thought to give rise to aggressive feelings," to "neurobehavioral levels," where the "prefrontal damage has been found to result in risk taking, irresponsibility, rule-breaking, emotional and aggressive outbursts, and argumentative behavior which can also predispose to violent criminal acts," to damages in personality levels, social levels, and cognition levels.[147] These results come from the scanned brains of "41 murderers pleading not-guilty by reason of insanity," which in turn were compared "to the brains of 41 normal controls who were matched with the murderers on sex and age."[148] Raine concludes that these brain dysfunctions "may be essentially a predisposition only requiring other environmental, psychological and social factors to enhance or diminish this biological predisposition."[149]

For Barrón, then, Barraza's biological attributes are evidence that she is a pathological serial killer. His book merges photographs of Barraza

Figure 2.6. Barraza being interviewed by Freggy Ostrosky.

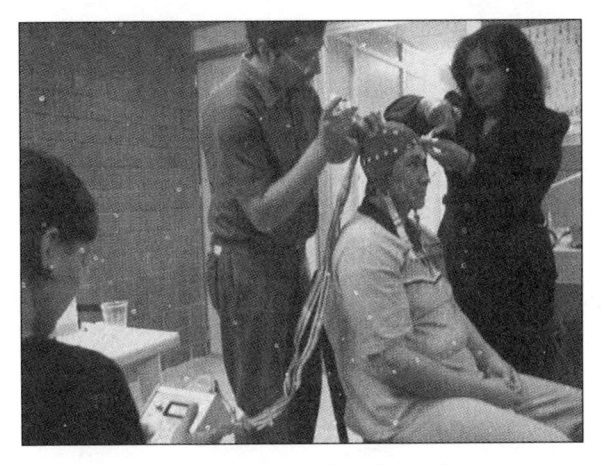

Figure 2.7. Barraza having an EEG performed.

and the police sketches as if to show similarities in the physiognomy there to figures 2.8, 2.9, and 2.10. Such "scientific" interpretations of Barraza's brain waves and physiognomy is problematic, to say the least. First, it presumes that an individual can possess certain "inner characteristics" and "physiognomy" that reveal her innate criminality. Second, both Barrón and Ostrosky have a capacity for "objectively" interpreting Barraza's "feelings, emotions, [and] behavior," revealing the "truth." Finally, it simplistically pathologizes Barraza because of her physiognomy, reducing her to a "species of person."[150]

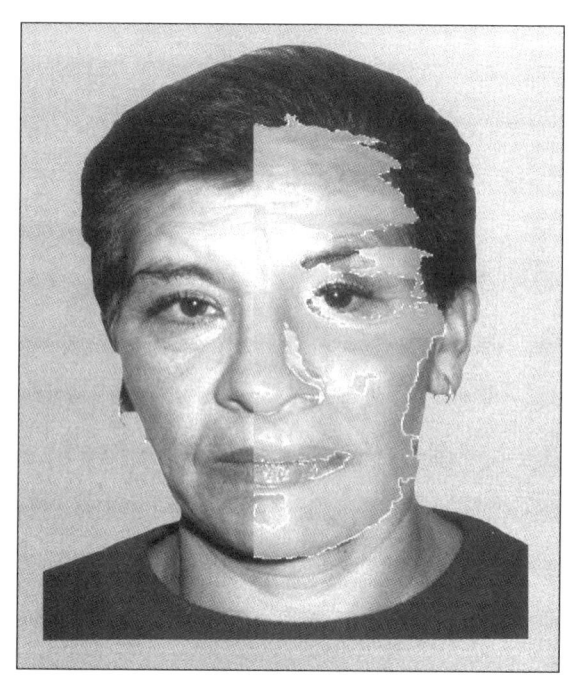

Figure 2.8. Superimposition of photograph of Barraza and bust created by Patricia Payán, published in Martín Barrón's *El nudo del silencio*.

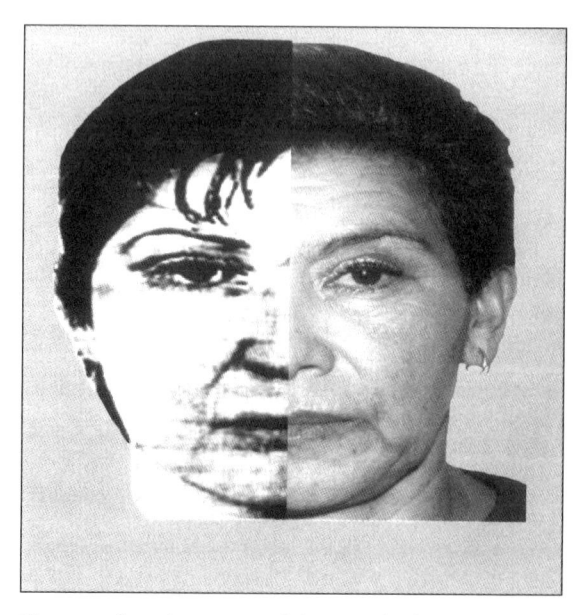

Figure 2.9. Superimposition of photograph of Barraza and police sketch, published in Martín Barrón's *El nudo del silencio*.

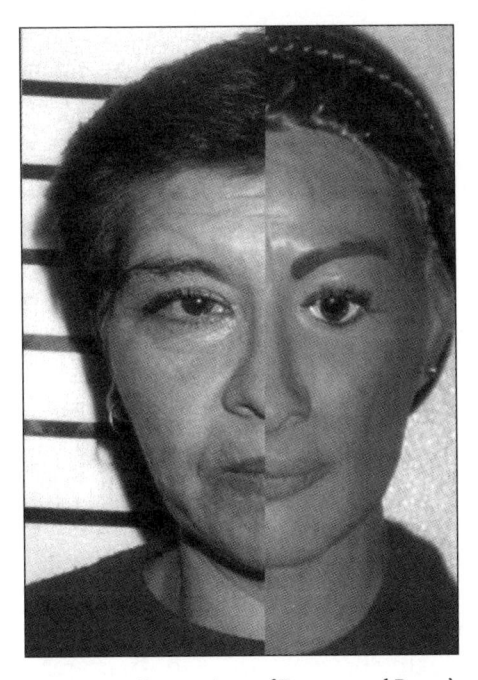

Figure 2.10. Comparison of Barraza and Payan's bust, published in Martín Barrón's *El nudo del silencio*.

Ostrosky also found that Barraza "shares with many serial killers psychopathic tendencies that could have been avoided if she had had a better life."[151] Ostrosky's analyses of Barraza's cerebral and psychological tests are not very far from Rougmanac's studies of criminals in 1904. Rougmanac believed criminality was a result of environmental circumstances. Both Ostrosky's and Rougmanac's studies of the brains of criminals reveal their belief that the ways in which killers' brains are different from those of noncriminals can be taken as evidence of their innate criminality.

As I've argued, the assumptions of Mexican criminology have changed little since the field's emergence and still serve as a "scientific" justification for sexist, classist, and racist prejudices. For example, consider the nineteenth-century belief in "harmony between moral beauty and physical beauty: every good person looks beautiful, while the morality of a bad person, a criminal, renders her 'ugly.'"[152] Barraza's face has been analyzed by criminologists following these standards so as to "prove" her criminality. Barrón and criminal psychologist Isabel Bueno, just like Roumagnac and Martínez and Vergara, have stated that Barraza's lack of "beauty," which for them is apparent in her features and facial expressions, reveals her criminality, thus rendering her an innate criminal and serving as further evidence of her pathology.

For Bueno, Barraza "has a problem with feminine identity, since 'she has a very marked virile appearance.'"[153] Bueno is following the criminal physiognomic classifications of Martínez and Vergara, who in support of their conclusions cite a Spanish proverb from the colonial period: "Never trust . . . a woman who talks like a man.'"[154] And just like Martínez and Vergara, Bueno presents her subjective interpretations of Barraza's physiognomy as scientific. What is problematic about this pseudoscientific use of physiognomy is that Barraza's criminality then extends far beyond her crimes. Even more than the homicides, Barraza's crime is her falling outside of the normative roles of femininity. In a significant sense, her crime is that she is literally perceived as "ugly" and "masculine." Bueno criminalizes and pathologizes Barraza for transgressing the norms of mexicanidad, for not "embellishing" her home with "her beauty"—an expectation placed on Mexican women since Porfirian times.[155]

Ostrosky was also interested in Barraza's face, and analyzed her facial expressions to "prove" her innate criminality. For Ostrosky, when Barraza expresses "remorse," it is just a simple imitation of a situation that she does not understand. During one of their interviews, Ostrosky asked her, "Is it bad what you did?" Barraza answered, "Yes, it's bad what I did . . . because no one has the right to take the life of someone else."[156] To Ostrosky, this answer came from a place that is rational and not emotional; "in reality she did not experience in that moment, or after, any feelings of remorse or guilt for her misdeeds."[157] Ostrosky's interpretations of Barraza's personality and EEG results supported the idea that she has no emotional sensations. Just like Rougmanac, who in 1904 asked prison inmates if they felt remorse, if they knew what remorse meant, and if they believed in God, Ostrosky deduced from their interview that Barraza was simply "faking it." According to Ostrosky, Barraza does not even understand what remorse is—on what basis, her text does not reveal. In sum, both Ostrosky and Barrón maintain the classist interpretation of criminality established a century earlier. It is also worth noting that Barraza did not know how to read and write, like many of the prisoners interviewed by Rougmanac, long an unacknowledged subtext of classism.

The face is seen not only as representing feelings and emotions, it effectively *becomes* the person.[158] A face *does*, more than represents, and what a face does is to "reshape the world so that we think or feel the world differently. When confronted by a face, whether reflective or intensive, we must recoordinate our view of the world and subsequently our actions in that world."[159] It is not only what is represented in the face that gives an indication of who a given person is, but what that face is *doing*—which would seem, invaraibly, to be a matter of subjective interpretation. Yet Ostrosky's knowledge of positivist science implies a certain knowledge that most people might not have access to. She can thus provide a "scientific" explanation of Barraza's face (along with her cerebral activity), which allegedly derives from an innate criminality.

America's most notorious female serial killer of recent decades, Aileen Wournos, worked as a sex worker in Florida. In 1989 and 1990 she killed six men, whom she alleged had raped her or attempted to rape her; she was sentenced to death and was executed in 2002. Wournos's case was portrayed in several TV shows, documentaries, and independent films, and became world renowned after Charlize Theron won an Oscar for playing her in the 2003 movie *Monster*. Like Barraza, Wournos came from a lower-class background and had a troubled childhood; abandoned by her mother and abused by her stepfather, she left home at a young age.

Wournos's history of marginalization was cited as "evidence of her pathology and inherent criminality."[160] Similarly, Barraza's history of marginalization and abuse, and her work as a wrestler and maid, have been used to pathologize her. Barraza was sold by her alcoholic mother in exchange for three beers to José Lugo when Barraza was only thirteen years old. She was sexually abused and gave birth to her first son at the age of sixteen. When Barraza was twenty-four, she witnessed the violent murder of her twelve-year-old son by a group of drunk young men. Criminologists, media, and officials point to this history of abuse as evidence that Barraza killed out of "rage and hatred" toward a female figure (but seemingly not, to Ostrosky, as evidence that Barraza might prefer an image of a chair to one of a woman).[161] In this view, elderly women triggered Barraza's uncontrollable anger because of the abuses perpetrated by her mother.[162]

Like the Wournos case in the United States, that of Barraza highlights the arbitrary nature of the category of serial killer. According to Seltzer, the FBI defines serial murder simply "as involving an offender associated with the killing of at least four victims, over a period greater than seventy-two hours."[163] Wournos was convicted for the killing of six men and Barraza has confessed to one murder, and though prosecutors estimated at the outset that she had committed twenty-four to forty-nine homicides,[164] she was ultimately convicted of a total of sixteen murders and twelve robberies.[165] In contrast to Wournos, Barraza did not kill men, and thus her crimes were not made a feminist issue. Barraza killed other women, elderly women, making her crimes yet another transgression. As noted in chapter 1, victims represent bodies that bring society into crisis; the conception of a victim is shaped by personal and social values,[166] and as such, elderly women are seen as victims in Mexico's conservative, moralistic, misogynist, and traditional culture, while younger women, travestis, and homosexuals are further stigmatized. The fact that Barraza killed women, grandmothers, who were *victims* made her, in turn, a *criminal*. Hers is a criminality based not solely on the homicides, but on moral prejudices and understandings based on ideologies of mexicanidad.

The "Look" of the Serial Killer

In *El nudo del silencio*, Barrón published a set of three photos focusing on Barraza's eyes under the rubric "Miradas que matan" (Looks that kill) (fig. 2.11). All three photos were taken on the day that Barraza was captured and identified as La Mataviejitas; what differentiates them is the lighting, angle, and closeness. All three are low resolution and pixelated. In the first—the caption reads "The look of Barraza at the moment of her detention"—Barraza's eyes are looking to the right; the gaze is not directed at the camera. The photo, purposefully or not, has a blurry effect that renders the eyes unidentifiable. In the second—"The look of Barraza the day of her capture"—the lighting is especially yellow so as to reflect the detention room; the viewer can appreciate more detailed features of Barraza's eyes, getting a glimpse of her makeup. Again, the

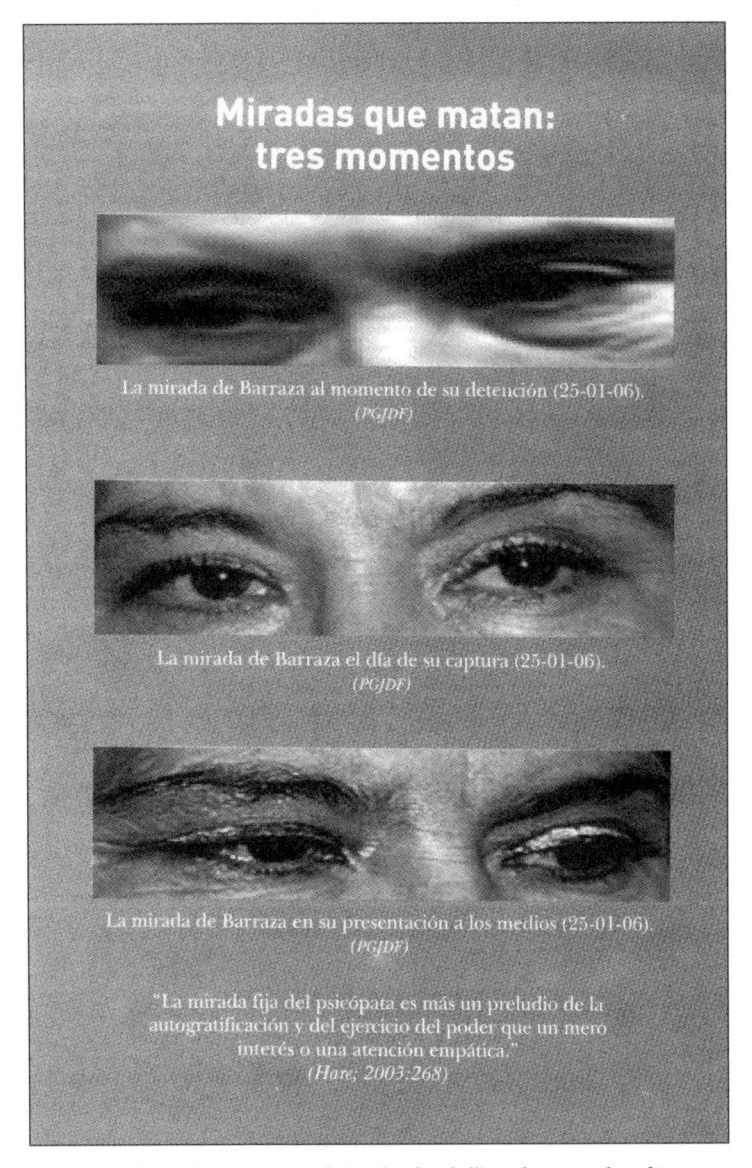

Figure 2.11. "Miradas que matan" (Looks that kill)—photographs of Juana Barraza's eyes, published in Martín Barrón's *El nudo del silencio*.

gaze is not directed to the camera but slightly askew, giving the impression that she is looking nowhere. The final photo—"The look of Barraza at her presentation to the media"—provides a close-up of Barraza's eyes: once again, her gaze is not directed at the camera, while the image further highlights her skin tone and texture.[167]

No information is provided as to the times at which the photos were taken, but they do claim to differentiate "the look" of the serial killer at three different moments. The lighting and the manner in which the photos were shot are embedded within the history of photography and criminality, where photographs of criminals are supposed "to prove the existence of the innate, visible traits in deviants or to serve as a dispassionate document of their deeds."[168] The cultural circumstances under which these photos were taken necessarily influence the personal perceptions of both the viewers and the photographer about Barraza's criminality. Knowing that the photos are those of the recently profiled La Mataviejitas predisposes viewers to distinguish the inner "pathological" traits of the serial killer in Barraza.

As David Green observes, photographic images' "intelligibility as representations cannot be judged from the correlation with a reality of appearances but with regard to the functions they were intended to facilitate and the objectives which they serve in social activity." That is, photographs "have to be regarded in every case as actively manufactured or constructed renderings of reality, produced within the limits of pictorial and technical conventions and subject to cultural and material resources."[169] The photos of the three "looks" of Barraza are published in a book whose sole concern is to demonstrate scientifically that Barraza is a serial killer, La Mataviejitas, despite the fact that up to the moment of her arrest, police were looking for a man. These same photos published in another book, with another title, might be perceived differently. While their objective is to serve as evidence of Barraza's innate criminality, they demonstrate, rather, that the *use* of photography as "scientific" evidence necessitates certain assumptions—specifically, understandings of criminals by viewers—and above all should be considered in the context in which they are presented. As presented by Barrón, these photographs follow the tradition of criminal photography initiated by Martínez and Vergara and Rougmanac in Mexico over a century ago. In fact, Barrón cites Rougmanac in his book, stating that the latter's studies are still relevant.

Barrón frames the three "looks" with a quote from Robert Hare, a researcher on pathology and criminality, who claims that "the fixated stare is more a prelude to self-gratification and the exercise of power rather than simple interest or empathic caring."[170] This "scientific" explanation follows the nineteenth-century field of physiognomy that, "under the banner of scientific theory," developed the idea that the "*innate nature of the criminal*" was identifiable through a "reading" of facial features and expressions.[171] According to Hare, the "look" of a psychopath and serial killer—like that of Gary Tison, a convicted murderer as described by James Clarke in his book *Last Rampage*—is "cold," "empty," "hard," and "with a malign intensity";[172] Barrón, in turn, was able to testify to the coldness and harshness of Barraza based on his interview of her. I am sure coldness, hardness, and malign intensity describe the look of many people who have perpetuated violence; however, these words also describe the look of many individuals who are not serial killers or anything of the sort. Criminalizing Barraza because of her "look" as a serial killer presupposes the ideology that criminals have a distinct "look": an "animal-like gaze" that translates into their expression of emotions.[173] This follows the nineteenth-century notions of criminality established in Mexico by Martínez and Vergara, with their claims that killers can be identified by their "glossy, cold, and haughty look."[174] Both historically and today, the unacknowledged subtext is the anxieties of elites related to gender and lower-class criminality.[175] Even Hare warns against the "false belief that we can reliable spot a psychopath by his or her eyes. It is all too easy to misread the eyes of others and to draw erroneous conclusions about character, intentions, and truthfulness."[176] Determining the qualities of a look is an inescapably subjective process, but through photography we seem to "know the criminal and the details of the violent crime in a way that is profoundly mysterious and ultimately reassuring."[177] Our knowledge of the "look" of the serial killer is predetermined in this case by our knowledge that Barraza has been declared La Mataviejitas.

On the one hand, Barrón determined that Barraza had a "cold" and "hard" look. But on the other hand, to police officers Barraza's look seemed "tranquil" and "serene" when she was arrested—which also translates into a revelation of her pathological inability to feel emotions, rendering her a criminal. The sketches produced using CaraMex software, the three-dimensional bust, and the three photographs of the "looks" of Barraza appear to be more a testament that "scientific theory" is susceptible to cultural bias and the product of circumstances than a testament to her innate criminality, let alone to careful, professional police work. Rather than any "evidence" or her "similarities" to the sketches, it is the narration and discourses around Barraza's detention that makes her La Mataviejitas

I am not arguing that Barraza is not La Mataviejitas or that she should not be held responsible for her crimes. My purpose is to problematize the resources used by police as evidence of Barraza's criminality. The photos of the "look" of Barraza as La Mataviejitas serve less as "scientific evidence" of her innate criminality and pathology and more as a weak reassurance to the public that police and criminologists have captured the serial killer and that there will be no more homicides of elderly women in Mexico City.

3

Performing Mexicanidad I

Criminality and Lucha Libre

Wearing a red sweater and looking like a true lucha libre aficionada, Barraza started by stating her name, "Yo soy la señora Juana Barraza Samperio." Just one week before her detention and consequent identification as La Mataviejitas, she was being interviewed on TV Azteca at the Arena Coliseo, a wrestling amphitheater located in downtown Mexico City. Asked, "¿Ruda o técnica?"—that is, whether she identified more with those wrestlers who lack proper schooling and act on impulse, or those who perform with technique and play by the rules—she replied: "Ruda del corazón," ruda from the bottom of my heart. She was smiling, showing her love of and dedication to lucha libre. "¿Y dónde es más ruda, aquí o en su casa?" (And where are you more of a ruda, here—in the wrestling arena—or in your home?)—"Ah, pues en los dos lados" (Well, in both places), Barraza answered as she shyly withdrew from the microphone, still smiling. It was 2006 and news about El Mataviejitas was already all over the country, with sketches ubiquitous in government offices and public transportation. Yet, that Sunday, as she talked on national TV as a lucha libre enthusiast, no one recognized her as La Mataviejitas. She was sweet and kind—the total opposite of a cold, harsh serial killer.

One week later, Juana Barraza was caught red-handed and declared the first female serial killer in Mexico. She was again wearing a red sweater, but this time it was proof of her aggressiveness (figs. 3.1 and 3.2). The public perception of Barraza changed dramatically from that interview; from January 26 onward, there was no doubt she was La Mataviejitas, despite the earlier arrests of at least two other people who were suspected of being the serial killer.[1] In April 2004, Araceli Vázquez García was detained as a suspect in ten house robberies and the homicide of an elderly woman.[2] Vázquez had "pretended to be a nurse" to gain access

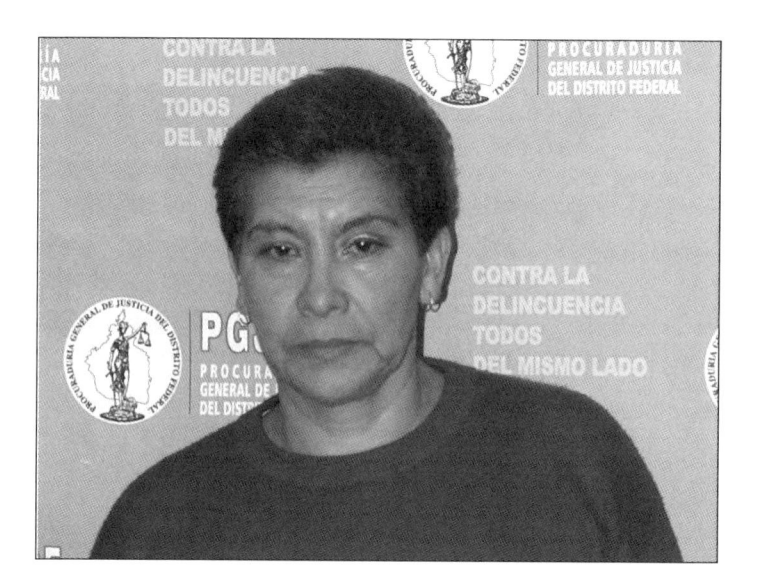

Figures 3.1 and 3.2. Barraza on the day of her capture.

to the homes of older women. As noted, police had described this as the modus operandi of El Mataviejitas, but neither the media nor authorities identified her as the serial killer. Vázquez, who was sentenced to forty-two years in prison, is currently detained at Santa Martha Acatitla.[3] One can argue that because police could not conceive of a woman as having committed the crimes, they were unable to see her as La Mataviejitas. Yet among the images provided to me by Comandante Moneda, one specific sketch is circled to indicate Vázquez was indeed La Mataviejitas (fig. 3.3). The question arises: Why wasn't Vázquez *called* La Mataviejitas?

Similarly, five months after the arrest of Vázquez, on September 12, 2004, police arrested Jorge Mario Tablas Silva for killing two elderly women. Tablas, a man, had also dressed as a nurse, wearing women's clothing and a wig, and had suffocated one of the women with a pair of tights, which matched the modus operandi that police attributed to El Mataviejitas. He had even pretended to work for the city's assistance program for older citizens, Sí Vale. Tablas was convicted and sentenced to sixty-one years in prison for the murders.[4] Neither the media nor police paid much attention to Tablas. One might presume that because he was not a travesti, or a homosexual, he did not fit the profile of the serial killer police were looking for—yet the profile of the serial killer as a homosexual appeared only after Tablas's arrest. In a journal Tablas had left at a crime scene, which police used to find him, he had written, "I know I am the Apostle Juan, the ghost of whom my mother told me about through a spiritualist session"; he also described his crimes as the acts of a third person, named El Maligno (The Evil).[5] I am not qualifying these statements as pathological, but why did the media and police not consider that Tablas might be El Mataviejitas, the "pathological" serial killer?[6]

Neither Vázquez nor Tablas caused the media uproar that Barraza has. I argue that Barraza offered media and authorities the perfect sensationalist story. Specifically, her wrestling practice and nonnormative body sexually transgressed the codes of normative femininity established for women through ideologies of mexicanidad, thus leading criminologists, police, and journalists to justify reading her body as that of a pathological serial killer, the one and only La Mataviejitas.

After Barraza's arrest, what really captured the media's attention was the fact that she had been a professional lucha libre wrestler. Headlines

Figure 3.3. "Les voisins et La Mataviejitas" (The neighbors and La Mataviejitas)—sketch compendium provided by Comandante Moneda.

emphasized that before Barraza was identified as La Mataviejitas, she was "in the public world of the lucha libre known as La Dama del Silencio [The Lady of Silence]."[7] As soon as this was discovered by police, La Dama del Silencio and La Mataviejitas became one: "La Mataviejitas assaulted her victims using the strength she acquired in the lucha libre";[8] "La Dama del Silencio of the lucha libre is the woman accused of killing elderly women."[9] This merging of personas, La Mataviejitas (the serial killer disguised as a nurse) and La Dama del Silencio (the wrestler disguise of Barraza), has been used by criminologists, media, and police as evidence that Barraza is La Mataviejitas. The Mataviejitas case was officially closed after the arrest of Barraza, despite the fact that even police recognized that more than thirty homicides "still need to be solved."[10] There is no talk of who killed the other thirty women, and while I have not been able to determine whether there have been unsolved killings of elderly woman in Mexico City after January 2006, the police stated at the time that "there might be other copycats on their way," again drawing on international patterns of serial killings.[11]

I argue that, in public perception, the wrestler La Dama del Silencio became the serial killer La Mataviejitas, more than the woman Juana Barraza did. Discourses of criminality and the spectacle of lucha libre intersect within Mexican culture and establish the parameters of mexicanidad, reinforcing but also revealing the limits of Mexican masculinity and femininity as subject to redefinition. This chapter focuses on this intersection as a potent site for denaturalizing Mexican masculinity and femininity and redressing the raced, classed, gendered, and sexualized limits of mexicanidad and criminality that have determined who is regarded as a criminal and who counts as a victim.

As noted in the introduction, Octavio Paz has limned mexicanidad as a pervasive ideology of Mexican national identity based on an idealized myth of masculinity, whose main characteristics are the figure of the mestizo and the macho. This discourse of mexicanidad has been mobilized by Carlos Monsiváis, among others, asserting that the male figure compensates for inferiority through the assertion of his virility.[12] Paz further argues that the idealized Mexican was the mestizo, whose image became entangled with the macho in the Mexican imaginary. Noting how the notion of mestizo has been more recently problematized by scholars as having served to justify the persistent racism in Mexico,

Roger Bartra has argued how the myths of mexicanidad respond to a historic construction of postrevolutionary Mexican identity that exclusively served the elite in power.[13]

In this chapter, I use the notion of performativity, defined through the work of Judith Butler[14] as a methodological tool with which to account for: (1) not single or deliberate acts, but practices of citationality that, through their reiteration, "produce the effect that it names" (that is, "the reiterative power of discourse to produce the phenomena that it regulates and constrains," in this case, is not only the intelligibility of subjects but also the discourses of mexicanidad and broader international accounts of criminality);[15] (2) "the [u]nderstanding of performativity not as the act by which the subject brings into being what she/he names, but, rather as that reiterative power of discourse to produce the phenomena that it regulates and constrains";[16] and (3) "a rethinking of a process by which a bodily norm is assumed, appropriated, taken on as not, strictly speaking, undergone *by a subject*, but rather than the subject, the speaking 'I,' is formed by virtue of having gone of such a process of assuming a sex."[17] It is through the notion of performativity that genders are constituted as materially "intelligible," constructing a "subject" while disavowing as "abject" those who do not maintain relations of coherence and continuity among sex, gender, sexual practice, and desire.

As noted in the introduction, I contextualize the notion of gender performativity within the pigmentocratic sociocultural system of Mexico. Furthermore, I use the notion of the performative act in a sense that refers to two different discourses, the first having to do with theatricality (performance) and the other referring to "speech act theory and deconstruction," that is, as both intentional and carrying with it the power of citationality and iterability.[18]

Criminologist Martín Barrón and neuropsychologist Feggy Ostrosky, who played central roles in determining Barraza's culpability through scientific evidence, based much of their scientific observations of her supposedly innate criminality on her wrestling persona, La Dama del Silencio. Building on this, I discuss how lucha libre contributes to the production of mexicanidad through an analysis of the performative acts that constitute it, paying particular attention to news reports of Barraza's wrestling practice. I go on to examine the challenges that Barraza, both as La Dama del Silencio and as La Mataviejitas, poses to the notion of mexicanidad. Finally, I look at how the identities of La Mataviejitas and La Dama del Silencio are displaced and circulate in popular culture, through a song and music video by underground singer Amandititita, a novel by Victor Ronquillo entitled *Ruda de corazón: el blues de La Mataviejitas*, and a video exhibited at the Police Cultural Center.

Born Mexican: Born Criminal, Born Wrestler

Ostrosky, director of the Neuropsychology and Psychophysiology Department laboratory at UNAM, merged the figure of the wrestler La Dama del Silencio with that of the serial killer La Mataviejitas to pathologize Barraza. Two years after Barraza's arrest, in 2008, Ostrosky's book *Mentes asesinas: la violencia en tu cerebro* (Killer minds: violence on your brain) was published, in which she dedicates a whole chapter to the case. Ostrosky begins by narrating what she imagines were Barraza's movements and thoughts the morning of January 25, 2006, the date of her capture. According to Ostrosky, Barraza looked at herself in the mirror and saw La Dama del Silencio, while listening to the news about El Mataviejitas.[19] Barraza then met Ana María Reyes Alfaro in her apartment, where there was an altercation over how much Barraza should get paid for her work as a domestic employee. Then, "inexplicably," inside Barraza's mind "all the images of previous suffering came back, the abandonment of her father, the constant abuse of her alcoholic mother that gave her away at age 13 in exchange for three damn beers."[20] Barraza could not control herself and strangled Reyes with a stethoscope. The victim was helpless before the "corpulence" of Barraza. After killing Reyes, Barraza had to regain "some air for that incomprehensible internal beast that used to come back once in a while."[21] As Foucault explains in "The Dangerous Individual," at the beginning of the nineteenth century, with the psychiatrization of criminal danger, crime was understood to "arise out of a state which one might call the zero degree of insanity."[22] That is, criminality was inherent to an individual who was biologically predisposed to insanity. For Ostrosky, La Mataviejitas was a "beast" that came out of Barraza, that "inexplicably" strangled elderly women using the "force and corpulence [*corpulencia*] of La Dama del Silencio."[23] In this narrative, Ostrosky is displacing the identity of the serial killer, La Mataviejitas, onto the identity of the wrestler, La Dama del Silencio.

Ostrosky deduced from the neuropsychological tests she performed that Barraza "had difficulties in some motor functions like alternative movements with both hands," thus suggesting a "pathology that affects frontal areas of the brain."[24] This diagnosis was further corroborated by the results of EEGs, which showed that Barraza demonstrated a "significant deceleration in electroencephalographic activity" when showed certain images.[25] This kind of scientific language is taken as justifying Ostrosky's subjective interpretations.

Ostrosky's interpretation of Barraza's neuropsychological test results echoes the nineteenth-century psychiatrization of crime, in which individuals were believed to be born with certain cerebral characteristics or biological conditions that appear suddenly as a result of their monomania or insanity. Ostrosky continues this nineteenth-century practice as, in the words of Foucault, she "emphasizes the character of the criminal" rather than the crimes that Barraza allegedly committed.[26]

Criminologist and police advisor Martín Barrón similarly merges La Dama del Silencio into La Mataviejitas. The title of his book, *El nudo del silencio*, translates as "the knot of silence," making reference to wrestling—in particular, to a lucha libre lock known as the knot, a move used to finish off an opponent. I read Barrón's use of the term "silence" as a reference to Barraza's wrestling persona. In combination with the subtitle, *Tras la pista de una asesina en serie, La Mataviejitas* (Following the tracks of a female serial killer, La Mataviejitas), it implies that it was through the locks used in lucha libre that the elderly women were silenced.

The book constantly merges Barraza the woman with the figure of the wrestler. The subheadings of the chapter entitled "La identidad" (Identity) suggest a wrestling match in which La Dama del Silencio is put into combat with different criminologists: "Barraza ante los escanogramas de Ostrosky" (Barraza before Ostrosky's scanograms), "La Dama del Silencio y la escala de Hare" (The Lady of Silence and Hare's scale), "La Dama del Silencio enfrenta los criterios de Skrapec" (The Lady of Silence against Skrapec's criteria), and, finally, "Barraza afronta los axiomas de Ressler" (Barraza faces Ressler's axioms).[27] The whole book is presented as though the merged persona of Barraza and La Dama del Silencio is in an international wrestling match, as a ruda fighting against the *técnicos*—those with proper technique. It is no surprise that she loses this match, and ends up *desenmascarada* (unmasked), as another chapter title suggests.

To determine if Barraza is a psychopath, Barrón follows the Canadian criminal psychology researcher Robert D. Hare, an FBI advisor on psychopathology. Hare developed the Hare Psychopathy Checklist–Revised (PCL-R), widely used to assess psychopathy in serial murderers. Barrón, in his chapter "The Lady of Silence and Hare's Scale," attempts to establish links between the PCL-R and the results of Barraza's psychological tests, "in order to detect the possible presence of a psychopathy in Barraza."[28] Point number nine on Hare's checklist, "the need for excitement," states that psychopaths "have an ongoing and excessive need for excitement—they long to live in the fast lane," which drives them to either "use a variety of drugs" or to even commit crimes "for excitement or thrills."[29] Barrón asserts that this point applies based on his own interview of Barraza, writing that "aside from the excitement that came from robbery and homicides in the history of Barraza, another point of excitement is found in the fact that at age 30, she started to practice Lucha Libre."[30] Barraza's wrestling practice attracted Barrón's "attention" because, according to him, she "lacked physical preparation"; instead, "her wrestling knowledge was assimilated through TV or going to the arenas to watch the spectacle."[31] It is interesting to highlight how, on the one hand, criminologists (including Barrón) pathologize Barraza because of her "muscular body," her "corpulence," using it as evidence that she is indeed La Mataviejitas, while on the other hand, Barrón pathologizes the same "muscular" body as lacking the "physical preparation" needed to perform lucha libre. Many lucha libre wrestlers have learned how to wrestle from experience and practice, especially if they are rudos. In fact, the point of being a rudo is precisely that one has neither had the "proper schooling" in wrestling technique, nor follows the rules.

Here I want to focus on how Barrón not only merges La Dama del Silencio into La Mataviejitas but also further pathologizes Barraza because of her wrestling practice, rather than for her alleged homicides of elderly women. Like Ostrosky, with his "scientific" evidence of Barraza's "pathology," Barrón criminalizes her by stressing attributes of her character and physique more than the crimes she allegedly committed. In his effort to fit Barraza into a checklist, he sees the "need for excitement" as demonstrated by her "wrestling body," and its use for lucha libre in a manner learned through spectatorship and experience. By this logic, almost any rudo could be made to fit point number nine in Hare's checklist.

In total, Hare's checklist comprises twelve points by which to detect a possible psychopath, including a "simple and superficial mind, lack of commitment, problems during childhood, antisocial behavior, lack of remorse and empathy and impulsivity."[32] Barraza is criminalized, for example, because when she explained her modus operandi to Barrón, she did so "without showing any emotion, coldly narrating the way in which she selected her victims"—and even for "not being able to remember her jobs as a maid."[33] Barrón presents his interview with Barraza in a way similar to how Carlos Rougmanac presented his prison interviews 102 years earlier, in 1904. In the last chapter of Barrón's book, "Reflexiones finales" (Final reflections), he presents his analysis of his interviews with Barraza and his conclusions, which are presented as "objective," not as interpretations. For Barrón, his objectivity is drawn from his criminological understanding of Barraza's facial expressions, activities, and emotions displayed in their interview—closely paralleling claims made by Rougmanac. Instead of presenting his results as interpretative, he claims that his readings of the interviews constitute neutral and objective "evidence"—evidence "that Barraza fulfills . . . the twelve principal criteria of [the PCL-R psychopathy] classification" and therefore is classifiable as a psychopath.[34] This evidence includes, for example, Barraza's aforementioned "hard" and "calculating" look and the fact that, as Barrón writes, "the only moment when Barraza looked away was when I extended my hand to thank her for having talked with me."[35] This "objective" analysis of Barraza's demeanor brings to mind the interviews conducted by Martínez and Vergara, who concluded that murderers "avert their eyes when spoken to."[36] I am not arguing that Barraza is or is not a psychopath; rather, I am problematizing Barrón's "objectivity" in criminalizing Barraza, as it perpetuates nineteenth-century criminological discourses that suggested criminality is both innate and visible in the face. For Hare, "the psychopathy that produces the serial killer originates in biological predispositions and social factors."[37] For Barrón and Ostrosky, Barraza is rendered a born criminal by her social circumstances, but mostly by biological factors. As such, they sustain the nineteenth-century belief in innate criminality.

Foucault suggested in "The Dangerous Individual" that the criminal is responsible for the crime by his very existence: the "crime is linked to the risk of criminality that the very personality of the individual constitutes."[38] By pathologizing the criminal, more than attributing responsibility, penal law defines the criminal as incorrigible. Both Ostrosky and Barrón considered Barraza's crimes to have been committed "without reason" and pointed to a link between her childhood environment and alleged pathology. Both Ostrosky and Barrón cast Barraza as an example of the "dangerous individual" whose criminality is explained by her pathology, which in turn is proven by the measurement of her brain waves. Barraza's characterization as a pathological serial killer renders her a criminal not for the crimes for which she was charged but for her supposed nature.

Both Barrón and Ostrosky framed their interviews with Barraza in a way that is seen in other, similar accounts: "through their personal narratives of travelling to the heart of darkness" in what Philip Jenkins describes as the "language of shamanism rather than psychology."[39] Like Rougmanac, they have continued a discriminatory practice of long-standing and international sway, adopting both Italian (biological) and French (environmental) approaches to criminality to develop a typology of the innate criminal in Mexico.[40]

Not only do Barrón and Ostrosky render La Dama del Silencio a born criminal, but they do so according to long-standing discourses that serve to delimit the characteristics of the criminal Mexican and the modern Mexican. The modern Mexican, again, ideally looks more "Spanish"—that is to say, white—while the criminal Mexican, whose face reflected his criminality, is mestizo—that is, lower class and with darker skin.[41] Like earlier criminologists, Barrón and Ostrosky classify only lower-class offenders, revealing racist and colonialist prejudices because the lower classes in Mexico were commonly indigenous and mestizo, that is, not *criollos*. Barrón and Ostrosky aligned Barraza, through scientific discourses of criminality, within the normative standards for lower-class women further secured through notions of mexicanidad. Because Barraza was a born criminal, she was not a born wrestler. According to Barrón, "it can be affirmed that the triggering moment to incursion in the homicidal practice was [Barraza's] retirement from lucha libre."[42]

Lucha Libre

Lucha libre, best described as a sport-spectacle, has been enormously popular in Mexico since the 1930s among mostly working-class spectators. It is also very popular with the many foreigners who visit Mexico City and consume professional wrestling as a local attraction for its "colorful masks, flamboyant personalities and a whole lot of spandex."[43] The actual fighting that takes place is a well-choreographed mix of judo, Greco-Roman wrestling, and boxing. Lucha libre in is not only a constitutive element of Mexican popular culture, it has become a social phenomenon,[44] offering a "spectacular performance" to its audience.[45] In this section I will look into the ways in which lucha libre constitutes a performance of mexicanidad.[46] As discussed in the introduction, mexicanidad is a porous notion and by looking at how the performances of lucha libre reiterate performances of mexicanidad, it is possible to see the disarticulation of machismo through the specific performance styles of women and *exóticos*. Exóticos are male *luchadores*, professional lucha libre wrestlers, who appropriate feminine aspects in their wrestling personas, from their movements to their costumes. The term "exótico" can be translated as "exotic"; in reference to exótico wrestlers, though, it means "weird, different, strange."[47]

According to Mary-Lee Mulholland, "one of the most important strategies in the imaginings, performances and productions of *mexicanidad* are the nostalgic narrations of certain origin myths."[48] These origin myths always refer back to the majestic indigenous civilizations and the horrific colonization "that led to the creation of the *mestizo* nation."[49]

One of the myths in which the Mexican identity is rooted is the Aztec myth—the origin of the *Mexica* civilization in what is now Mexico City. The story is that, around the 1300s, the Aztecs were nomads looking for a place to settle, until they found a sign from their god Huitzilopochtli: an eagle perched on a nopal cactus devouring a serpent. Aztecs saw this sign in the middle of Lake Texcoco and founded their city on its banks.

There is also the powerful myth of La Virgen de Guadalupe. In 1531, in the north of Mexico City, on a hill where indigenous populations worshiped their goddess Totonatzin, a brown-skinned manifestation of the Virgin Mary, appeared to an indigenous man, asking him—in the indigenous language of the region—to build a church in her name. La Virgen Morena or Virgen Mestiza (The Dark-Skinned Virgin) was worshiped by mestizos from then on; a church was indeed built on that hill, facilitating the Spanish evangelization of Mexico. I return to this in chapter 4.

Alongside such origin myths, Muholland also argues, for example, that "[m]ariachi is a national myth" that delimits and produces mexicanidad through the authenticity of its performance and performers.[50] Building on her observations, I make the case that other national mythical figures also contribute to the delimitation and production of mexicanidad—including professional wrestlers.[51] Like mariachis, wrestlers "perform their authenticity through the blood, sweat and tears of its performers and its performance."[52]

Professional wrestlers constantly draw upon origin myths rooted in colonization. For example, Perro Aguayo, among the most successful luchadores, stated in an interview that Mexicans identify with him because he is the "classic *indio*, that race of bronze that goes forward despite all adverse circumstances."[53] Aguayo is drawing on the notion of the ideal postrevolutionary Mexican, the mestizo and macho, Vasconcelos's race of bronze that will save us from the "white supremacist." Aguayo also stated that "one is born to be a wrestler."[54] In this way, he is contributing to notions of mexicanidad much as mariachis do, for whom being Mexican and feeling Mexican is in the blood. Similarly, another very well-known wrestler, Konnan, has affirmed that "wrestling is in my blood."[55] From El Santo in the 1940s to Místico in the 2010s, professional wrestlers in Mexico have contributed to the idea of authenticity (being born a wrestler, having it in the blood, dying if not been able to wrestle) that constitutes a pillar in the production of mexicanidad.

Another performative act essential to mexicanidad is the enactment of machismo, which is central to lucha libre. In a typical wrestling match, the luchadores are introduced by pretty women wearing bikinis, who escort the wrestlers as they enter the arena amid flashing lights and loud music. Wrestlers embody machismo through their muscular bodies, animal-like shouts, and displays of territoriality within the ring. They occupy center stage—not only because they are about to fight, but, precisely, because they are male and macho.

Another trait of machismo can be read in the unmanning of conventional wreslters by exóticos. Heather Levi has argued that lucha libre's theatricality challenges mainstream machismo in Mexico through the performance of exóticos, wrestlers (normally rudos) who fight in bright costumes, are sometimes associated with homosexuality, and appropriate feminine symbology in their wrestling personas—yet are taken seriously, which does not necessarily happen in any other sport or popular-culture medium in Mexico.[56] Exóticos like El Bello Greco, who fought during the 1980s and the first half of the 1990s, have described how their mere presence enraged spectators, who would threw urine and garbage at them, and shout slurs like "puto, puto, puto." At the time exóticos did not wear makeup or sequins and flashy outfits, but featured a visual style that was relatively "elegant."[57]

As a slur, "puto" is comparable to how "queer" was used during the 1970s and 1980s in the United States. The term is use to describe men who take on the passive role during the sexual act, that is, are the ones penetrated, *pasivos*. "Puto" further connotes effeminacy and working- or lower-class status. The effeminate male who occupies the passive role during the sexual act is also known as a *chingado*, according to Octavio Paz.[58] The opposite of the *chingado* is the *chingón*, who demonstrates his power of masculinity as he penetrates, playing the active role in the sexual encounter. ("Chingón" is a term commonly used in Mexico to signify the "winner," the "victorious.") The *chingado/chingón* dyad has been studied as the active/passive model for understanding male homosexuality in Mexico by researchers like Joseph Carrier (1985). In most cases, however, it is impossible to know about sexual practices in accurate detail, to understand what really happens in bed during sexual encounters. Many vestida sex workers have stated that it is in fact "men" who want to be penetrated by them since "they have the fantasy" of having a sexual encounter with a "woman that has a penis."[59]

Levi argues that exóticos "contest the dramatic representation of machismo" in lucha libre, as they successfully unman their opponents in the ring while also "rejecting the outward signs of manhood."[60] In this way, exóticos reinscribe the production of mexicanidad as they challenge the ideal mestizo/macho heterosexual wrestler, at the same time that they provide a space for the macho probado. Some wrestlers do not accept exóticos or their way of wrestling, but they are an important part of lucha libre.

May Flowers, one of the most important exóticos, believes that they "offer a spectacle that is in between virile and exótico."[61] Exótico wrestlers' presentations have changed over time; today, most of them wear makeup during their performances, as well as elaborate outfits with feathers, sequins, and flashy leotards. An important part of the exótico performance is the ¡beso!, ¡beso!, ¡beso! (kiss, kiss, kiss), shouted by the audience as an exótico such as Cassandro or Pimpinela Escarlate enters the ring. "If the public asks for a kiss, who are we not to please them?" asks Pimpinela.[62] Similarly, for Cassandro, one of the most important exóticos, "if he feels like giving a peck" to an opponent, or if the public ask for a *beso* even before the exóticos go into the ring "since they know their way of being," why would he not do it?[63] Part of the exótico performance is to actually give a small peck to the opposing wrestler. This performative act, the kiss, is supposed to be read as a fantasy for the exótico, but a "punishment" for the opponent, who are so "macho" they could never stand to kiss another man. One can read this kiss as a sort of macho probado performative act in which machismo is reinscribed precisely because there is a macho that has "tested" homoeroticism.

As noted, the most macho of all machos is the macho probado, the macho calado, he who has already tried same-sex relations only to prove that he is not tempted to continue on that path, or to "realize" that it is not for him, or to establish that he has the "permission" to take advanatge of such relations in case of necessity, such as being in jail. Rodrigo Parrini has noted on his work on the construction on masculinity at the Reclusorio Preventivo Varonil Norte (Northern Preventative Male Prison), how "masculinity admits no denial, only failures, falls and remains."[64] In his analysis of what masculinity entails for men in prison, Parrini concludes that what is said is much more important than what is done.[65] These findings echo what has been pointed out earlier in relation to mexicanidad and machismo.

Since the 1920s, the national discourse of mexicanidad promulgated by both the conservative elite and the Left emphasized the values of Catholicism and machismo. Under the ideology of mexicanidad, "expressions of sexuality that did not conform to the rules imposed by the institution of marriage" were condemned.[66] Conversely, at the same time, this ideology "also tolerated alternative male sexual behaviors that took place in an underworld of bordellos and drinking places where men can come in contact with 'bad women' and 'effeminate men.'"[67]

Héctor Carrillo, writing on the perceptions of homosexuality in the contemporary Mexican cultural landscape, argues that "the role of hybridity must be taken into consideration in the construction of sexual identities."[68] By hybridity, Carillo means the "co-existence of the new with the old," that is, the traditional gender-based categories which in Mexico "are not only alive but also constitute viable options . . . for individuals' interpretations of their own desire towards members of their own sex, particularly among the working classes.[69] Many of the men that Carrillo interviewed saw no contradiction between for example, being married and having kids and at the same time having a boyfriend, and not identifying necessarily as bisexual, gay or homosexual; or a man identifying as heterosexual and not being attracted to women.

Carillo's research focused on Guadalajara, a conservative state in the west of Mexico, where he interviewed mostly "middle-class homosexuals." Parrini, by contrast, interviewed fifteen men in prison, many of them sex workers, making it safe to assume most if not all were from working- and lower–class backgrounds. It is interesting to note that in both instances, the construction of masculinity in men (there has been little study of the construction of masculinity in Mexican women) allows for a fluidity in which practice does not necessarily go hand in hand with self-identification, as it commonly does in Anglo North America.

Carillo found that for men who were having sex with other men in Guadalajara, "trying to have it both ways—to be gay and at the same time, to maintain their affiliation to the larger society—they end up perpetuating a second-class status for homosexuals in Mexico. They do not make bold statements or assert the power to be unapologetically and openly gay because they feel they have too much to lose."[70] Carillo speaks about "culturally accepted patterns of silence"—if those are broken, "relationships with their families will be jeopardized, with whom most of them live"; they also risk being "fired from their jobs" and are likely to "experience considerable discrimination."[71]

The culturally accepted pattern of silence can be summed up in the phrase *lo que se ve no se pregunta* (what you see you don't ask, or you don't ask the obvious) made famous by beloved singer and songwriter Juan Gabriel (1950–2016), known as El Divo de Juárez (note that the term "diva" is masculinized) or Juanga (short for Juan Gabriel, but also making this nickname a feminizing diminutive alluding to his sexual ambiguity). Juan Gabriel's songs are gut wrenching and heartbreaking; a study of their lyrics would constitute a study of mexicanidad itself. Loved and adored by all social classes, he was celebrated for his melodramatic performances and his flashy outfits, very much like those of an exótico. Appearing on the TV program *Primer Impacto*, an interviewer spoke about how Juan Gabriel had "broken with many sexual barriers" on stage, since he explored the "feminine side of art," to which Juan Gabriel replied, "Art is feminine." The interviewer then posed a very direct question:

> FERNANDO DEL RINCÓN: Juan Gabriel, Juan Gabriel, dicen que eres gay. Juan Gabriel es gay? (They say you are gay. Juan Gabriel is gay?).
> JUAN GABRIEL (LAUGHING AND GESTURING): A usté le interesa mucho? (Are you very interested? [using the formal voice in Spanish]).
> FERNANDO DEL RINCÓN: Yo pregunto (I'm only asking).
> JUAN GABRIEL: Yo le respondo con otra pregunta, dicen que lo que se ve no se pregunta, m'hijo (I answer with another question, they say that you don't ask the obvious).¿Qué ve usted? (What do you see?).
> FERNANDO DEL RINCÓN: Yo veo a un cantante frente a mi, veo a un triunfador (I see a singer before me, I see a winner).[72]

This interview can be read as a wrestling match, a power struggle between mexicanidad and machismo. Juan Gabriel was an established and recognized artist, someone who might not have too much to lose if he were openly gay, one might think. Juan Gabriel never came out publicly, either to maintain his "affiliation to the larger society," or to protect his family, or simply to maintain his right to privacy. Asked about his sexual orientation, he answered with another question.

Annick Prieur has pointed out how in Mexico it is common for men to self-identify as straight although they practice homosexual intercourse. She differentiates gays from vestidas according to their economic status, finding many ways of being a homosexual man between the "middle-class gays" and the "lower-class vestidas."[73] Similarly, Nesving argues that "active partners in Latin America are not considered 'truly gay.'"[74] The constitution of machismo thus creates an intriguing figure:

the man who has, or *has to have*, sex with other men but does not identify as homosexual.

The symbolic significance of the exóticos, some of whom are openly gay, lies in showing how machismo works through its inclusion of the macho probado figure. In its reiteration of the performances of mexicanidad, wrestling allows for exóticos like May Flowers who "feel ostracized from society but not from lucha libre."[75] One of the most successful lucha libre duos is that of Rudy Reyna, a gay exótico, and Rizado Ruiz, a very "macho" wrestler.

Similarly, machismo is reinscribed and resisted at the same time through the history of female wrestlers. Lucha libre debuted in Mexico in 1933, and by the 1940s luchadoras were participating, if only in smaller venues outside the capitol. Women's lucha libre is a story of great endurance by now living legends who over the decades gained respect from the fans. During the 1960s, they began to appear in films, first in secondary roles and then as protagonists, for example in *Las luchadoras contra el médico asesino* (1962), with La Güera Solís, Magdalena Caballero, La Tapatía, Irma González, and Chabela Romero; *Las luchadoras contra la momia y las lobas del ring* (1964), with Caballero, Marina Rey, and Refugio Cervantes; and *Las mujeres panteras* (1966), with Betty Gray, Guadalupe Delgado, and Rey. Still, they were barred from performing in Mexico City arenas for more than forty years, until 1986. The following year, a female referee and promoter, Toña La Tapatía, was allowed to take the ring in the so-called cathedral of lucha libre, Arena México. Since then, luchadoras have increasingly overcome resistance from promoters, authorities, and colleagues, and carved out an important place for themselves in the world of lucha libre.[76]

In 2016, the Universidad Autónoma Metropolitana presented a conference and exhibition on women's lucha libre. The legendary Lola "Dinamita" González gave a lecture and performed in an exhibition match along with other legendary luchadoras like Lady Apache, Esther Moreno, and Rossy Moreno. Their outfits, as well as accessories were presented as part of the exhibition, *Lo mejor del ring* (The best of the ring).[77] A year later, in 2017, as part of the celebrations of three decades of female professional wrestling in Mexico City, similar events, conferences, and self-defense workshops took place at the National Autonomous University of Mexico, in the Museum of Contemporary Art.[78]

Like exóticos, female wrestlers can also be read as posing a challenge to the conventional meanings of lucha libre performance. Traditionally, although women wrestlers fight only other women[79] and cannot literally unman male opponents in the ring, they do so culturally, transgressing the codes of normative femininity both inside and outside the ring. For example, Martha Villalobos, a now retired luchadora but active promoter and two-time champion of the Reina de Reinas (Queen of Queens) competition has spoken about the tensions of being a strong, robustly built woman; although her physique has contributed to her success in the ring, outside, it is seen as "unusual for a woman to handle such weight" and she is "confronted regularly with questions regarding her sexual orientation."[80] Villalobos, like other female wrestlers, has transgressed the normative codes of femininity, embodying masculinity through their robust bodies and challenging ideas regarding their sexual orientation and interest in motherhood. Villalobos came out publicly in September 2009, through a widely circulated celebrity gossip magazine called *TVyNovelas*, stating not only that her partner was a woman but also that she was very happy raising their two children together.[81] It is interesting to note that Villalobos retired from the lucha libre in 2005 when her mother died, saying she felt she could not enjoy it anymore.[82]

It is important to underscore the fact that women like Barraza, as La Dama del Silencio, and others such as La Dama Enmascarada, Lola González, and Martha Villalobos—are full-fledged wrestlers in contrast to the objectified "hostesses" wearing small bikinis whose sole role is to introduce the male wrestlers to the audience before a match. The luchadoras demonstrate how Mexican women have resisted traditional and hegemonic cultural traditions, opening new doors for Mexican women's roles and identities.

Another important element in lucha libre is the melodramatic combat by wrestlers whose personalities are based on their nicknames—El Santo, Blue Demon, Perro Aguayo, Místico. Wrestlers fight *máscara contra cabellera* (mask against hair); not only are the losers defeated physically, but they also lose their lucha libre identity, either through revelation of their identity or through the cutting of their hair. Winning represents an unmanning of the opponent, in what might be seen as a repetition of the victory of colonization. Losing and winning are themselves performative acts; losing reenacts colonization in so far as the unmanning of the loser symbolizes the unmanning of the indigenous people. This reference to colonization is performed reiteratively in a manner that underscores the performativity of mexicanidad. The mostly heteronormative framework for these male, macho, mestizo wrestlers—the masks, the *cabelleras*, the melodramatic combat, the shiny and colorful costumes—are all constitutive elements of mexicanidad.

Added to the mix of judo, Greco-Roman fighting, and boxing are the different types of *llaves* (locks) performed by the wrestlers, with the ultimate goal of defeating the opponent at the count of three—the final win comes when the opponent has two "falls" out of three attempts. The spectators also participate in the performance, shouting to the wrestlers over and over, within an endless stream of curses, "Blood!" and "Kill him/her!" and "Finish him/her!"

In the performance of the melodramatic combat of lucha libre, a wrestler is either a rudo or a técnico. The *luchadores rudos* (rude wrestlers) are commonly the bad guys, who fight without proper technique or training and fuel the "hatred of the public."[83] One of the most famous Mexican wrestlers, now a legend, was Rodolfo Guzmán Huerta (1917–84), who performed as El Santo, El Enmascarado de Plata (The Saint, The Silver Masked). He started his wrestling career at seventeen years old as a rudo "doing forbidden things" that were not officially permitted in lucha libre, such as "knees to the stomach, really low blows, *llaves de rendición* [locks of surrender]."[84] When the image of El Santo became a symbol of justice in films and comic strips during the 1950s, Guzmán became a técnico, the good guy who fights with technical skill and does not need to "play dirty" to win.

The combat between técnicos and rudos is the fight between good and evil. As such, Barraza's identity as La Dama del Silencio, a ruda, was a sign to media and criminologists that she was La Mataviejitas. Being a ruda was a testament to her lack of schooling and proper technique, and fighting as one supposedly evidenced her "lack of morality," because the rudos are the bad ones, the evil in combat against the good.

I have attempted to demonstrate how the reiteration of lucha libre's performative acts, within the heteronormative framework of these authentic mestizo, macho wrestlers (in melodramatic combat), perform and produce a discourse on mexicanidad in which the postrevolutionary idealized Mexican is born mestizo and macho. This ideal Mexican is in direct opposition to that other ideal Mexican, the post-independence Mexican who is white and of European ancestry.

Whether as La Dama del Silencio or as La Mataviejitas, Barraza challenges both of these heteronormative frameworks for understanding mexicanidad and criminality. She falls outside both the postrevolutionary and the post-independence ideal Mexican, because she is a woman who is "muscular." The discourses of both media and criminology have displaced the figure of the serial killer onto that of the wrestler, in order to prove that Barraza is indeed La Mataviejitas.

Nicknames, Masks, and Disguises

Both despite and because of gender and sexual bias on the part of the police and the media in their search for El/La Mataviejitas, Barraza's nonnormative femininity led officials to represent La Dama del Silencio as La Mataviejitas. The merging of nicknames, La Mataviejitas and La Dama del Silencio, helped to pathologize Barraza—not for the homicides against elderly women but because her wrestling body sexually transgresses the codes of female normativity, thus leading observers to read Barraza's body as that of a pathological serial killer.

The nickname El Mataviejitas was coined by the media and adopted by the police to refer to the alleged serial killer of elderly women. The nickname, as in the case of Jack the Ripper in 1888, itself became a "media event."[85] As the only case in Mexican history in which a nickname preceded the identification of a serial killer, it is an example of a kind of dynamic nominalism. Ian Hacking defines dynamic nominalism as the phenomenon in which "a kind of person [comes] into being at the same time as the kind itself [is] being invented."[86] I argue that in the case of El/La Mataviejitas it is the naming of the serial killer that has defined and determined the police responses and public reaction. As soon as the name was coined, a search was started. As previously observed, other Mexican serial killers in Mexico have been given nicknames by the media, but only *after* their arrests. There is no account of how many gay men in the Zona Rosa, Mexico City's gay enclave, had been murdered, dismembered, and stuffed in suitcases before police detained Raúl Osiel Marroquín Reyes—who confessed to killing four homosexuals in a month and "feeling no remorse, and if he had the opportunity he would do it again more intelligently so as to not get caught"—yet there was no search for El Matagays before his arrest.[87]

The significance of the category of "serial killer" became pivotal at the same time prosecutors decided there was a serial killer in Mexico, and as Hacking points out, such categories are bound up with the "possibilities" that limit the subjectivity of a categorized individual.[88] These possibilities are defined by the beliefs as to who the criminal is and what he does, did, and will do.

Neither the news media nor the police paid much attention to Marroquín, who was arrested the same day as Barraza. Marroquín, twenty-five years old at the time and ex-military, kidnapped, tortured, killed, and dismembered gay men with the help of an accomplice, Juan Enrique Madrid. After the kidnapping of a man from a major TV station for a ransom of 120 thousand pesos, police started a search for the kidnapper in November 2005. There was, however, no mention of a serial killer, no profile, no nickname. Nor did the homosexual men who had been killed count as victims. It was only after an upper-class TV personality went missing that a search for that specific person started. It is not clear how Marroquín was finally captured, but he was arrested the same day as Barraza by federal authorities in Mexico City. He was convicted and, depending on the source, sentenced to either 128 years[89] or 280 years in prison.[90] Marroquín is currently housed in the same prison as Barraza, Santa Martha Acatitla.

Similarly, police arrested José Luis Calva Zepeda, aka El Poeta Caníbal, in October 2007. Not only did Calva Zepeda kill his girlfriends, he dismembered, cooked, and ate them. Yet there was, again, no police search for a serial killer, even though at least five dismembered bodies following the same pattern were found.[91] The number of women Calva Zepeda killed is unknown; he was convicted of for the murder of his ex-girlfriend Alejandra Galeana Garavito before he committed suicide in prison two months after his detention.[92]

Why were there no police investigations, sketches, informative pamphlets, or media reports that warned gay men in Zona Rosa or young women in Estado de México that they might be in danger? After their arrests, El Sádico and El Poeta Caníbal became just two of the many criminals in Mexico City; there are no songs, music videos, criminology books, or exhibitions about them. I argue that Barraza, as La Dama del

Silencio, became the one and only Mataviejitas despite the high number of still-unresolved murders in the case because Barraza's wrestling practice gave the police, criminologists, and media—mainstream news outlets and nota roja alike—the perfect sensationalist story. Barraza's criminality goes far beyond the murders of elderly women. In the following sections I emphasize how, as in criminological accounts, the displacement of La Dama del Silencio onto La Mataviejitas in popular culture has served to criminalize Barraza for the homicides of elderly women but also, and equally, for falling outside the normative roles of femininity in discourses of mexicanidad and criminality.

As noted, as soon as police had declared the existence of El Mataviejitas, they "knew" certain characteristics of the killer, most saliently that it was a man, despite the accounts of witnesses that pointed to a woman. Right away, police had access to a whole set of ideas about how a serial killer behaves, what a serial killer does, and who a serial killer is in terms of gender, sexuality, and class (and we can argue skin color, too, since they created sketches of the killer using CaraMex, which draws on a database of profiles that are 90 percent indigenous men and darker mestizos). Clearly, these assumptions and descriptions were not based on police experience with serial killers in Mexico, as there had officially been only one: Goyo Cárdenas, in 1942. As noted in chapter 1, Mexico City deputy prosecutor Renato Sales Heredia offered a serial killer profile that corresponded to virtually every other international account of such criminals.

The profiling of El Mataviejitas in terms of gender, sex, and sexuality may be understood in relation to the power of performative acts within discourses on criminality. Practices of citationality carry within them a historical legacy such that the interpellation of a subject, El Mataviejitas, precedes and conditions the formation of this subject, a male serial killer. Existing authoritative discourses on serial killing made it impossible for police to imagine a female serial killer. Barraza, as a female, challenged internationally naturalized assumptions of the male character of serial killers.

Despite cases such as those of El Sádico and El Poeta Caníbal, it is La Mataviejitas who has been profiled in criminological accounts and media reports as an extreme case of stranger violence. During their search of Barraza's house, police found a photo of Barraza in her wrestling costume.[93] The photograph shows La Dama del Silencio posing with the World Women's Wrestling Championship belt across her shoulder and waist, standing against a blue background with one hand on her hip, displaying her muscular arm. She is wearing a bright pink Power Ranger–style suit with silver details, and her face is covered by a silver-and-pink butterfly mask. Barraza's wrestling photograph thus juxtaposes markers of her physical strength with those of femininity, codified through butterflies and the vivid pink color of her suit. In doing so, the photo creates what Anne Balsamo calls a "gender 'hybrid' that invokes corporeal codes of femininity as well as of masculinity."[94] This gendered hybrid challenges the norms of femininity established by discourses on mexicanidad and at the same time aligns Barraza with international discourses on female criminals.

Barraza as La Dama del Silencio doubly transgresses Mexican female normativity. Not only is she strong, she performs lucha libre, a spectacle mostly reserved for men. As previously noted, although women wrestlers have performed around Mexico since the 1940s, they have been allowed in Mexico City arenas only since 1986.[95] Consequently, for the media and criminologists, Barraza's wrestling practice and nonnormative feminine gender became the weapon she used to commit her alleged multiple crimes.

In contrast, news reports of El Sádico and El Poeta Caníbal make no reference to the men's bodies, faces, or physical appearance. Nor was I able to find references to the bodies of Tablas or Vázquez, the other two potential El/La Mataviejitas. Yet media depictions of La Dama del Silencio made repeated reference to her face, body, and physical attributes: for instance, "Her facial features, her hair style and red hair color [are] common to a certain class of women recognizable in Mexico City."[96]

Through such descriptions, media narratives reinforce class stereotypes implicit in cultural understandings of wrestling practice and in historical descriptions of criminals that point to the entangled relationship in Mexico and between Mexicans to class and skin tonality. In this relationship, the privileged and desirable subject position is that which whiteness offers, associated with lighter skin color and economic affluence, while the darker skin is associated with lower socioeconomic status. Such narratives further align Barraza's socioeconomic class to that of a criminal, following discourses of criminality established two centuries ago, and through discourses of mexicanidad.

Barraza's wrestling body disobeys the established gender and sex roles socially defined for women, thus defying traditional productions of mexicanidad. The physical strength that she displays in the photograph as La Dama del Silencio resists historical and biological notions of the properly feminine body constituted as "weak" and pathological and the culturally dominant codes of femininity that exclude women from sports that serve as "cults of masculinity,"[97] especially in a Mexican cultural context. Female bodies are culturally accepted if "naturally" feminine—that is, if they do not threaten the dominant codes of the idealized Mexican, be it the mestizo and macho, or the more "European" and upper-class Mexican.

Barraza's body is interpreted by authorities and media not as a sign of resistance to normative feminine roles or as a challenge to the norms of mexicanidad, but on the contrary, as further evidence of her innate criminality and of the status of her body as a murder weapon: "physical force is the instrument by which she pays her bills and killed old women, until yesterday, when she committed an error that resulted in her capture."[98] There are numerous accounts that point to Barraza's features, body, and strength in this way: her "virile features," "humongous height," and "short hair" are taken as manifestations of her "repressed sexuality."[99] The discourse on mexicanidad that makes La Dama del Silencio's body the weapon she used to commit her crimes is aligned with the discourses of criminality noted above and in the next chapter. Her body is her weapon: outwardly, through her nonnormative gender and physically features, and internally, as seemingly confirmed through her EEGs.

Barraza's corporeal strength and wrestling practice have been seen as the reason police assumed El Mataviejitas was a man. Because police could not imagine a woman serial killer they deduced the murderer was a travesti, since witnesses had described a person dressed in women's clothing but also with "physical strength," someone "broad-shouldered, strong, around 1.70 cm tall" who "could have suffered childhood abuse (sexual and psychological)."[100] Since police had established a profile of the serial killer that was not consistent with Barraza, criminologists instead profiled La Dama del Silencio. First, police stated that because Barraza was "tall," "robust," and "strong," police thought the killer was "a man dressed as a woman"[101]—thus suggesting that Barraza was La

Mataviejitas, but serving to criminalize La Dama del Silencio instead of Barraza.

Second, the photograph of La Dama del Silencio proudly posing with her championship belt became evidence that, "like the rest of the serial killers in the world, Juana Barraza Samperio, La Mataviejitas, was egocentric and fetishist."[102] Third, for Ostrosky and Barrón, that La Dama del Silencio wrestled as a ruda was evidence that Barraza had an "aggressive nature,"[103] which she was able to vent through lucha libre—an aggressiveness that is also a common trait of serial killers and, as discussed earlier, is seen as "unnatural" in women. Fourth, criminologists deduced that Barraza wrestled to become famous, another common cliché in serial killer narratives; it is often suggested that they kill to "become somebody."[104] Finally, Barraza's succession of disguises, as a nurse and a "power ranger," testified to the "chameleon-like quality"[105] often attributed to serial killers.

In brief, serial killers are like wrestlers. They need a different persona to perform their trade. With the new persona, the serial killer either kills or blends into the crowd; the wrestler performs the fight between good and evil. It is this new persona that each acquires, either through media narratives or in the ring, that renders both the serial killer and the wrestler into mythic figures, celebrities. Serial killers wear a "sanity mask" that allows them to act like "normal" individuals in between crimes.[106] Wrestlers wear a mask to wrestle. Both inspire films and songs and have T-shirts made in their honor.[107]

In their merging of nicknames and personas, media and authorities followed this reasoning: Barraza dressed as a nurse to fool elderly women into letting her into their houses to then kill them. Similarly, Barraza deceived the public that all she wanted from wrestling was to be famous, echoing the principle that serial killing is performed in an effort to "become someone." Finally, and most importantly, Barraza tricked the police for over three years, and it was her fault for being so tall, strong, and robust that police expected her to be a man. For the media and police alike, Barraza existed only through disguises, either as a nurse or as pink-clad Power Ranger. In order to kill, Barraza became La Mataviejitas, and in order to wrestle, she became La Dama del Silencio. She could not exist any other way. Her lack of coherence with the gender norms established for women by discourses on both criminality and mexicanidad rendered her body materially unintelligible, abject.

A nickname is as crucial in lucha libre as it is in the narrations of serial killers: the name defines the persona. In lucha libre, the nickname is invariably associated with a mask. Masks have a historical significance in Mexico; they recall pre-Hispanic times, invoking images of animals, gods, and ancient heroes, and drawing upon origin myths. Most importantly, they disguise the wrestler's persona in the ring. El Santo, the greatest legend of Mexican wrestling, always maintained his anonymity—no one ever saw his face.

Barraza explained that she chose the wrestling nickname La Dama del Silencio because her personality is "reserved and quiet."[108] Note that she also chose to call herself *dama*, "lady." She completed her wrestling persona by wearing a butterfly mask. As analyzed in the previous chapter, in its merging of personas between La Dama del Silencio and La Mataviejitas, the title of Barrón's "Desenmascarada" (Unmasked) chapter suggests that he himself was in a wrestling match with La Dama del Silencio and had won, thus "unmasking" her. In lucha libre, to unmask a wrestler is "not only to defeat but to humiliate the opponent."[109] Barrón thus means to convey that he not only defeated a serial killer through his criminological investigation and deployment of international criminologists' "scientific" metrics, but, further, was able to humiliate La Mataviejitas by corroborating Barraza's innate criminality.

Considering that within the norms of mexicanidad as described by Paz, "Mexicans considered women an instrument" for men and for society, it is not a stretch to argue that Barraza's life without *máscaras* (masks) did not exist, especially considering her lower-class status.[110] According to Paz, women do not create but transmit or conserve the values of society. As I have argued, Barraza as La Dama del Silencio instead challenges the parameters of mexicanidad insofar as she defies normative roles of femininity. Barraza as the alleged La Mataviejitas challenges criminality discourses on serial killing but aligns La Dama del Silencio with international accounts of women murderers. As one newspaper suggested, "nobody was ready for Juana Barraza."[111]

Killing as Performance
The Music Video: "La Mataviejitas"

The displacement of personas from La Dama del Silencio to La Mataviejitas that has persisted in police, media, and criminological accounts has also circulated through different popular cultural sites. The year after Barraza's arrest, Amandititita, an underground singer from Mexico and self-proclaimed "la reina de la Anarcocumbia" (the queen of the *anarcocumbia*), released a song entitled "La Mataviejitas." On September 12, 2007, a music video that accompanies this song during Amandititita's live performances was uploaded to YouTube.[112]

The video starts with an image of Barraza sitting in a police car, presumably after being arrested, looking at the camera. Her face is covered by the title "La Mataviejitas," which proceeds to flash on and off against red and yellow backgrounds. The song starts with a heavy bass line as the title "La Mataviejitas" continues to flash. A rapid collage of images of Barraza follows: Barraza's face next to the three-dimensional bust done by police, Barraza being interviewed by police after she was caught fleeing the crime scene, the sketches used by police in the search for El/La Mataviejitas, a mug shot of Barraza—then, for a split second, the image of a face screaming.

In the next scene, a woman dressed as a nurse with a red sweater is walking down the stairs of the government institute for social health; we then see her walking on the street, evidently careful to not be followed. She takes some black tights out of her very feminine blue purse and smells them, fetishistically. In the next scene, someone is cleaning a house, caring for plants, eating cake, and preparing tea. Viewers are led to assume she is an elderly woman. The rapid sequence of images from Barraza's detention and the sketches of El/La Mataviejitas repeats before we see a young nurse in the elderly woman's apartment. The nurse is forcing the older woman onto a couch, trying to asphyxiate her with her bare hands and then throwing her to the floor as in a wrestling match. The nurse applies the *llave voladora* (a move in which one wrestler falls on top of the other) and then another *llave*; the elderly woman moves her hands to signal she is "giving up" (in lucha libre, moving the hands back and forth rapidly means a wrestler is surrendering). The nurse then starts counting to five, again as in a wrestling match to declare a winner. The wrestling performance continues, with the nurse taking out the pair of black tights and strangling the elderly woman, who is comically pretending to defend herself. The nurse leaves the apartment and experiences a sort of ecstasy as she skips down the street, turning with her hands flying, more like a ballerina than a professional wrestler. The last scene underscores her fetishism (a characteristic assumed typical of serial killers), as she sits on a park bench secretively smelling the black tights while making sure she is not being watched.

What is interesting about what gets reproduced culturally by an independent production such as this video is the casting of the characters. While the nurse is dressed in a white skirt and a red sweater (letting the public known she is La Mataviejitas), she is played by a very feminine woman who sits in the park cross-legged with her hands on her knees, displaying a very normative femininity—the lack of which has characterized other media representations of Barraza. A man, meanwhile, plays the elderly woman.

In this video, the persona of the nurse merges with that of a wrestler, as the killer uses wrestling techniques to defeat and kill the elderly woman. La Mataviejitas is La Dama del Silencio but not Juana Barraza. What this implies is that the killing of elderly women becomes a wrestling performance, which works to dehumanize the victim; the serial killer, La Mataviejitas, becomes a wrestler and the victim might not be really dying but just giving up. This performance of killing renders comedic the actual homicides of elderly women.

The constant repetition and recreation of the killings are also performed in the lyrics of Amandititita's song. The catchy chorus repeats over and over: "La Mataviejitas, La Mataviejitas, La Mataviejitas, La Mataviejitas se quiere echar a tu abuelita" (La Mataviejitas wants to do your grandmother). The use of the verb "do" rather than "strangle" or "kill" lends a sexual double entendre to the performance of killing. This double entendre is also prevalent in serial killing discourses, as the figure of the serial killer is commonly also that of a sex criminal. Similarly, lucha libre performances use many *llaves de rendición* that "leave the losing wrestler not only helpless, but in a position of marked sexual vulnerability."[113]

The lyrics further render the performance of wrestling/killing comedic as they claim, for example, that La Mataviejitas wants to kill elderly women because she collects false teeth, or that La Mataviejitas hates elderly women because they do not invite her to their INSEN (National Institute for Elderly Citizens) parties.

For Monsiváis, "machismo is also a complaining demand for recognition. . . . Having been dispossessed, the never-quite-adult macho from the popular classes offers up the credulity of his puerile, deteriorated and sacrificial ego for commercialization."[114] This exploitation of the dispossessed "popular classes" is at work in the consumption of machismo in Mexican wrestling practice, paraphernalia, and commercial culture. Following Monsiváis, we can read the increasing popularity of lucha libre (and its demonstration of machismo) among middle- and upper-class Mexican and global consumers of "third world" kitsch as a way of reveling in the spectacular disenfranchisement of the increasingly visible poorer classes in Mexico.

This video might only accompany Amandititita's live shows, but I take it as representative of the fantastic element of killing as performance. Furthermore, while it might only circulate among a small niche, the middle-class "alternative" sector of Mexico City, it shows how different socially stratified public opinions process La Mataviejitas and how the figure of La Dama del Silencio is that of the serial killer—a displacement of identities that I have shown is similar in police and criminological accounts.

The Novel: Ruda de corazón

Journalist Victor Ronquillo wrote a novel, published in 2006, based on the case of La Mataviejitas. In it, as in Amandititia's video, Barrón's and Ostrosky's accounts, and news media reports, Barraza's identity as La Dama del Silencio becomes one with that of La Mataviejitas.

First, the title of the novel, *Ruda de corazón*, makes reference to Barraza's declaration on TV Azteca that she is an enthusiastic devotee of lucha libre, or a "ruda from the bottom of her heart." Second, the novel narrates, in the third person, the life of La Dama del Silencio, including her difficulties training in a gymnasium, being a female wrestler, and working with a promoter who never really believed in her. The narrative places special emphasis on the photograph of La Dama del

Silencio posing with the championship belt and imagines the wrestler's pride.

Ronquillo's book merges La Dama del Silencio and La Mataviejitas when he introduces two fictional cops, Luciano Nuñez and Gerardo Silva, who visit La Dama del Silencio. Nuñez is extorting her and stops by her house to collect his payoff. The wrestler pays him with a ring that has "a shiny stone." Years later, Silva, now a taxi driver, looks at the photographs of La Mataviejitas published in the newspapers and realizes that he had met her with Nuñez years before—that she was La Dama del Silencio—and he would never forget "the hands of the wrestler."[115] In reality, Barraza had indeed been extorted by police officer Moisés Flores Domínguez, who in 1996 discovered that Barraza had been burglarizing houses and demanded twelve thousand pesos in exchange for not arresting her.[116] Except for one news report, this extortion, which probably lasted years, is rarely mentioned. Domínguez was supposed to be in police custody, but I have not been able to find out if he has been convicted.

Ruda de corazón mixes journalistic reports into the fictionalized story, tracing the life of La Dama del Silencio, the victims, the killings, and the police response as the years progressed. This is a rare instance in which Barraza's life is used not as an explanation of her pathology but as way to show that she herself was a victim too, as Ronquillo explains, of a "society that is enormously machista, exclusive and unequal."[117] Ronquillo stated that he is not interested in "denying the legal responsibility" of Barraza but in showing that the serial killer of elderly women is a "lamentable result of the social degradation that Mexico City experiences."[118] The novel is, in his own words, a response to the "stigmatization and media lynching" of Barraza.[119]

Although Ronquillo sees Barraza as a victim and not only a victimizer, he, too, displaces the identity of La Dama del Silencio onto that of La Mataviejitas as evidence that Barraza is the serial killer. In the novel, the killings of elderly women are, in contrast to Amandititita's video and song, not comedic performances but a result of the victimization characteristic of a machista society.

The Police Cultural Center Exhibition

In December 2006, the Police Cultural Center in downtown Mexico City opened an exhibition on serial killers that continues to date. It resembles the *casa de los sustos* (house of horrors) found at any fairground, designed to frighten children with macabre staged scenes and the display of props. The exhibit starts with the sixteenth-century "blood countess," Elizabeth Báthory, passes through 1880s London with Jack the Ripper, and of course ends with Juana Barraza, La Mataviejitas. In the thirteen different areas of the exhibit, visitors may listen through earphones to a narration that recounts each crime as a story, complete with background sounds. The objective throughout is for the visitor to travel into the mind of the serial killer.

The part of the exhibit devoted to La Mataviejitas showcases the original three-dimensional bust created in 2005 by Patricia Payán. Also behind glass are photographs of La Dama del Silencio and of Barraza out of costume, and official police documents featuring her fingerprints. The most interesting prop in this area is a video, presumably produced by police, that re-creates the killings of elderly women. The video starts with the face of Juana Barraza. The next scene shows an elderly woman sitting in a chair, while another woman appears from behind and starts suffocating the victim, with what could be tights or a stethoscope. The elderly woman dies of suffocation while the younger woman, who is bigger and stronger, angrily stares at the camera. The video lasts only a couple of minutes and then starts over again.

Unlike news reports, criminological accounts, Amandititita's video, and Ronquillo's novel, this video alludes to Barraza but makes no reference to La Dama del Silencio as La Mataviejitas. Like Amandititita's song and video, however, it renders the killings of elderly women a performance. The video is part of an exhibition that already poses serial killers as notorious characters; the sound and staging render the crimes theatrical, rather than realistic. The most important feature, I think, is the constant repetition of the killings, played over and over again in a neverending loop.

Robert Ressler, the special FBI agent credited with coining the term "serial killer" in the 1970s, talked about "naming the event" as not a "big deal at the time" but just an "effort in trying to get a handle on those monstruous crimes."[120] For Ressler, "serial killing" made more sense than "stranger killings" in that it seemed a "highly appropriate way of characterizing the killings of those who do one murder, then another and another and another in a fairly repetitive way." Also, it had a personal resonance for Ressler. As a child, he would watch "serial adventures" at the movies every Saturday, and every week he was "lured back to see another episode, because at the end of each one there was a cliffhanger. In dramatic terms this wasn't a satisfactory ending, because it increased, not lessened, the tension." He proposes that "the same dissatisfaction occurs in the minds of serial killers. The very act of killing leaves the murderer hanging because it isn't as perfect as his fantasy."[121] Seltzer takes this further and points out that for Ressler, the "real meaning behind the term 'serial killer' is the internal competition between repetition and representation."[122] The video of the killings in the Police Cultural Center exhibition is in an internal competition, between (a) representing La Dama del Silencio as La Mataviejitas and (b) constantly repeating the strangulation of an elderly woman. Seltzer makes an analogy between "addiction to representation" and "acts of killing" that is "an equation between acts of violence and the relative passivity of 'just looking.'"[123] As such, the video brings the act of killing (the repetition of the strangulation) on par with the addiction to representation (the act of looking by the visitors).

Drawing on Seltzer's ideas, I suggest that these videos are possible only in a wound culture addicted to violence, where "scenes of spectacularized bodily violence are inseparable from the binding of violence to scene, spectacle and representation."[124] This spectacle of killing—repeated over and over until the day ends, only to start again the next day—incites a distanced fascination with the killings and the killer, rendering the homicides against elderly women an eerie performance.

The repetition of the killing of elderly women in this video is in itself a performative act; it is through the repetition of the crimes, the reiteration of the gender and sex of the serial killer in the video, that spectators come to know the sex and gender of both the killer and the victim. The spectator can then rest assured that Barraza was indeed La Mataviejitas and that elderly women in Mexico City have nothing to worry about anymore.

I take this video to be a signifier of how the police want the public to understand Barraza. Following critiques of serial killer narratives, one can conclude that this video works to create "a dominant understanding of a serial killer as inhuman"—an understanding prevalent in cinematic and media representations.[125] La Dama del Silencio as La Mataviejitas is a comedic performance for Amandititita, a mirror of an unequal and unjust society for Victor Ronquillo, and part of an eerie, fantastic world in the Police Cultural Center.

4

Performing Mexicanidad II

Criminality and La Santa Muerte

On top of a small, two-tiered wood dresser there are four skeleton figures wearing capes. The one in the middle is wearing a bright red cape; behind her there is a vase with three yellow flowers. Another figure is holding a scythe and a blue globe. Behind that skeleton there is a photograph of the same figure, also with a scythe and a blue globe. There is also a plate with apples, one burned-out glass candle, and two Styrofoam cups. The walls surrounding the altar are painted bright red. This is an altar found at Juana Barraza's house. A photograph of it is shown in Martín Barrón's book; the caption reads "Altar to La Santa Muerte found in Juana Barraza's house the day of her arrest." La Santa Muerte (The Holy Death) is a popular Mexican personification of death as a *calavera* (skeleton or skull)—a folk saint commonly associated with marginalized communities, mostly lower class. The altar also has a figure of Jesús Malverde, commonly known as the saint of narco dealers, and fake bills of various denominations. The altar and the photograph that proves its existence serve as evidence of Barraza's criminality, as the cults of La Santa Muerte and Jesús Malverde are associated with delinquents, sex workers, narco traffickers, and drug addicts (fig. 4.1).

News reports stated that, in addition to the Santa Muerte altar and framed image of Jesús Malverde, there was also a figure similar to that of a Buddha. At the feet of these figures, there were quartz stones, an apple, a serpent, and snails as offerings, and a small, barrel-shaped container with the phrase "for abundance" written on it. The discovery of this altar led to media headlines such as "Barraza entrusted herself to The Holy Death as to not be detained by police" and "La Mataviejitas practiced black magic to avoid being discovered."[1] A "figure of white resin of La Santa Muerte in her bag" was also found, yielding the headline "Amulets fail."[2] That Barraza had in her home an altar with the figures of La Santa

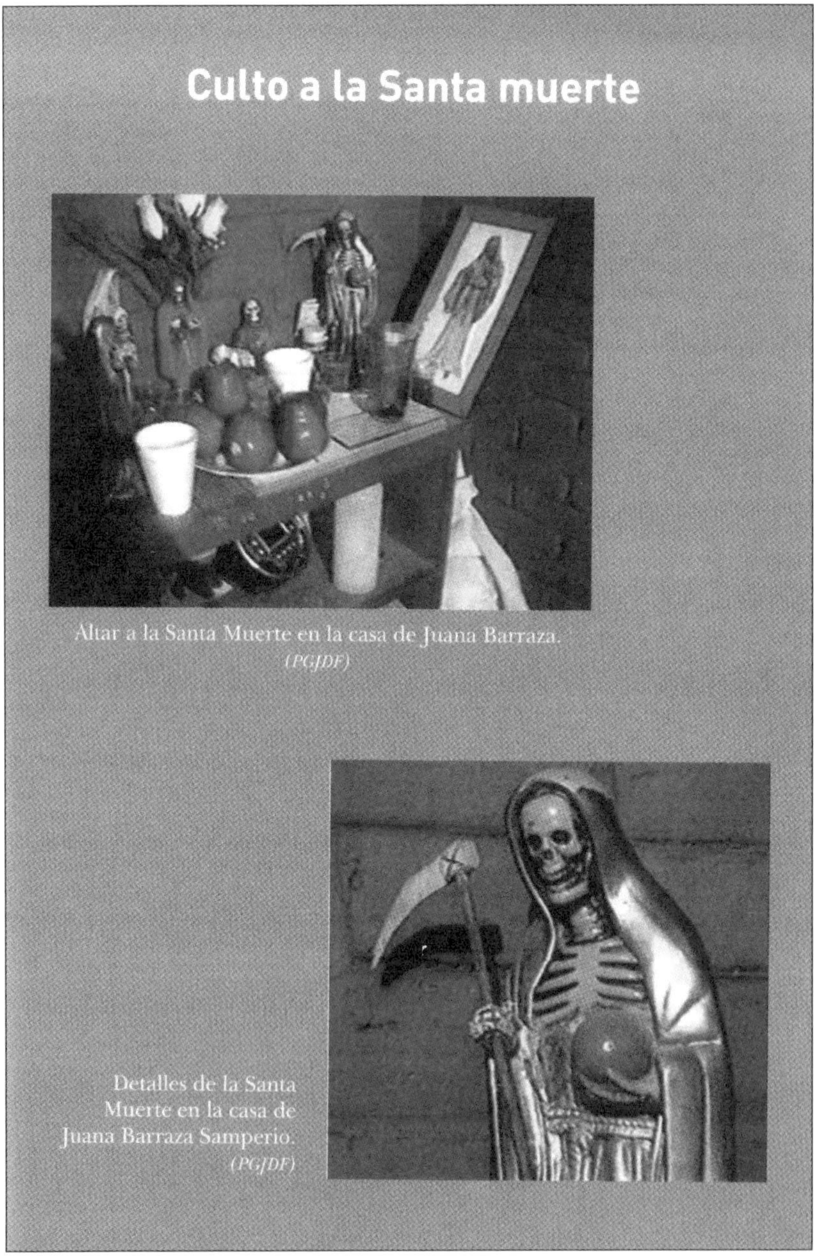

Figure 4.1. Barraza's altar to La Santa Muerte.

Muerte and Jesús Malverde was immediately exploited in criminological and media narrations to pathologize her as an innate criminal.

These two figures of devotion were used in police and media narratives to criminalize Barraza as La Mataviejitas, establishing who constitutes a "morally good" Mexican versus an "evil" Mexican, based on religious and cultural beliefs. These notions further reinforce cultural understandings and perceptions of who is a criminal and who counts as victim—conceptions that have been delimited through understandings of mexicanidad, in terms of gender, sexuality, and class/skin tonalities.

I am interested in understanding how the cult of La Santa Muerte since its origin has been linked to criminality and delinquency in comparison to one of the main myths in the construction of mexicanidad: that of the virgin mestiza, La Virgen de Guadalupe. It is through the archetype of La Virgen that discourses on mexicanidad have determined who is an ideal (and sacred) woman/mother, thus delimiting what "type" of women is deemed worthy of the attention of the government. By comparing the origins of and rituals around these two motherly figures, I establish how constructions of mexicanidad have delimited notions of femininity, of who constitutes a morally acceptable and ideal Mexican woman versus an immoral, criminal, and evil Mexican woman.

I ask in my analysis how ideologies of mexicanidad are intertwined with religious values, which have been translated into moral values that in turn have influenced criminal discourses and, most importantly, have determined which bodies are grievable and which bodies matter as cause of national concern. I do so through analyzing how Barraza has been further criminalized through her personal religious and cultural beliefs, along with her socioeconomic class. Media and criminological narrations of Barraza's religious beliefs not only construct her as a criminal but also reveal why the bodies of young poor and brown women and the bodies of indigenous women—victims of feminicide and police sexual abuse—are not deserving of the recognition of the government.

Through examinations of the religious and moral constructions of mexicanidad, I question why the bodies of the young mestizo women and indigenous women killed violently in places like Estado de México (the same place where Barraza lived) and Ciudad Juárez (known internationally for its feminicides) do not count as victims to the government. Why are their bodies not deemed worthy of shocking the nation?

There are other figures like that of La Santa Muerte in Mexican popular culture, like that of the calavera known as La Catrina. In the early 1910s, world-renowned lithographer José Guadalupe Posada created an etching, *La calavera Catrina,* to satirize those Mexicans who aspired to the status of the European aristocracy. Government discourses and popular-culture narratives transformed this image into a symbol of mexicanidad, promoting it as an icon of the Day of the Dead. While both La Santa Muerte and La Catrina are female skeletons widespread in Mexican popular culture, their representations and significances are quite different. In this chapter, I compare how the historical representation and promotion by official, media, and popular discourses of these two figures reveal classed, gendered, and sexed constructions of mexicanidad that have had actual effects on the construction of criminal discourses, in terms of femininity, masculinity, class, and skin color.

Finally, I am interested in the rituals related to La Santa Muerte in contempory Mexico City, to explore the cult's social stigma and association with the criminalization of the marginalized and poor. I discuss the relationship between Santa Muerte and Jesús Malverde, analyzing how they are associated with criminality in general and drug-related trafficking and narco culture in particular. Examining the cultural beliefs around these figures can shed light on how Barraza was further criminalized in the media, not only for her alleged crimes, but for her religious beliefs, rendering her "evil" by nature—again, a natural-born killer.

After Juana Barraza was apprehended in January 2006 and declared the one and only La Mataviejitas, everything about her was scrutinized. As I have shown, this included her body, her brain, her face, and her emotions. According to police authorities and criminologists, Barraza's physical appearance, physiognomy, psychological profile, and even brain functions and emotions all fit the modus operandi, the psychological profile, the physiognomy, and the neuropsychological profile of the serial killer that police and criminologists had developed. The only things that fell outside the authorities' profiling of El Mataviejitas was Barraza's sex and sexual preferences, since police authorities had been looking for a man, possibly a man with homosexual tendencies. But as we have seen, police did not perceive this inconsistency as an inaccuracy on the part of their profile of the serial killer, but as yet more evidence of Barraza's inner criminality—it was her fault for looking so "manly" and "robust" (for a woman) that police thought she was a man.

My analysis further problematizes these discourses through the notion of pigmentocracy. As explained in earlier chapters, I use the concept of pigmentocracy to designate the entangled relationship in Mexico and among Mexicans between skin color and social stratification, a relationship first defined during Spanish colonization that continued in the subsequent colonial period and persists to the present day. Within this relationship, skin tonality has been a marker of class. Here, skin color works not so much as a simple marker of race or ethnicity or class but as a power mechanism—interdependent and reproducible.

I am especially interested in why police and news media chose to focus on Barraza's altars as further evidence that she was the pathological La Mataviejitas but failed to contextualize her alleged crimes with others in the same neighborhood where she lived. Barraza's house is located at 101 Abetos Street, on the outskirts of Mexico City in Izcalli, Ixtapaluca, a poor Estado de México banlieue that is a mix of a small provincial town and shantytown. Surrounding Mexico City, Estado de México is known for its social and economic precarity, having the highest number of people in the country living in poverty: 9.46 million, according to *Forbes* in 2015.[3] Barraza's neighborhood of Ecatepec has been called the worst place to live in Mexico, lacking in infrastructure, security, and basic services.[4] Most importantly, it is the municipality with the highest number of feminicides in Mexico—7 in 100,000 women killed every day between 1990 and 2011.[5] It is crucial to analyze the feminicides in Estado de México alongside those in Ciudad Juárez, which gained more international attention, following pressure by feminist activists and nongovernmental organizations. Police and media treatment of the feminicides in Ciudad Juárez is echoed in that of feminicides in Estado de México; that is, the state responds to gender violence—and specifically to the killing of young mestizo women—in similar ways.

The Spanish term *feminicidio*, which can be translated as "feminicide," was adapted and adopted in Mexico from the English term "femicide," defined by Jill Radford and Diana Russell as "the misogynous killing of women by men," which is a "form of sexual violence."[6] In 1994, anthropologist Marcela Lagarde adopted the term *feminicidio* as opposed to *femicidio* (that is, "femicide"), because in Castilian, femicide is homologous to homicide, simply meaning the killing of women. Lagarde recasts the term *femicidio* as *feminicidio* to imply that the misogynous assassination of women is performed by men with the complicity of the state. The term thus highlights the structural impunity with which the endless feminicides in Mexico have been committed.[7]

The news in January 2006 focused on showing how Barraza was indeed La Mataviejitas. Yet only four months after her arrest, at the beginning of May, an event of horrific police brutality and gender violence against indigenous women took place in Salvador Atenco, a municipality in Estado de México. I analyze this event as it sheds light on determining which bodies are deemed grievable by the nation and which are not in terms of gender, sexuality, class, and skin color. It further shows how indigenous women continue to be part of the "Indian problem" defined since the building of the nation.

Feminicides in Estado de México and Ciudad Juárez

In 2017, Estado de México was named the "capital of feminicides," the epicenter of the killings of women in Mexico.[8] According to Humberto Padgett and Eduardo Loza's *Las muertas del estado* (The [female] deaths of the state), between 1993 and 2005—roughly the same period that El/La Mataviejitas allegedly operated in Mexico City—4,379 feminicides took place in Estado de México.[9] During those same years, in Ciudad Juárez, at least "382 girls and young women" were violently killed, after being tortured and raped; "some of them were mutilated, calcined, and their cadavers thrown into inhospitable places and in the desert that surrounds the city."[10]

During the late 1990s, before the mass feminicides in Estado de México were at last publicly recognized, Ciudad Juárez came to be known internationally for its feminicides, thanks to the pressure of family members who brought the crimes to the public eye. Those who were killed or disappeared were "predominantly young women, brown, students, industry workers, girls and all of them . . . marginalized economically."[11] Many worked at the maquiladoras, whose numbers expanded rapidly around the period of the negotiation and 1994 signing of the North American Free Trade Agreement, linking their deaths to the transnational economy.[12] It was in 1993 when activist Esther Chávez started taking account of how many young, poor women had been disappearing without any interest or action taken by the state government of Chihuahua or police.[13] Three years later, the Coordinadora de Organismos no Gubernamentales en Pro de la Mujer (coordinator of nongovernmental organizations in favor of women) was formed, representing sixteen different civil organizations demanding justice for the victims of feminicides in Ciudad Juárez.[14] Bodies of young women—killed after being raped, tortured, and mutilated—had been found, often several at a time, dumped in deserts, empty lots, and cotton fields, yet police took no action to solve these violent murders.[15] Again, most of the women were "poor and brown";[16] within Mexico's pigmentocratic system, their bodies were treated as disposable and their muders not worth investigating.

Academic María Socorro Tabuenca has analyzed the visuals and text in various crime prevention campaigns put into place by the government of Chihuahua, and concluded that the conception of women trapped in a dichotomy of virgin/whore and Eva/María is what informs their understanding of the victim. For Tabuenca, there is a clear differentiation between women who are "decent," "pure"—which also reads as white and middle or upper class—who do not go out at night, do not accept a "beer" from anyone they do not know, and the victims of feminicides, who are poor, young, brown, and depicted as more inclined to "fall into temptation," going out very late at night with men they do not know or "falling into drugs."[17]

The now well-known phenomenon of Las Muertas de Juárez reached international notice thanks to the work of activists and family members who continue to look for the more than three hundred victims. It is not because the government or police authorities started investigating these disappearances of young women that the public learned of these cases. On the contrary, what has characterized the feminicides in Ciudad Juárez is the lack of interest, the corruption, the profound lack of will to solve the murders—the incapacity of the Mexican state to find the people responsible.[18] Berlanga Gayón has analyzed specifically the way the photographs of the victims of feminicides are presented to the public, which is invariably in a violent fashion that further denigrates and humiliates them.[19] The images normalize and naturalize the horrors of feminicide, showing the victims almost naked, as they were left on the pavement, in the open fields, with their bodies uncovered. According to

Berlanga Gayón, these photographs contribute to the way feminicides are treated by the state, that is, through a patriarchal power structure inscribed in a society that permits, remains silent about, and justifies violence against women.[20]

The number of women reported to have been killed in Ciudad Juárez varies, from 257 cases reported by the Inter-American Commission of Human Rights, to 370 reported by Amnesty International, to 382 reported by the database Feminicidios by Julia Monárrez of Colegio de la Frontera Norte, to 470 reported by journalist Diana Washington Valdez.[21] In 2003, the number of registered missing women according to a National Human Rights Commission report was 4,587.[22]

Academic and activist Julia Monárrez created a database for analyzing these feminicides, since the numbers given by the government cannot be trusted; evidence has been tampered with and anomalies identified in those few investigations that have been conducted.[23] Monárrez classifies the feminicides, taking into consideration the way young women have been found and under what circumstances. Because many died following similar patterns, involving sexual violence, Monárrez's studies in the early 2000s suggested that many of the feminicides could have been committed by serial killers,[24] following the work of Jane Caputi and of Deborah Cameron and Elizabeth Frazer, who understand serial killing as sexual killing.[25] Indeed, it is not a stretch to conclude that the feminicides in Ciudad Juárez are the result of serial killing, since the hundreds of young women of low economic resources murdered violently were raped, mutilated, and/or tortured and then left in deserted areas of the city and in vacant lots, their bodies sometimes disposed of in big containers using either cement or corrosive acid, a practice known as *entambalar*.[26]

Press reports on the case, according to Monárrez, have focused "on giving the total number of victims murdered in the same fashion, feeding a morbid curiosity and creating a stereotype of a serial killer."[27] Ten years later, however, Monárrez's work avoids the term "serial killer"; the feminicides, she writes, could also have been perpetrated by "'multihomicides,' copycat killers, 'spontaneous killers' and they could also be national or foreigners," and she now considers it outside her scope "to determine who the murderers are."[28]

In fact, there might have been several serial killers in Ciudad Juárez, considering the similar patterns and the numbers of bodies found in the same place on the same day or during a specific time with similar mutilations, leading journalists such as Sergio González and Diana Washington Valdez to suggest that the persistent, organized, and systematized manner of the murders spoke of serial sexual crimes.[29] For instance, in 1995 in Lote Bravo, eight women were found dead; in 1996 in Lomas de Poleo, nine bodies were found. These were both the results of searches by academics and activists who, to compensate for the authorities' lack of interest, took the task of investigating the feminicides into their own hands.[30] Criminologist Óscar Máyrez Grijalva concluded that a serial killer was responsible for the feminicides and stated that the chief of police in Chihuahua, Francisco Molina, was not interested in investigating or following up on these findings.[31]

The purpose of my analysis is not to determine whether or not there have been serial killers in Ciudad Juárez, but to highlight that neither the government nor the media have nicknamed or sought, let alone found, one—in contrast to the case of El/La Mataviejitas. As discussed in chapter 1, the murdering of elderly women spoke of a society in anomie, yet during those same years, young women in Ciudad Juárez and in Estado de México were being murdered, quite possibly "for the pleasure of killing" and out of "sexual pleasure," yet police and government authorities never spoke in that context of a serial killer or a society in anomie.

On the contrary, in 2006, the same year that Barraza was apprehended, "the doctor Mario Álvarez Ledesma, who submitted the final report of the Fiscalía Especial para la Investigación de Homicidios de Mujeres [Special Prosecutor Office for the Investigation of Homicides of Women]" stated that "in Ciudad Juárez there are no feminicides, no serial killers, the number of women disappeared is insignificant, there is a severe problem of intradomestic violence and everything is a myth created by women of nongovernmental organizations and academia."[32]

The pattern in Estado de México is similar. There, in 2006 as well, sixteen women were found strangled, dismembered, and tortured, all of them sexually attacked, and their bodies left in empty lots.[33] The media have talked about sexual crimes following similar patterns and the possibility of a serial killer. In Estado de México, the press referred to El

Asesino del Bordo de Xochiaca (The Killer of Xochiaca) after the capture of Francisco Galván in 2006, who was convicted of the murders of six young, marginalized brown women.[34] On April 24, 2006, three months after Barraza's arrest, the bodies of five to seven young women between fifteen and twenty-four years old were found in a construction site in Chimalhuacán, Estado de México; all had been murdered just weeks apart, kidnapped between 5 and 6 a.m. while on their way to work. The news media have raised the possibility of serial killers in Estado de México—sometimes reporting a modus operandi, since most of the murders are sexual crimes. A newspaper article even reported that the Procuraduría de Justicia of Estado de México, while waiting for the results of DNA testing in five homicides, had announced that if the results showed the same DNA, then the murders were most definitely the work of a serial killer.[35] As usual, the feminicides in Estado de México prompted no task force, no criminal sketches, no memorable nickname.

Padgett and Loza argue that the feminicides in Estado de México were not committed by only one serial killer, but in any case, as Monárrez points out, it is the complacency of the state that enables these feminicides to take place—so much so that it is the state that can be named the serial killer: a serial-feminicide nation.

It is important to underline that although many cases in both Ciudad Juárez and Estado de México suggest the possible culpability of a serial killer—taking into consideration the similarity of circumstances in which young women were murdered, the fact that most feminicides are sexual crimes, and that it seems that the killer, in many instances, did not know the victims—there has not been nearly the same national interest, let alone the will and effort to find one or more serial killers, as in the Mataviejitas case. La Mataviejitas continues to stand alone in terms of the naming of and search for a serial killer in Mexico. There has been no national preoccupation with the "killing for the pleasure of killing" that has plausibly taken place in Estado de México and Ciudad Juárez. The rampage of feminicides in those places has caused no shock to the nation. To this date, young women continue to disappear, to be killed with impunity by men who know they are not going to be investigated, much less held responsible for their crimes. In 2006, Abel Villicaña, chief of the Procuraduría Federal de Justicia in Estado de México, declared that a woman could feel safe there, despite the high rate of feminicides, if she "knew how to behave," if she took "precautions, and [was] alert to the aggression that she can be subject to and has the character and personality to take decisions." If they take these steps, he said, young women will be "less vulnerable."[36]

In Ciudad Juárez, in particular, very few feminicides have been solved. In 1995, an Egyptian man, Omar Sharif Latif, and members of a gang known as Los Rebeldes were arrested. Sharif widely thought to be responsible for the deaths of at least twenty-five women, an alleged "serial killer," was convicted for just three murders.[37] He died in prison in 2006. Of the members of Los Rebeldes who were arrested in 1996, five were sentenced in 2004 to forty years in prison and one was sentenced to twenty-four years.[38] In 1999, five members of the Toltecas gang were arrested and, in 2004, sentenced to forty years in prison for the homicide and rape of seven women in Ciudad Juárez; one gang member—who had a private lawyer—was later found innocent.[39] Two bus drivers, Víctor Javier García Uribe and Gustavo González Meza, were arrested for the killings of eight women found in Lote Algodonero; Amnesty International and the Inter-American Commission of Human Rights considered both to be scapegoats and maintained that they had been arbitrarily detained and tortured by the Procuraduría to confess. In 2003, Gonzáles was murdered in his prison cell. García was released in 2005.[40]

The press has reported that members of Los Rebeldes as well as García and Gonzáles were tortured to confess, along with other irregularities. Luis Miguel Hernández, formerly of Chihuahua's Comisión Estatal de Derechos Humanos (State Human Rights Commission), had quit in 1998, arguing that many of the members of Los Rebeldes had been torturados and isolated, that witnesses had been fabricated to link them to Sharif, and that the police had physically tortured two women to compel them to link Los Rebeldes to the feminicides.[41] Oscar Maynez, forensic specialist of the Fiscalía Especial para Crímenes de Mujeres en Chihuahua (Special Office for Crimes against Women in Chihuahua), stated that he could not identify five of the eight bodies he had examined, even after DNA testing.[42]

In total, only twenty-four cases have apparently been solved; more than sixty cases remain unsolved and more than thirty victims have still not been identified; in fact, the supposed body of Elizabeth Castro García, for which Sharif was arrested, turned out to be that of another person.[43]

Monárrez has argued that the feminicides in Ciudad Juárez need to be studied using an analytical tool she calls systemic sexual feminicide, which considers the gender, social class, and skin color of the women killed in the context of the hegemony of patriarchal and capitalist violence as well as permitted legal transgressions.[44] The tool of systemic sexual feminicide considers that what is murdered is not only the women themselves but also what has been signified as erasable by the toxic masculinist state.[45]

Most of these feminicides involve women between the ages of eleven and twenty-two, with the plurality of victims aged seventeen.[46] Though it has become general knowledge that women who work in maquiladoras have been the main targets, Monárrez found that women working in bars, sex workers, and students have also been victims of feminicide.[47] Economic need and a lack of infrastructure puts young women at risk because they are forced to walk long distances alone at night or take night shifts; there are no buses that can take them directly home and no public transportation. Monárrez and Fuentes have found that is the victims are more likely to have lived in the western zone of Ciudad Juárez, where there is the greatest deficit of urban infrastructure in terms of electricity, potable water, drainage, pavement, and also where the immigrant population is concentrated.[48] Their murdered bodies are classed and racialized as factory-worker bodies, owned as capital by the maquiladoras in Ciudad Juárez and readily disposable.[49] At the same time, both in Ciudad Juárez and in Estado de México, these young women are also targeted because they transgress public norms by becoming the primary domestic providers. As politician, academic, and activist Teresa Incháustegui has stated, women who transgress the traditional and conservative norms of being women in order to occupy predominant economic roles in their families are punished.[50]

In Ciudad Juárez, many of the family members of the women killed have to pay for private investigators or even bribe authorities to investigate. The situation in Estado de México is similar, with a "code of silence and intimidation from the authorities" who are supposed to be solving the feminicides there.[51] For the most part, in the almost total absence of official investigations, families are responsible for looking for their missing relatives. In 2012, the term "feminicide" entered penal law, and although it has been essential in terms of language to differentiate between a homicide and the misogynist killing of a woman by a man with the complicity of the state, the naming of the term and its use in penal law has not translated into the prevention of, or a decrease in, these types of murders.[52]

The truth is that the number of young women killed in Ciudad Juárez and Estado de México is unknown. No credible government body has investigated the feminicides. The high number of young women who have disappeared in Ciudad Juárez and in Estado de México contrasts dramatically with the forty-nine elderly women killed in Mexico City. And the contrast between the task force deployed to capture the killer of those elderly women in Mexico City, on the one hand, and the lack of interest by the government in investigating the feminicides in Ciudad Juárez and Estado de México, on the other, sheds light on the understanding of which bodies matter to the nation and whose deaths are worthy of bringing it into crisis. This is crucial to show how constructions of mexicanidad and pigmentocracy, in relation to womanhood/motherhood, have determined which bodies are deemed grievable to the nation.

Researchers and activists who since 1999 have been analyzing the feminicides in Ciudad Juárez have remarked on how police and government officials blame the young women for their deaths. In the collective volume *El silencio que la voz de todas quiebra: mujeres y víctimas de Ciudad Juárez* (The silence that shatters the voice in all: women and [female] victims in Ciudad Juárez), the authors aim to bring readers closer to the women who have been killed, not as statistics, but by showing how they lived. They also note the various official statements that rationalize the women's deaths by suggesting they led "double lives."[53] Chihuahua's deputy police chief, Jorge López Molinar, for example, stated that "many women work in maquiladoras, and because it is not enough to live on, from Monday to Friday they work and weekends they are dedicated to prostitution."[54] Many of the narratives around the women killed in Ciudad Juárez center on the idea that what actually killed them was a "lack of values, going out at night, going dancing to a bar, or that they dressed in a provocative way."[55] If it could not be corroborated that the young women were sex workers, authorities still insisted that they were very familiar with "nocturnal centers."[56] This narration was justified "scientifically" by criminologists such as Antonio Parra, who declared that a fraying of family values contributed to Ciudad Juárez becoming a target for murderers.[57] The "double life" narrative also responds to constructions of mexicanidad, in which an ideal woman dresses in a "decent" fashion and fulfills her role as the "guardian angel of the home"; she never goes out of the house alone, much less during the night, because to do so is to invite rape, especially if she "dresses provocatively."[58] In statements by religious leaders like Bishop Renato Ascencio and politicians such as Chihuahua governor Patricio Martínez and Senator Genaro Borrego, the "lack of family values" and a "youth with no limits" are to blame for the feminicides; no differences in gender and class are mentioned in the disappearances and killings of young women.[59]

These opposing narratives of the "double life" and of strong family values show how ideas of womanhood are determined through hegemonic notions of mexicanidad, which in turn have defined whose bodies matter, who counts as a victim, and who does not. Elderly women—seen as the grandmothers of the nation—count as victims and their bodies are deemed grievable since they hold the family together. In contrast, the idea of a "fragmented family," a "disintegrated family," renders the bodies of young women insignificant to the nation. Monárrez has noticed how "the social discourses on disintegrated families are the foundation of the precarious socialization of women and the consequence of feminicide."[60]

These narratives and ideologies of mexicanidad and their relation to womanhood become visible every time the family members of a missing woman deal with the authorities. Police officials, and even the private investigators to whom family members turn, commonly "imply that the young woman missing ran away with a boyfriend or a lover or escaped the household."[61] It is the "sexual conduct" of women violently killed that is placed under scrutiny; as Monárrez points out, "it is their sexuality which is the object of punishment," rather than the "criminal atrocities of the murderers."[62]

Elderly women killed in Mexico City were considered vulnerable, not due to their age or physical state, but because they lived alone, which in turn was perceived as the result of abandonment by their families. In contrast, young women in Ciudad Juárez, who were forced to walk alone because of the lack of infrastructure and thus put at risk, were not only not considered vulnerable but were blamed for being attacked. In other words, they brought it upon themselves. Arturo González Rascón, State of Chihuahua attorney general, stated that "unfortunately there are women that due to their life conditions, the places where they perform their activities, are at risk; because it would be very difficult for someone who went out when it's raining to not get wet."[63] And Patricio Martínez, governor of Chihuahua from 1998 to 2004, said, "Well, these women were not coming back from mass when they were attacked."[64] Through these comments, we see how "moral" values intertwine with Catholic discourses of how a woman should be—if a woman is "decent" and goes to mass, she will not be sexually attacked. Holding women responsible for their own tortures, rapes, and tragic deaths ignores that (a) these ideologies of mexicanidad have determined what constitutes ideal mother/womanhood, which in turn has determined which bodies bring the nation into crisis; (b) the severe socioeconomic crisis and lack of infrastructure that cannot support these women renders them already and always exposed; and (c) when women are held responsible for being murdered, the responsibility is lifted off of the government and police to prevent and investigate their deaths.

Even after international attention and pressure were put on the issue of the feminicides in Ciudad Juárez, prevention campaigns focused on blaming the victims. Campaign pamphlets stated that if a woman was at a party, if she stayed out until sunrise, if she dressed provocatively and drank, then it was very possible that her "guardian angel" would not always be present to protect her.[65] As noted in Tabuenca's study of prevention campaigns, young female victims were not only racialized as brown and classed as poor, but that differentiation from the "pure" and "decent" middle- and upper-class white women put them at fault. Young, brown, poor women were to blame because they had decided to go out dancing at night on clandestine dates with upper-class men whom they did not know.[66] Asma Jahangir, the United Nations special rapporteur on extrajudicial executions from 1998 to 2004, observed in her 1999 report on feminicides in Ciudad Juárez that "the arrogant behaviour and obvious indifference shown by some state officials in regard to these cases leave the impression that many of the crimes were deliberately never investigated for the sole reason that the victims were 'only' young girls with no particular social status and who therefore were regarded as expendable."[67]

As Monárrez has pointed out, government authorities' responses to feminicides have legitimized, normalized, and naturalized the killings.[68] In Ciudad Juárez in 1998, the right-wing Partido de Acción Nacional (PAN) deputy Javier Corral Jurado stated that the killing of women in the city was not exclusive to that municipality and that many women were also raped in Mexico City, but without the same media attention.[69] The following year, state attorney general Arturo González Rascón argued that despite the focus on Ciudad Juárez, the same events would not be noticed if they happened in Torreón, or Durango, or Sinaloa.[70] Two years later, in 2001, after meeting with the mother of a missing young woman, González stated, "I'm drowning in a glass of water. Dead women are everywhere"; he added, "This is the situation in all the county and we should not be so worried."[71] The then governor of Chihuahua, Francisco Barrio, stated that the number of feminicides in Ciudad Juárez was not higher than in other municipalities in the state and that "it could be considered normal."[72] Similarly, in Estado de México, the secretary of the state government, Eruviel Ávila, commented, "Is Estado de México where more crimes against women are? Yes! But it is also where more women are."[73]

Despite national and international feminist organizations' great efforts to bring attention to the serial killing of women in Ciudad Juárez and Estado de México, feminicides continue to happen with impunity. In Ciudad Juárez, Fiscalía Especial para la Investigación de Homicidios contra la Mujer (FEIHM—the Special Government Department for the Investigation of Homicides against Women), was established in 1998; it has been so ineffective that the officer in charge has been replaced at least nine times.[74] In 2002, the Instituto Chihuahuense de la Mujer (Chihuahua Institute of Women) was created to promote equality between men and women; at the federal level, a special commission to prevent and eradicate violence against women in Ciudad Juárez was created in 2003, but the officers in charge of both organizations were criticized for their extravagant salaries and minimal work ethic.[75]

As in the case of the killing of elderly women in Mexico City, there were tensions between the local and federal governments regarding the feminicides. In the Mataviejitas case, however, there was no question that it was imperative to find who was responsible—local and federal officials agreed that the killing of elderly women had crossed the line. In the case of the feminicides in Chihuahua and Estado de México, the total opposite occurred. Jorge Madrazo Cuellar, attorney general of Mexico from 1996 to 2000, as well as his successor, Rafael Macedo de la Concha (2000–5), stated that there were no elements that warranted bringing the cases to a national level.[76] Finally, as international pressure mounted, then president Vicente Fox Quesada created an office at the federal level to investigate the feminicides. Even after reports to the contrary from Amnesty International and the UN High Commissioner for Human Rights, Fox stated that there was no corruption and that progress was being made in the investigations.[77] In fact, while Enrique Peña Nieto was governor of Estado de México (and already a potential presidential candidate), Columbia Law School professor Edgardo Buscaglia stated that high-level agreements were in place between the federal and the local governments to keep the feminicides under the radar, and outside the jurisdiction, of federal authorities in Mexico, the DEA, and the FBI.[78]

Peña Nieto, who would serve as president of Mexico between 2012 and 2018, was governor of Estado de México from 2005 to 2011; 922 homicides of women were officially reported across the state between 2005 and 2010[79]—independent researchers believe the actual figure is many times higher. Humberto Padgett and Eduardo Loza, in their analysis of the feminicides in the state, note how Peña Nieto's presidential campaign promoted the idea "that he was a sort of boyfriend of the women of Estado de México and later the boyfriend of Mexican women."[80] Padgett and Loza describe how Peña Nieto ignored the "more knowledgeable and prestigious voices in matters of violence against women," who in "public forums, social networks, newspaper articles, and reports of Human Rights" were letting him know that the number of feminicides in Estado de México had surpassed the tragedies in Ciudad Juárez.[81] With the help of the local press, Peña Nieto denied the growing number of feminicides,[82] even as many young women were paid to support him and to chant at his campaign rallies: "¡Enrique Bombón, te quiero en mi colchón! ¡Peña, mangazo, contigo me embarazo! ¡Enrique, amigo, mi vieja quiere contigo!" (Enrique, sweetheart, I want you in my bed! Peña, you are like a mango, with you I get pregnant! Enrique, my friend, my wife wants you!)[83] In

2010, Peña Nieto married a soap opera star, Angélica Rivera, and much of his campaigning resembled a telenovela, from the couple's wedding to Rivera's press statements to the reporting by Televisa, the main national TV broadcaster.[84] Once elected president, Peña Nieto stated that he had brought the PRI (Institutional Revolutionary Party) back into the Pinos (the Mexican equivalent of the White House) specifically thanks to the "women's vote."[85] Padgett and Loza argue that the feminicides in Estado de México in fact were denied and covered up to benefit Peña Nieto's presidential campaign and to maintain the construction of him as the "candidate of women."[86]

In July 2015, in response to growing outrage from civic organizations and the public, the Estado de México government put in place the Alerta de Violencia de Género contra las Mujeres (AVGM—Alert of Gender Violence against Women), targeting eleven municipalities. According to a government press release, the AVGM "consists in implementing a set of emergency governmental actions to confront and eradicate the femicide and/or the existence of a comparative wrongdoing. Its fundamental objective is to guarantee the security of women and girls, the end of the violence against them and/or to eliminate the inequalities produced by a legislation or public policy that breaches their human rights."[87] The state also pledged to "integrate a database of violence against women" to "generate citizens and inter-institutional networks of prevention and attention of violence against women and girls" as well as to support the "training and professionalization of the public service in terms of gender perspective and women's human rights."[88] In brief, the existence of the AVGM acknowledges the high number of feminicides in Estado de México but does little in practical terms. The "gender alert" has left many wondering what this mechanism actually means, how it is actually going to help to find the people responsible for past feminicides, and how it will actually prevent more. In the more than three years since the AVGM was announced, its provisions have yet to be enacted, despite multiple requests from nongovernmental organizations.[89]

While the news in 2006 focused on showing that Juana Barraza was La Mataviejitas, an event of horrific police brutality took place only four months after her arrest in Estado de México, where she lived. This event, which took place in the municipality of San Salvador Atenco, came to be known simply as Atenco. According to reports from the National

Human Rights Commission of Mexico, 700 preventive police officers and 1,815 national riot police brutally attacked what began as a group of "60 flower vendors" who had resisted police efforts to try to stop them from selling flowers.[90] Houses were raided and at least two people were killed by police, including a fourteen-year-old boy. Protestors were indiscriminately detained and tortured: 206 in total, including at least 45 women, mostly indigenous.[91] Twenty-six of these indigenous women were sexually abused by police, some repeatedly.[92] Years later, "none of the officials responsible for their abuse ha[d] been held accountable."[93]

In 2006, early in Peña Nieto's tenure as governor, researchers estimate that 1,997 women were murdered in Estado de Mexico.[94] The events of Atenco took place that same year. Yet what captured the attention of the news media and authorities was the arrest of a female wrestler serial killer. None of the rapes or murders of young mestizo and/or indigenous women have been granted the attention of the government. Why not? Why has the killing of these young women not brought the nation into crisis? These killings happened around the same time that elderly women were being killed in Mexico City, between 1998 and 2006. To date, the indigenous women attacked and raped by police officers in Atenco have not counted as victims to the government, in particular the federal Department of Justice. For the most part, media narrations also have not considered them victims—not enough to warrant the sensationalist stories inspired by the killing of elderly women in Mexico City.

Indigenous women in Mexico, *indias*, "have always been raped by ladinos," a practice that has been accepted for centuries.[95] Through this practice, according to anthropologist Olivia Gall, Indian women are marked as an inferior sex and race, which does not let them reach full citizenship or equality; as such, their bodies continue to belong to the elites, whose contempt for the women is made legitimate and, in circular fashion, translated back into the violence of rape.[96] This practice continued in Atenco, where Indian women were raped by police officers with total impunity. And it is against this backdrop of endemic violence against young, poor, and brown women, mestizo and indigenous, that police and news media instead sensationalized Barraza's story.

The researchers, academics, and activists who have brought the feminicides in Estado de México and Ciudad Juárez to the public's attention have highlighted how the victims lived in very precarious conditions.

As mentioned earlier, many resided in—and their bodies were often left in—areas with no infrastructure. How bodies relate to infrastructure, how they are or are not supported by it, and the relationship between precarity and faith, and in turn with constructions of mexicanidad, are important questions. In the next section, I continue to trace constructions of mexicanidad in relation to womanhood and precarity that have defined who constitutes a morally good woman in terms of class and skin color. I start by comparing two myths of mexicanidad: that of La Virgen de Guadalupe, and that of her evil sister, La Santa Muerte.

Spiritual Sisters: La Virgen de Guadalupe and La Santa Muerte

A skeleton is dressed all in white, in a wedding gown. Only the face and hands are exposed. The white veil that covers the head leaves visible the skeletal face, with two black holes where the eyes must have been. Although it does not look like she is smiling, her mouth is open and we can see all of her teeth. In her hands, the tall figure carries anything from a scythe to a globe or flowers; sometimes, her gown is not white but brightly colored.

This skeletal figure, which literally represents death, is La Santa Muerte. It is seen as holy by about ten million people, mostly in Mexico City, despite the prohibition of the Catholic Church. Although the cult of its glorification took hold beginning in the mid-1990s, many researchers have traced the idolization of La Santa Muerte back to the pre-Hispanic cult of the Aztec deities of death, Mictlantecuhtli and Mictecacíhuatl, the Lord and Lady of Mictlán, the land of the dead for men and women who have lost their lives to natural causes.[97] Many researchers concur that the worship of La Santa Muerte is a result of syncretism, pastiche, or bricolage[98]—that is, a mix of the imposed Catholic religion and pre-Hispanic traditions, an assemblage of pre- and postcolonial cultures and belief systems. The cult of La Santa Muerte involves rituals and symbolism taken from both Catholicism and pre-Hispanic traditions. For example, rosaries are common in the Catholic practice of using beads to count the components of the prayer; devotees of La Santa Muerte have adopted this practice. Similarly, the symbols of the apple and the serpent, which in the Catholic Church represent the original sin and temptation, are also used in the worship of La Santa Muerte—as noted earlier, these figures appeared in Juana Barraza's domestic altar.

The rituals related to La Santa Muerte involve "shamanic and *santería* practices" such as the offering of flowers, food, tobacco, and marijuana, elements that can also be traced back to pre-Hispanic traditions.[99] In a typical "mass" to La Santa Muerte, devotees will draw on a cigarette or cigar and blow the smoke toward the skeletal figure, a practice known as *purear*.[100]

In Mexico City, the adoration of La Santa Muerte—a figure also known as La Santísima (The All Saint), La Niña Blanca (The White Girl), and La Flaquita (The Skinny One)—is performed at vitrines placed on various street corners in mostly poor and precarious neighborhoods. The space of the cult is the street (fig. 4.2). A small house with concrete sides and a glass cover, or just a box of plain glass, typically about one meter tall, contains the skeletal figure of La Santa Muerte. In the altar, she is surrounded by dozens of flowers, candles, photographs, alcohol, and tobacco. Dollar bills are sometimes pinned to her gown. Octagonal mirrors cover the entire altar to "contain" La Santa Muerte. Devotees will bring their offerings and gather in the street to pray the rosary. Most believers have their own private figure that they keep at home and bring to the public rituals. Another important characteristic of these altars is that a figure of Jesús Malverde often features at the side of La Santa Muerte.

The adoration of La Santa Muerte is commonly associated with delinquency and marginalized communities, attracting adherents mostly from the lower socioeconomic classes: "narco traffickers, delinquents, prisoners or prostitutes." In her study of the cult of La Santa Muerte, however, Perla Fragoso finds a much more diverse group of devotees, who, in spite of the stigma, are drawn from a population that "shows a state of social vulnerability" and use the cult to cope with their precarious social situation. These "vulnerable sectors" comprise participants in "informal commerce, independent workers, taxi drivers, migrants, homosexuals, police men, military men, delinquents, housewives from poor neighborhoods and prostitutes."[101]

Similarly, Anne Huffschmid states that among members of La Santa Muerte's cult, "sex-workers, travestis, consumers or dealers of illegal substances" are not the only subjects who are economically marginal-

Figure 4.2. La Santa Muerte altar on a city street.

ized, abandoned, and in emotional need. This "temporal space" also includes, more and more, "common men and women, neighbors, traders, adolescents and elderly people."[102]

As the cult of La Santa Muerte grew rapidly in the mid-1990s, organized crime was also expanding, creating "the impression that the icon [La Santa Muerte] belongs to a coherent 'narco-culture.'"[103] During this time, as well, a neoliberal economic crisis hit the nation even as the industrialization of Ciudad Juárez created the maquiladoras and the experience of womanhood changed in the state of Chihuahua. The experience of precarity became an everyday reality for many in Mexico due to the "socioeconomic crisis, violence and insecurity," creating in turn a crisis of faith and credibility in the Catholic Church. La Santa Muerte emerged as a sort of deity of the crisis.[104]

The first known public altar to La Santa Muerte (as opposed to an altar in a private home, as was customary for its clandestine adoration) was set up on Calle Alfarería in the Mexico City neighborhood of Morelos. Also referred to as Tepito, Morelos is widely considered a dangerous neighborhood, known for drug trafficking and open trade in pirated goods from DVDs to luxury items and stolen electronics (iPhones are among the hottest commodities). This altar, placed on October 31, 2001, would become the cult's most important.[105]

Enriqueta Romero, known as Doña Queta, is the main figure behind both the cult of La Santa Muerte and the public altar in Tepito. There are no priests or sermons—Queta (a term of endearment) can be considered its main authority. Queta created the Tepito altar and has been attending to it ever since. She stated in one interview that she had been a devotee of La Santa Muerte, or La Santísima, "since she was a little girl, about 49 years ago," that is, since the early 1960s.[106] On the first of every month, a sort of mass is held for La Niña Blanca at the altar, which is about two meters tall. Hundreds of devotees show up for the mass, which involves praying the rosary and *purear* with a cigar to the figure of La Santa Muerte. Some of the prayers are the same as those used in the Catholic Church, such as the Hail Mary and the Glory Be, but many others are specially dedicated to La Santa Muerte, for example, "Oh santísima muerte / angel de dios / te doy las gracias, infinitas y sinceras / por los favores que nos has concedido" (Oh, holy death / angel of God / I thank you, infinitely and sincerely / for the favors given) and

"Oh santísima muerte / vive y contempla / el dolor de quien te respeta y te venera" (Oh, holy death / live and contemplate / the pain of those who respect you and venerate you). During a ritual, it is common to see people crying, begging, and crawling on their knees for blocks until they arrive at the altar, where they touch with great devotion the saintly figure.

According to Perla Fragoso, there are three main features of La Santa Muerte: she is egalitarian and righteous, a protective spiritual being, and the mother of all cycles of life, of changes and transitions.[107] Since her veneration is forbidden by the church and stigmatized, a way of making it less evident is "to place, instead of an image, a white carnation surrounded by white candles."[108]

Without priests or formal methods of worship, devotees are more spontaneous in their shows of faith, bringing different types of offerings out of personal inspiration. Since there are no churches, and no official sites of worship, the cult of La Santa Muerte goes beyond the private altars and the street-corner vitrines deeper into the public realm, "in markets, streets, bodies (tattoos, T-shirts, and clothing with the merchandising of the Santa Muerte)," practices that have expanded to other places in Mexico and across the US border.[109]

I have found, to date, five altars to La Santa Muerte around Mexico City, mostly in lower-class neighborhoods. It is interesting to note the parallels with the tradition of altars to and worship of La Virgen de Guadalupe. Almost every neighborhood has at least one street corner featuring an altar to La Virgen. Their purposes vary: as a deterrent to people throwing garbage on the street (which works, because the adoration of La Virgen is so strong that it is seen as disrespectful to discard garbage where she is present), as a site at which to pay homage to an individual killed at that corner, or simply as a means of expressing gratitude toward La Virgen. The adoration of the figures of La Virgen de Guadalupe inside these altars is different from that of the figures located inside churches—there are no street-corner masses for La Virgen—but their spiritual function seems to have the same significance for their devotees. Most believers will make the sign of the holy cross on their bodies whenever they pass one of the public altars.

La Santa Muerte, unlike La Virgen de Guadalupe, embodies a "spiritual resource" that "addresses the vulnerability of the devotees," offering her followers guidance through the country's economic, social, and religious crisis.[110] La Santa Muerte, like La Virgen, is a godsend, an intermediary between God and mortals; yet La Santa Muerte is believed to be a more fair, just, and egalitarian mother to her followers than La Virgen de Guadalupe. La Santísima will not judge you or punish you, but simply take you sooner or later, whether you are rich or poor, a Mexican enjoying the privilege whiteness offers or a darker mestizo, evil or good.

In this way, La Santa Muerte is closer to her devotees, and she can be approached for everyday needs relating to economic and social survival. Believers ask La Santa Muerte for a range of favors: to increase revenues from informal business (which might involve the selling of illegal or stolen objects), to help with the risk of skirting the law, to help with their drug addictions. As such, the cult of La Santa Muerte is pragmatic, the object of utilitarian devotion, and has had a sustaining effect on the frail "national psyche."[111] As one researcher puts it, La Santa Muerte is seen as an "effective hope because the state is not capable of guaranteeing justice or access to basic human rights. What are the chances to continue to live and not become a statistic?"[112]

One of the most important myths in the construction of mexicanidad is the myth of the brown, mestizo virgin, or La Virgen de Guadalupe. The myth of La Virgen largely traces a well-established Spanish, and more broadly European, narrative of the apparition of the Virgin Mary. Certain differences in the story, however, point to creole and indigenous appropriation of Christian symbols.[113]

In 1531, on Tepeyac Hill in the north of Mexico City, La Virgen de Guadalupe appeared, three times in total, to an indigenous man named Juan Diego, asking him to build a church in her name. After Juan Diego failed to convince the bishop Juan de Zumárraga of the truth of his experience, La Virgen appeared again, giving Juan Diego roses as a testament to her presence. The myth assures us that roses were hard to come by on that hill, especially as it was winter. At the moment when Juan Diego was about to present the bishop with the roses, which he had kept on his lap, an image of La Virgen de Guadalupe appeared imprinted on his clothing. Spanish missionaries decided to build a church for La Virgen on the same hill, which "coincidentally" had been used by previous indigenous populations as a ceremonial site for the goddess Tonantzin. According to one of the Spanish missionaries, Bernardino de Sahagún, Tonantzin was related to the Aztec goddess Cihuacóatl, a name that means "serpent woman."[114] Among Tonantzin's other epithets was Coaxtlaxopeuh—also meaning a woman with dominion over serpents—which evolved into Guadalupe.

The story of La Virgen de Guadalupe is explained by most researchers as a myth created by the Spanish colonizers to evangelize the indigenous populations. Evangelization, bringing the Catholic religion to the New World, became a primary justification for colonization and one of its main tools. Yet leading missionaries had contradictory policies regarding the elimination of indigenous cults. On one side, the Franciscan prelate Zumárraga had no tolerance for the adoration of any indigenous gods. On the other side, the Dominican friar Alonso de Montúfar allowed traditional indigenous offerings to La Virgen de Guadalupe and even allowed missionaries to talk to indigenous people about Tonantzin when referring to the Virgin Mary.[115] These strongly opposing views illuminate the limits of spiritual colonization. In the same church, indigenous people might very well have worshiped Tonantzin alongside the Spanish who prayed to La Virgen de Guadalupe. The figure might have changed but there is no guarantee that indigenous people changed their internal way of honoring and worshiping their goddess.

Another important characteristic of the myth of La Virgen de Guadalupe that contributed to the construction of mexicanidad is the state-sponsored notion of mestizaje. La Virgen was brown, not white like the Virgin Mary, and she spoke the indigenous language of the region, not Castilian Spanish. Symbols of the Aztec capital of Tenochtitlán—such as the eagle perched on a cactus devouring a serpent, now depicted on the Mexican coat of arms and flag—were appropriated for representations of La Virgin by Miguel Sánchez, a creole priest considered by some to be the inventor of the apparition of La Virgen de Guadalupe.[116] The myth of La Virgen was a crucial device, helping Spanish colonizers both to justify the violence they perpetrated on the indigenous populations and to control them through religious means.

Long after colonization, at the start of the War of Independence in 1810, La Virgen de Guadalupe became a symbol of national identity. The Catholic priest Miguel Hidalgo y Costilla, now known as the Father of Independence, used her image to arouse support among mestizos and Indians. At the Sanctuary of Nuestra Señora de Guadalupe (Our Lady of

Guadalupe), Hidalgo affixed an image of La Virgen Morena and added a proclamation: "Long live religion! Long live our most Holy Mother of Guadalupe! Long live Ferdinand VII! Long live America and death to bad government!"[117] The use of La Virgen for the insurgency movement represented a call for a religious sensibility and, ultimately, the creation of Mexican nationalism.

For centuries, the colonial casta system had relied on a social stratification regime based on skin color, in which being "black or indigenous was bad, being white was good."[118] Legal mechanisms were put in place that prevented social mobility, such as the certificate of *pureza de sangre* (purity of blood). This document was intended to serve as proof that the subject in question was of a pure lineage, with no contamination from inferior castes.[119] This document of *pureza de sangre* was commonly offered among the ecclesiastical authorities and members of the artistocracy when they wanted a marriage certificate or a bureaucratic position.[120]

Miguel Hidalgo y Costilla's ideology regarding legal equality among the population was key in the War of Independence. For Hidalgo, the only solid base for "our common happiness" lay at "the general union between Europeans and Americans, Indians and indigenous."[121] This ideology is not very different from José Vasconcelos's idea of the "cosmic race," discussed in chapter 1. The mestizo identity was supposed to better the race through the eventual elimination of Indian blood. Hidalgo (who had once himself acquired a *gracias al sacar*, or certificate of pure blood) demanded the immediate abolition of the casta system and slavery that had been in place in New Spain during the colonial period.

The use of La Virgen de Guadalupe was a crucial element in Mexico's independence struggle, uniting a nation that was otherwise fragmented by the casta system. La Virgen came to signify mestizaje—she was at the same time indigenous and creole, a mestiza herself, that is, Mexican. The *sistema de castas* and slavery were officially abolished in 1821, but this did not translate into an erasure of skin-color-based divisions in the imaginary of the state or among the elites in power. The relationship between skin color and economic and social status transformed into notions of mexicanidad that established who, after independence, would constitute the ideal Mexican: the Spanish, making whiteness the desirable and privileged position.

Even though both La Santa Muerte and La Virgen de Guadalupe can be analyzed as products of syncretism in the construction of a "mestizo nation," they respond to different national purposes. La Santa Muerte is not officially a saint. In fact, not only is she not recognized by the Catholic Church, she is often demonized by it. Yet both La Santa Muerte and La Virgen de Guadalupe offer their believers an intimate relationship, with no need for clerical intermediaries, and both work as spiritual mediators before God. They are depicted wearing similar gowns, and there are similarities in the rituals of their worship, such as rosaries and novenas. Yet while the adoration of La Virgen was promoted (maybe even invented) by the Catholic Church and the government, the cult of La Santa Muerte is forbidden.

In constructions of mexicanidad, La Virgen de Guadalupe represents the ideal feminine mestiza woman. She is the ideal mother and the role model for women in Mexico. She is typically represented in popular culture as self-abnegating, self-sacrificing, feminine, and always forgiving. Through state-promoted ideologies of mexicanidad, in popular-culture discourses and media narratives, she upholds the ideal of female sexuality, that is, to remain a virgin until marriage. Ideally, women would want to be like her, and men would want to have a mother like her and to marry someone like her. Devotees of La Virgen de Guadalupe not only have good morals but are upstanding citizens. Like Miguel Hidalgo, many politicians have used the image of La Virgen to gain the population's trust. On the other hand, devotees of La Santa Muerte are of dubious morality; they are the dispossessed and marginalized lower classes. These believers not only defy the state-promoted Catholic religion, they are also dishonorable members of the Mexican society.

Both La Santa Muerte and La Virgen de Guadalupe are motherly figures, and both are called *santísimas*, or "holy saints"—the addition of the superlative suffix "-ísima" casts both figures as the holiest of all saints. These godsends and mediators between God and humanity offer a direct relationship to God, without intervention by a priest, a defining characteristic of spiritual practice for indigenous populations that persisted through evangelization. But where the myth of La Virgen de Gudalupe, the brown Virgin, served as a means of evangelization, a tool for colonization, La Santa Muerte is a maternal figure selected by her own followers, not imposed on them.

While La Virgen de Guadalupe is the ideal mother, always forgiving and sacrificing herself for her children, La Santa Muerte is, as Homero Aridjis writes in his novel *La Santa Muerte: sexteto del amor las mujeres, los perros y la muerte*, her "sinister" sister.[122] La Santa Muerte is the ultimate protector, the mother who at the end of the day, for those constantly criminalized in popular, media, and criminological discourses, can really be trusted. La Santa Muerte takes everyone with her in the end, privileged or disadvantaged. In this way, La Santa Muerte is ultimately a less discriminatory figure than La Virgen de Guadalupe; she offers a more transparent faith and deeper comfort. While it is not clear how La Virgen de Guadalupe helps and rewards her believers, La Santa Muerte offers true consolation. You will die, she will take you with her to the dead—there is no other option.

Many of the believers of La Santa Muerte are also devotees of La Virgen de Guadalupe, but for different reasons. Many come to La Santa Muerte for favors that are morally condemned by society or punishable by law. Many believe that La Santa Muerte has alleviated or ended their addictions, or has helped with their business, often conducted at the edge of, or beyond, the law. The cult of La Santa Muerte believes she protects those who are not protected by the law and are marginalized by society in their everyday lives. La Santa Muerte, moreover, seems to hold her devotees responsible for their actions. Unlike the state-promoted image of La Virgen de Guadalupe, La Santa Muerte is not always a forgiving figure. On the contrary, she is a sometimes-terrifying mother, one who will punish her devotees and make them accountable for their actions.

It has long been a common practice in Catholicism to pay to reserve a place in heaven. The payment, called *diezmo* (a tenth), was collected by the civil servants of the Spanish crown to maintain the church, and although it was officially abolished after independence, the government took over this sort of tax collection from the church. The ideal Mexican, rich and with good morals, continued to give a *diezmo*. The cult of La Santa Muerte eliminates these beliefs and enables justice and equality for the marginalized poor. Whether you are rich or poor, mestizo or *criollo*, La Santa Muerte will take you, allowing for the feeling that equal justice is ultimately served despite the economic inequalities between whiter and more indigenous Mexicans.

Notions of mexicanidad delimited what constitutes a morally good woman, modeled after La Virgen de Guadalupe, at the same time that the notion of an evil woman was being constructed. As analyzed in chapter 1, since colonization La Virgen de Guadalupe provided a refuge to the raped mother, La Malintzin. La Virgen was further used to establish the ideal of the always-loyal and desexualized role for women and mothers in Mexico. The ideal woman, then, is the one who, modeled after La Virgen, even though she is brown, aspires to occupy the space of privilege that whiteness offers in Mexico.

The ideal woman in constructions of mexicanidad is middle class, well mannered, feminine, and heterosexual; if single, she will remain a virgin until marriage, and once married, she will become a self-abnegating wife and self-sacrificing mother. As La Virgen de Guadalupe can be a mother to the nation, the ideal mother can be forgiving of her family, the ultimate protector, and the intermediary between her children and the nation. The killing of elderly women in Mexico City brought the nation into crisis because, in a powerful sense, El/La Mataviejitas was killing La Virgen de Guadalupe. State-sanctioned notions of mexicanidad also determine not only what constitutes a good woman but also what types of women are criminalized. The women (and men) who adore La Santa Muerte are already morally condemned, more by what they believe than by what they do.

The altar to La Santa Muerte found in Barraza's house was not treated by the news media and criminologists as an individual's response to the everyday experience of precarity, a sign of devotion to an alternative motherly figure who brings justice to the marginalized. On the contrary, the presence of this devotional figure was seen as further proof not only of Barraza's criminality, but of her "evil nature."

La Catrina and La Santa Muerte

La Santa Muerte stands in contrast to another skeletal figure, another calavera prominent in Mexican popular culture: La Catrina. Created by illustrator and lithographer José Guadalupe Posada, his original 1910–13 etching, *La calavera Catrina*, depicts a skeletal head and upper torso—atop the grinning skull is an enormous hat overflowing with flowers and giant fronds. Intended by Posada to ridicule those Mexicans who exalted the traditions and styles of the European aristocracy La Catrina has been fully co-opted into discourses of mexicanidad. As either a full-length skeleton or skull, La Catrina is often represented in works of a decorative art through *papel picado*, clay or edible sugar, as part of the celebrations of the Day of the Dead.

Although these two skeletal figures, La Santa Muerte and La Calavera Catrina, are very similar aesthetically, they have an opposite relation to constructions of mexicanidad. The modern-day image of Mexicans as having a close relationship to death to the point of celebrating and mocking it was propagated by Diego Rivera (known for surrounded himself with images of death in his studio, including many Posada-like skulls) and Octavio Paz, whose classic essay on mexicanidad states that an essential trait of Mexicans is to laugh at and mock death. This internationally familiar and unthreatening relationship between Mexicans and death is celebrated as the Día de Muertos, the Day of the Dead. In his study of death in Mexico, Claudio Lomnitz argues that the place that postrevolutionary intellectuals gave to the dead legitimized an "authoritarian political regime that naturalized its own penchant to trample, mangle, and stamp out life and projected its own tendencies onto 'the Mexican's disdain of death.'"[123] Lomnitz suggests that this tradition of fiesta and mocking of death, the commercialization of the Day of the Death through sugary skulls, is "essentially the invention of an authoritarian state."[124] The skull had a different meaning in Mesoamerica than in Catholicism. In Mesoamerica, the skull "was a sign of early rebirth as much as dead and the transposition of live flesh and skull was a reminder of the duality and interdependence of death and birth, or of death and power, rather than a sign of the brevity of life or its vain passions."[125] For the Catholic Spanish, the skull represented the Final Judgment, the moment of truth, when one is either condemned to hell for eternal punishment or granted eternal life in heaven in the company of God.

As noted earlier, in the postrevolutionary period, anxiety over the US cultural presence in Mexico inspired both the political left and the conservative elite to strengthen a sense of national identity. The Day of the Dead, rooted in historical indigenous practices, was recuperated in the popular imagination and disseminated as a purely Mexican tradition (even in parts of the country where it had never been celebrated before). Lomnitz describes how, later in the twentieth century, intellectuals increasingly concerned about US cultural influence—in this regard, particularly the celebration of Halloween—came to view the Day of the Dead as "essential to national identity." By the late twentieth century, the celebration of the Day of the Dead went "full circle, from being tightly controlled by the Church, to being a popular celebration that resisted the attacks of the modern and secular state, to being an officially promoted identitarian ritual."[126] As Lomnitz describes, the prevailing view in contemporary scholarship is that the Day of the Dead has "few or no significant pre-Columbian elements, that at the popular level [it is] a deeply Catholic festival, but that [its] most salient development has been as an invented tradition."[127] What is most relevant about Mexico's relationship to the dead, Lomnitz argues, is not whether it is or not an "invented tradition" but how, why and which place does dead play in Mexican political discourse, that is "the political control over dying, the dead, and the representation of the dead and the afterlife has been key to the formation of the modern state, images of popular culture, and a properly national modernity."[128]

Both prominent representations of death in Mexico, the skeletal figures of La Catrina and La Santa Muerte, can be traced back to pre-Hispanic origins. Just as researchers have traced the adoration of La Santa Muerte back to the cult of the Aztec death deity Mictecacíhuatl, popular images of La Catrina—whatever Posada's original intentions—can be linked to indigenous traditions. Although many indigenous rituals were concerned with death, through "elaborated funerary rituals and religious fiestas, such as [the Aztec month of] Miccailhuitontli," the association of a skeletal figure with death can be attributed to colonization. When Spanish colonizers found pre-Hispanic skeletons in rituals, they interpreted them under their "medieval conception" of death and skulls.[129] While human skulls were present in many indigenous funerary monuments, the skull was not exclusively associated with death. According to Matos Moctezuma, the calavera was employed as an ornament of everyday use, often adorning drinking vessels; its use alluded to the start of a new life cycle.[130] Calaveras were also, however, sanctified by indigenous peoples.

While both skeletal figures derive from pre-Hispanic traditions, they now represent very different religious and cultural beliefs. La Santa Muerte, as noted, is understood by most as dangerous and evil; condemned by the Catholic Church, she is also condemned to a certain extent by public opinion—as seen in the pathologizing of Barraza on the basis of her altar. On the other hand, La Catrina is promoted as a symbol of mexicanidad, appearing in tourism promotions and helping to identify Mexicans as Mexicans, while furthering the stereotype of mocking death. A good Mexican has a Catrina and celebrates the Day of the Dead with tamales and atole in an altar, but should be afraid of La Santa Muerte.

After independence in 1810, the calavera was taken up by official discourses and made a "national symbol."[131] One hundred years later, the revolutionary nationalism of 1910 returned to the popular-culture figure of the skeleton, especially as envisioned by José Guadalupe Posada, who made hundreds of engravings in which men and women of all social classes are depicted as skeletons in scenes from everyday life. After the revolution, artists and intellectuals "secularized and 'domesticated' the image of the Calavera and transformed it into an ecstatic representation of life on the other side, making it a sort of national totem."[132] As noted in earlier chapters, after 1910 there was a return to everything indigenous by the intellectual and artistic elites. Posada's most celebrated calavera, La Catrina, was reproduced in many venues, most famously the 1947 mural *Sueño de una tarde dominical en la Alameda* by Diego Rivera, in which Rivera himself holds La Catrina's hand.

During the 1940s, according to Lomnitz, death—especially its representation as a "playful, mobile, and often dressed-up skeleton—had become a recognizable Mexican sign."[133] Official discourses promoted the image of the calavera, which had been promulgated by modernist artists "in their quest to construct a hegemonic national identity."[134] Similarly, efforts were made to commercialize the "ritual of the Day of the Dead, which had previously scandalized the privileged sectors."[135] Ultimately, the Day of the Dead was completely nationalized, coming to symbolize something deeply Mexican.

According to Fragoso, the Mexican state trivialized the image of the calavera—previously sanctified by indigenous people during the pre-independence period—by promoting the figure of the skeleton or skull as playful, dressed in a *charro* costume or with a hairstyle like Frida Kahlo's.[136] Similarly, the state promoted the idea that all Mexicans have a certain playful familiarity with death. To this day, the idea that Mexicans have an intimate connection with death continues to be promoted by the state in tourism propaganda celebrating the Day of the Dead as an "authentic," age-old tradition.

For La Santa Muerte's believers, a close relationship with death is holy, and conceptualizing death as a saint, as a figure of devotion, is far from Catholic thinking, in which death is the end of life. La Santa Muerte incarnates death as a "benevolent saint, created by God, like the rest of all beings, and subjected to the divinity, a type of messenger or angel designed to help human beings have an easy transition to the other side."[137] These beliefs fall outside the notions of mexicanidad as promoted by the state and the Catholic Church.

La Santa Muerte and Jesús Malverde: The Saints of Narcos

The connection between La Santa Muerte and criminality was secured in popular discourse with the 1998 apprehension of Daniel Arizmendi, aka El Mochaorejas (The Ear Chopper). Arizmendi, an ex–police officer from Morelos, was a kidnapper notorious for chopping off the ears of his victims and sending them to their families, asking for ransom.[138] From his kidnappings, he gained close to five million US dollars, somewhere between forty-three and seventy-seven million pesos, and at least twenty-five houses.[139] When Arizmendi was arrested, police found an altar to La Santa Muerte in his home. The next day, media reports portrayed Arizmendi next to this altar, with headlines stating that La Santa Muerte had protected him for his illicit activities; thus, a relationship was established between criminality and the cult of The Holy Death.[140] There are different versions of what happened to Arizmendi's Santa Muerte figure after he was detained. According to Sergio Gonzáles, before he was sent to prison, Arizmendi (who had still been a police officer when he turned to crime) asked another officer for a favor, which was granted. Arizmendi took his figure of La Santa Muerte, covered it with his jacket, and asked that it be kept.[141] Another version of the story, by Desirée Martin, states that the police allowed Arizmendi to bring his Santa Muerte with him to prison.[142] In any case, what is important is that the media narrations focused as much on Arizmendi's relationship with La Santa Muerte —treated as proof in of itself that he was a criminal—as on the actual crimes he committed.

Another case of the press linking criminality to the cult of La Santa Muerte is that of Gilberto García Mena, aka El June, one of the leaders of the Gulf Cartel. When police captured him in 2001, they also found an altar to La Santa Muerte. Though a narco kingpin, El June was loved by the people, as he had built a church and helped his town through difficult times.

In his reporting on the case for one of the most reputable newspapers in Mexico, *El Universal*, journalist Alejandro Almazán describes the altar in great detail, as if breaking down a scene from a horror movie, making evident the link between El June's acts of criminality and his adoration of La Santa Muerte. According to Almazán, the altar contained "17 red candles with the image of La Santa Muerte," "tequila bottles and unopened beers," and a "plastic container with greenish water," which contained a special lotion to attract money, with a sticker that read "Ven dinero" (Money come to me).[143] Other journalists described El June's altar as well, citing the presence of phrases such as "Dinero, ven dinero" and "Muerte querida de mi corazón, no me desampares con tu protección" (Dearest death of my heart, do not leave me alone without your protection).[144]

Like many devotees of La Santa Muerte, El June also had affection for La Virgen de Guadalupe, an image of whom was half aerosol-painted on the wall of his hiding place. Meanwhile, the image of La Santa Muerte found at El June's altar was described as that of a figure who "frightens anyone that sees it, a mix between good and evil."[145] As in the case of Arizmendi, journalists focused their cover stories more on the relationship between El June and La Santa Muerte than on his crimes. In both cases, as well, news stories focused on how these criminals continued to idolize La Santa Muerte while in prison.

La Santa Muerte has been associated with drug lords in other regions, such as Michoacán, where Amado Carrillo, or El Señor de los Cielos (The Lord of the Heavens), is believed to have financed a shrine to The Holy Death.[146] The problem with these associations is that they continue to criminalize a certain kind of worship and, in doing so, cast all its practitioners as inherently evil, at least as much for their beliefs as for any crimes they might have committed. In many of the instances in which captured criminals worshiped La Santa Muerte, they also adored La Virgen de Guadalupe and Jesús Malverde; altars to and figures of La

Virgen were not linked to criminality, however, and devotion to her was not criminalized by the press or in official discourses.

Along with La Santa Muerte, police found a figure of Jesús Malverde and one of a Buddha in the altar in Barraza's house. Whereas the Buddha has not been cited in any reports as being associated with Barraza's criminality, the presence of the Malverde figure has. The story of Malverde is a version of the story of Robin Hood, in which the protagonist is a Mexican narco-saint. According to legend, Malverde was a "construction worker for the Western train in Mexico."[147] His parents died of hunger, victims of landowners' abuses, which motivated his hatred for the rich and sparked his criminal behavior.[148] He became known around the turn of the twentieth century in the northern state of Sinaloa, in the state of Culiacán, during the dictatorship of Porfirio Díaz, just before the Mexican Revolution.

Although there is no official documentation of his life, there is growing interest in Malverde, as seen in popular stories, paraphernalia, *corrido* songs, novels, and plays dedicated to his legend as the Holy Bandit.[149] Malverde became a hero for the poor and working class "because he challenged the Mexican government's authority and refused to comply with its laws."[150] Like Robin Hood, another holy bandit, he is invariably depicted as wearing green clothing to blend into his environment—hence the derivation of his name: *mal verde* (bad green).[151] In Malverde's case, green is also the color associated with dollars, thus associating him closely with financial benefits.

According to the legend, Malverde continued his criminal pursuits until 1909, when he died. There are various accounts of his death: in some, he was betrayed; in others, he died of illness; and in one version, a robbery went wrong and Mexican law enforcement officials captured and executed him.[152] Stories say that government officials left his body "hanging from a mesquite tree until the cord broke and his bones fell to the ground."[153] Because the government of Sinaloa forbade his burial, the legend says, the people of Culiacán threw stones at his body to cover it, and every time a stone was thrown, a wish was made. So many of these petitions were answered that an avalanche of hopeful stones created a sort of memorial to him. Since his mythic death, Malverde has represented hope to Mexico's underprivileged—to the poorest, the handicapped, pickpockets, thugs, prostitutes, drug traffickers, and addicts, in sum, the stigmatized, who do not find anyone who look likes them in civil or religious iconography.[154] The main shrine to Malverde, built in the 1970s in Culiacán, is the site of a celebration held every year on the supposed anniversary of his death. In many shrines dedicated to La Santa Muerte in Mexico City, a figure of Jesús Malverde can be found. Similarly, his image can often be found alongside that of San Judas Tadeo, traditionally the protector of thieves.

In Northern Mexico, within narco-trafficking culture, Malverde became known as "the angel of the poor," "the generous bandit," and "the saint of narcos."[155] His devotees include Mexican immigrants to the United States, as it is believed he offers protection to them. Malverde's association with Mexican drug traffickers is such that it is seen as a useful tool for the identification and arrest of criminals even in the United States. In a 2008 FBI bulletin, special agent Robert J. Botsch illustrates the importance of "recognizing subtle indicators, such as drug-related religious paraphernalia," specifically that of Jesús Malverde, since it "can give law enforcement personnel advanced warning of potential officer-safety issues and lead them to evidence that they otherwise may overlook."[156] Botsch argues that it is imperative that US police officers learn that "many Mexican drug traffickers acknowledged Malverde as their patron saint," and he relates the experience of a particular Utah Highway Patrol officer who "encountered items bearing Malverde's image in 6 or 7 of about 20 other successful drug interdiction stops."[157] In another case, an officer with the Nebraska State Patrol, searching a car, found "5 pounds of amphetamine concealed in a door panel and a phone card with a small picture of Jesus Malverde attached to it."[158]

According to Botsch, "traffickers often carried various items depicting Malverde's image hoping this paraphernalia would protect them further. If they successfully completed their drug-trafficking objective, they thanked Malverde for his guidance. If arrested, they continued to ask for his assistance throughout their court proceedings."[159] The purpose of Botsch's report is to let FBI agents known that recognizing the image of Malverde—be it on pendants, stamps, statues, cards, photos, tattoos, candles, or any other paraphernalia—is one of the "key factors" in the search for drug traffickers. He gives another specific example, in which an officer with the Wyoming Highway Patrol had pulled over a car because of a minor violation; after noticing that "both the driver and front seat passenger were wearing necklaces with a Jesus Malverde emblem on them" and that there was "a Jesus Malverde emblem hanging from the rearview mirror," the officer recalled Malverde's association to drug trafficking and searched the car, locating "9 pounds of marijuana and 7 pounds of methamphetamine."[160] The link between Malverde's image and drug-related activity is documented, featured in training courses, and can be used in court proceedings.[161]

That Juana Barraza had in her house an altar to both La Santa Muerte and Jesús Malverde was seen as further proof of her criminal nature, confirmation that she was indeed the serial killer that police had struggled to find. In *El nudo del silencio*, Martín Barrón analyzes Barraza in terms of Joel Norris's classification of the psychological phases a serial killer goes through: aura, trolling, wooing, capture, murder, totem, and finally post-killing depression.[162] According to Barrón, the aura phase is not fulfilled totally by Barraza because she did not plan out of a fantasy or obsession to end the lives of elderly women. Yet, he writes, she did "have a compulsion" to kill.[163] The trolling phase encompasses her modus operandi, including dressing as a nurse. The phases of wooing and capture—or stalking and courtship—are not completely identified in Barraza's case. The murder phase, in which "the fantasy of realizing the homicide" is completed, is also not totally met by Barraza; even though she told Barrón in interviews that many elderly women "resembled her mother," Barrón states that "the comparison between the memory of a mother that died around 40 years old and an elderly person is not convincing, and at the end is just a projection of her own fantasy."[164]

Barrón describes Barraza's house in detail, noting that it was painted "red" inside and out and there were several altars in the dining room and living room. As noted earlier, criminologist Isabel Bueno has argued that the color red signifies aggression. Barrón details the altar "dedicated to abundance, with a Buda surrounded by coins (different denominations and different countries), seeds, quartz stones, frogs and elephants"; and another altar with an "Apache [Indian] on his knees with [his] hands in a type of bowl and its interior diverse seeds, a sculpture of Jesús Malverde, the saint of narcotraffickers," making a point of explaining that the "altar or church" of Malverde is in Culiacán, Sinaloa. He explains how the police found a "painting of Sacred Jesus," a "representative figure of La

Virgen de Guadalupe," and, "the most significant of them all, an altar dedicated to La Santa Muerte . . . in different postures, dresses of different colors, as well as its respective offerings (seven apples, seven glasses of water, seven glasses with liquor, cigars, seven candles, also coins and bills from different denominations and countries)."[165]

For Barrón, these totems, mainly those dedicated to La Santa Muerte and Jesús Malverde—because it "has been corroborated that narco traffickers have in their houses an altar to La Santa Muerte accompanied by Jesús Malverde"—show that "the fact that [Barraza] had different representations comes to reinforce the strong totemic (fetishist) compulsion that [she] had to carry out her activities."[166] That is, because Barraza had altars to the two figures, there was no doubt that she fulfilled the serial killer's totemic phase identified by Norris. To further pathologize Barraza, Barrón states that for "Sigmund Freud, totemism was a product of a neurotic structure," ignoring that Freud said that everyone was neurotic, some more functionally than others.[167] Finally, to fit Barraza into the last phase, depression, Barrón notes that "according to the psychiatric report the hypothesis of suicide, as a line of research, was a viable option" for Barraza, because she "presented two suicide attempts."[168]

Of the seven phases of the serial killer, it seems that only one—the totemic or fetishistic phase—is completely fulfilled by Barraza, the most important evidence being the altar, which is enough for Barrón to prove that Barraza is a serial killer in terms of Norris's classification. Again, I am not stating that Barraza is not a serial killer, but rather that the evidence relied on by criminologists and police officers, and presented as objective, seems rather the result of subjective interpretations and discourses on mexicanidad and criminality that have historically defined who is a criminal.

Not all who believe in La Santa Muerte, of course, are fetishistic serial killers, nor are they necessarily connected to narco culture or drug trafficking. Researchers into her cult and that of Jesús Malverde argue that the adoration of both figures represents a resistance to the neoliberal economy in Mexico since the 1990s. As noted earlier in this chapter, the worship of La Santa Muerte has been stigmatized in news media and discourses of mexicanidad because it is prohibited by the Catholic Church and linked to criminality. Having raised the association with the violent drug trade, Barrón asks rhetorically, ominously, "What kind of favors did Barraza ask of La Santa Muerte or Jesús Malverde?"[169]

Researchers have pointed out how the recent emergence of these cults of La Santa Muerte and Jesús Malverde are linked to the impasse of neoliberalism, lack of infrastructure, socioeconomic pressure, and crisis of faith that contemporaneously emerged in Mexico. Yet this context is ignored by Barrón. Instead, devotion to these figures is presented as proof that Barraza is indeed an evil and fetishistic serial killer.

Conclusion

I started this project stating that I was interested not in Juana Barraza's culpability but rather in what the figure of a female wrestler serial killer said about constructions of criminality and mexicanidad in a pigmentocratic culture. In the course of writing this book, however, I realized that there is an aspect in which I feel I do want to defend Barraza. More than wanting to defend her as a victim of her circumstances, a victim of a patriarchal and machista society, I want to defend her right to transgress the normative roles established for women through notions of mexicanidad. I want to defend Barraza's right to not look "feminine," her right to look (as she has been described) "masculine," her right to be a masculine woman—and to a certain extent, her right to be held responsible for her crimes, as opposed to being criminalized for the way she looks, in both her appearance and her gaze. I want to emphasize the difference between what Barraza does and who she is. Barraza most definitely should be held responsible for her actions. But through the scientific language of criminality and the expertise of neuropsychologists like Ostrosky and criminalists like Barrón, Barraza has been criminalized for what she is, not for her alleged crimes. Responsibility lies in distinguishing what Barraza is and what Barraza has done.

Also, more than wanting to figure out whether Barraza committed sixteen or all forty-nine murders of elderly women, I have been interested in why the killing of elderly women brought the nation into crisis, in contrast to the hundreds of murders of young, marginalized, brown women in Estado de México and Ciudad Juárez.

Barraza most certainly had a horrible childhood. Her mother, Justa Samperio, an alcoholic who constantly beat her, sold Juana to an older man named José Lugo in exchange for three beers when the girl was just thirteen years old. Barraza related this story to Martín Barrón, who interviewed her twelve hours after she was arrested. Barraza recalled that at the beginning she thought it was not real—she believed that her mother would come to pick her up, or maybe her stepfather would come and get her. This did not happen, and Barraza was tied to a bed that first night and raped. She was never allowed to leave Lugo's house; she had to do all the domestic chores in the house and was raped repeatedly. She became pregnant and had an abortion; she became pregnant again and had a son. Five years passed before her uncles found her. Apparently, her mother had insisted that Barraza had left with Lugo on her own. Barraza believes her stepfather did not trust her mother and continued to look for her.[1] Her stepfather had shown her love and compassion and, unlike her mother, did not beat her. After Barraza was found, her stepfather helped raise her son.

When I learned this story, I was shocked by the tragic similarities between Barraza's life and that of Malinalli, the mother of the mestizo nation. Malinalli—La Malintzin, La Malinche—is the embodiment of betrayal, betrayal that is always feminine. To this day, the adjective *malinchista* in Spanish describes a Mexican who seems to prefer foreign cultures, denying their own heritage and ancestry. La Malinche later became the archetypical figure of La Chingada, the raped woman, the symbol of the raped nation by the Spanish colonization. Five hundred years later, it is as if Malinaili existed not in flesh and bone but only as a mythical figure.

But she did exist, and her life story is very similar to that of Barraza and to those of many other young women and girls in Mexico, especially in Tenancingo, Tlaxcala, "the capital of women's trafficking."[2] At an early age, no more than thirteen years old, Malinalli was also sold by her mother. Malinalli's father was an important prince, *tecuhtli*, named Topicazpe or Teotzingo. After he died, Malinalli's mother remarried. Malinalli had no place in this new marriage. In their hometown, a young girl died and Malinalli's mother pretended the girl was her own daughter. In the market of Xicalanco, she then sold Malinalli as a slave to Mayan merchants. They in turn sold Malinalli to the Señor de Potochán.

When Hernán Cortés landed in the state of Tabasco in 1519, the Aztecs welcomed him and his fellow Spanish travelers. As it was an Aztec tradition to travel with women, Malinalli was presented to Cortés along with nineteen other young *nahua* girls. According to Spanish law, marriage could take place only between single, Christian people, so Malinalli was baptized. Cortés was, in fact, already married in Spain, but he took on Malinalli as a mistress. She was renamed, Castilian-style, Marina. Already conversant in both Mayan and Náhuatl, Malinalli soon learned Spanish, and her translation skills became key to the conquest.[3]

When I learned this story, it was appalling to me that as a Mexican, I had based my national identity on the actions of a fourteen-year-old girl. I had grown up with this tension: not wanting to be *malinchista* and betray my heritage, yet presented with the notion that all things foreign are better. I was shocked that I had based my idea of mexicanidad on what a *nahua* girl, regardless of her terrible childhood, had done in her betrayal of the nation, even though there was no nation yet, even though three centuries would pass before there was a Mexico. Malinalli did exactly what the Tlaxclatecas, Texcocanos, Totonacos, Cempoaltecas, and Xochimilcas did—ally against the Aztecs:[4] "for Malitzin, as for the groups subjected to the Aztec empire over them, Moctezuma was as much as a foreigner as Hernan Cortés and, consequently, Malitzin owed no loyalty to any group; if they joined the Spanish, it was due to circumstances and encouraged by their internal desire for revenge."[5] Yet Malinalli is the only one held responsible for selling us out—yes, five hundred years later there is an "us" that feels betrayed by her.

I had learned in school about colonization. I grew up with notions of mexicanidad through which I learned to be resentful not only about colonization per se, but more importantly about La Malitzin, who had made colonization happen. If she had only not learned Spanish and sold us out to the Spaniards!

Barraza and Malinalli were both sold by their mothers when they were only teenagers. Neither had as a mother a guardian angel of the home, a self-sacrificing Mexican mother always giving unconditional love. Neither had a mother like La Virgen de Guadalupe, or a grandmother like Sara García. On the contrary, both Barraza and Malinalli found in the figure of the father a nurturing parent. It was Barraza's stepfather who showed her love and helped her raise her child. It was Malinalli's dad who protected her, even from her own mother; when he died, she was left to her own devices. Malinalli found in Hernan Cortés, twenty years older than she, a new father figure. This is extremely important in terms of the construction of mexicanidad. Although hegemonic and official notions of mexicanidad have depicted the ideal woman/mother as a self-sacrificing, always nurturing mother, there are these cases in which it is the father, or the father figure, who is the nurturer. Hegemonic constructions of mexicanidad seem to allow men only the traditional spaces of either the macho or the submissive *mandilón*.[6] While there are innumerable movies, telenovelas, songs, and other expressions of popular culture that feature nurturing mothers, such depictions of fathers are exceedingly rare.

Barraza and Malinalli have both become symbols of betrayal, treachery, and deceit to the nation. Barraza has been criminalized more for her "muscular" body and her "virile" appearance than for the homicides of elderly women of which she is accused.

Barraza is a modern La Malintzin—but unlike her predecessor, Barraza lived in extreme poverty. She did not know how to read and write. By contrast, Malinalli was an upper-class woman with a facility for languages. Yet she was punished for that, for learning Spanish and acting in complicity with Cortés, the man she was given to. She is condemned on the basis that she should have known better and never betrayed the nation that did not yet exist. The story of Malinalli that circulates is that of the betrayer, the treacherous woman, establishing an idea of mexicanidad in which women who decide for themselves what is best are selfish, betraying their families and their nation. These women are also sexualized, rendering them easy and disposable, not counting as victims.

Barraza was, and continues to be, punished for her betrayal of the ideal for Mexican women. She is constructed as the worse type of criminal, for she killed the most vulnerable of Mexicans, elderly women, the grandmothers of the nation. Barraza became La Malintzin, betraying the nation by killing the ideal Mexican women, the virgins, the desexualized abuelitas. And unlike Mario Tablas or Aracelí Vásquez, who also killed elderly women, Barraza looked like a "man" and thus further betrayed the female ideal, the image of the feminine Virgen de Guadalupe. Barraza was killing La Virgen de Guadalupe, the representation of the ideal, self-sacrificing, self-abnegating woman.

La Malintzin was killing La Virgen de Guadalupe.

La Malintzin (Barraza) was killing La Virgen de Guadalupe over and over.

Who counts as a victim in Mexico?

Women who represent the ideal of woman/mother as established through notions of mexicanidad. Women who are desexualized like La

Virgen de Guadalupe. Women who seem to not have agency, but are the idealized guardian angels of their homes.

Who does not count as victim in Mexico? Which bodies are not deemed grievable by the state?

The bodies of women who, like La Malintzin, are sexualized. The bodies of women who have agency. The bodies of women who transgress normative roles defined for women/mothers in Mexico. The bodies of victims of feminicides do not count and continue to be raped by the state. When young, poor, and brown women are killed or sold, their bodies are reinscribed into that of Malinalli.

La Malintzin and Hernan Cortés had a son who spent all his life in Spain and died there. Martín Cortés abandoned his home and mother and, like a good (first) Mexican, was a *malinchista*. La Malintzin stayed in Mexico, lamenting the loss of her son, and became the figure of La Llorona—the weeping woman, a ghost woman. She exists only as a ghost because she lost her children; in different versions of the story, either she drowned them in the river or she drowns herself in the river. In either case, La Llorona now cries eternally, and she always does so close to a river.

The figure of La Llorona has not occupied a place in national culture as central as that of the Malitzin or La Virgen de Guadalupe. The celebration of her legend is nonetheless popular and diverse.[7] La Llorona can be seen as a syncretic figure based in a European narrative-type with the following features: a woman with children, betrayal by an adulterous husband, vengeful infanticide, and the mother crying for her children in eternal, anguished repentance.[8] The characteristics of this European narrative are attached "to another distinctive Indian legend, that of Ciuacoatl, the Aztec goddess that according to Fray Bernadino de Saghún appeared in the night crying out for dead children."[9] This Indian woman is always crying "near a body of water (an important element in Aztec mythology), and confronting people, mostly men, who are terrified when they see her."[10] La Llorona is always dressed in white, much like the gown often worn by La Santa Muerte.

Although La Llorona has been read as representing Mexican women's fears and apprehensions about being mothers,[11] Limón suggests she is a more active female symbol than La Virgen de Guadalupe and La Malinche, subverting the "patriarchal norms for what women should do, namely take care of their children and preserve the nuclear family."[12] For Limón, La Llorona "kills because she is also living out the most extreme articulation of the everyday social and psychological contradictions created by those norms for Mexican women." Symbolically, she "offers us a fascinating paradox: the symbolic destruction of the nuclear family at one stage, and the later possible restoration of her maternal bonds from the waters of rebirth at a second stage."[13]

Tenochtitlán, now Mexico City, was located on an island near the Lake Texcoco, in the Valley of Mexico.[14] Since the settlement of the basin of Mexico, all the rivers started to dry out in the process of urbanization. There are no true rivers left in the region, only canals, mostly in Estado de México to the east of Mexico City. The Canal de Chalco used to belong to the River of Remedies. It runs through working-class districts in Estado de México. In recent years, this canal has served as a clandestine cemetery for the victims of feminicides. Indeed, while I was writing this book, the body of Valeria Mora was found in the Canal de Chalco. In 2014, seven thousand bones were found during a ten-mile-long dredge of the canal.[15] Officials denied the discovery was evidence of a massacre, stating instead that most of the bones belonged to animals. However, Octavio Vargas, head of Estado de México's public safety commission, claimed that the attorney general had admitted in private that at least sixteen cadavers had been found of women who had been tortured and killed.[16]

Close to this body of water, Canal de Chalco, which symbolizes birth and holds the bones of the victims of feminicide in the Estado de México, we can find La Llorona. La Llorona is read as lamenting the loss of her sons, but she might be lamenting the loss of her own life, thrown as expendable in the river. La Llorona is not La Malitzin, as hegemonic readings on mexicanidad—by Paz, for instance—have it. La Llorona *is crying for* La Malintzin, for the victims of feminicides left in the canal. For those who do not count.

This lack of infrastructure cannot support their bodies. And the canal has always signified a fluid space in which women are lost.

In Canal de Chalco, La Llorona is not only destroying the nuclear family, she is rebirthing herself, restoring the bonds of maternity, restoring her own life.

I want to defend the right of Mexican women to be La Llorona. To have agency over their own lives and bodies. And I want to defend Barraza because I want to know. I want resources to be put into investigating the serial killing of young mestizo women in Ciudad Juárez, in Estado de México, in all of Mexico. Of homosexual men, of every single person disappeared. Of the forty-three students missing and all of the unknown number of bodies that have disappeared with the complacency of the Mexican government. *Queremos la verdad, sin disculpas, dosificación o duda.* We want the truth with no apologies, doubts, or excuses. This is what the parents of the missing students of Ayotzinapa are fighting for. It is what the surviving family members of the women murdered in Ciudad Juárez and Estado de México are fighting for.

It is appalling that the only mass homicides that have shocked the nation—and therefore the only subjects that have counted as victims, the only bodies deemed grievable—are those of elderly women. Of course, I am not against counting elderly women as victims; on the contrary, I am advocating that all those killed with the complacency of the Mexican government be considered victims. Elderly women who lived alone counted as victims because they were considered grandmothers who had been abandoned by their families, by the nation. The abandonment of elderly women spoke of a nation in decomposition, a society in decay. If grandmothers and mothers have since Porfirian times had the role of holding together the family, the nation, then their killing was the killing of the nation itself. And their killing was, again, perpetrated by La Chingada.

La Chingada was killing La Virgen of Guadalupe.

La Chingada (Barraza) was killing La Virgen de Guadalupe over and over.

The responses to Juana Barraza as La Mataviejitas, by both Mexican authorities and in popular culture discourses, show how a sense of national identity and notions of mexicanidad powerfully influence everyday life, to the point of affecting even how public policy and the day-to-day responsibilities of the state are implemented.

I spoke in chapter 2 about the mestizos who were left out of the Cara-Mex archive—those mestizos and mestizas who can occupy spaces of privilege within the pigmentocratic system of Mexico. In constructions of the ideology of mexicanidad, what has been left out and consigned to the shadow archive is the sexuality of those women who transgress ideals of mexicanidad, ideals of how women should be and how their sexuality should be embodied. These are not only the mothers that killed or sold their children, but also the mothers that simply work and have agency over their own bodies.

Just as I was writing the conclusion of this book, in May 2017, a UNAM student named Lesby Berlin Osorio was murdered. Academics, activists, and others were infuriated when the Procuraduría General de Justicia del Distrito Federal tweeted that the young woman was "drinking alcohol and doing drugs" and that she was not a student of UNAM. This gave rise to the protest hashtag #SiMeMatan (if I get killed), with which thousands of women tweeted what they thought police would say about their private lives, blaming them for their own deaths and criminalizing them: "I was a whore," "I lived with my partner without being married," "I did not want to get married," "I wore miniskirts," "There was no man to take care of me," and so on.[17] These tweets also showed the reality of feminicides in Mexico—that there is no safe place and no way to know who will be next. This subject could not be more depressing and urgent.

I have attempted to demonstrate how cultural beliefs around who is a victim, who is not, what a criminal looks like, and how a criminal behaves have actual consequences. These cultural beliefs, as I have shown, stem from national discourses on mexicanidad, from ideologies of racism and classism, and from sexism hidden in the most obvious of places, such as in media narrations and popular cultural forms.

What I did not realize when I set out to write this book is that I was going to write about mothers and about the figures of motherhood in Mexico. La Santa Muerte, the evil twin and sinister sister of La Virgen de Guadalupe, functions as an alternative mother figure, one who can actually help in a crisis—like a crisis of faith against a state that cannot provide justice or security (financial or emotional), but on the contrary murders its citizens. A mother who, unlike La Virgen de Guadalupe, does not promote an image of a woman/mother that is desexualized, always virginal, and self-sacrificing and self-abnegating. La Santa Muerte is a mother that holds you accountable for who you are and what you do. La Santa Muerte is La Llorona.

What do not count, either, are the bodies of homosexuals, travesti, and transsexuals, many of them sex workers, who also are murdered with the total complicity of the state. Gay male users of the Grindr app say there has been a serial killer of gay men in Mexico City since the mid-2000s, that gay men have died in their apartments, strangled after sexual encounters.[18] Because of the lingering stigma of homosexuality and their families' shame, these crimes are rarely reported. And many know that reporting them would not make a difference.

As I was writing this manuscript and sharing these ideas with Mexican academics, it made sense that the killing of abuelitas is what brought the nation into crisis. Elderly women had a face, they were familiar to the nation. They were Sara García, our grandmother. The symbolic killing of Sara García shocked the nation. But that is not what shocked me. What shocked me was learning that García was a lesbian who had spent the last sixty years of her life in the company of Rosarito, her "companion," to whom she left everything she owned. I ascribe, however, to Eve Sedgwick's notion that it constitutes epistemological violence to "out" or to ascribe a gender-sex identity to any individual contrary to the one the subject ascribes to,[19] or even to assume a gender identity before asking, and I have opposed publicly the idea that a public figure must and should "openly" disclose their sexuality. Carlos Monsiváis (1938–2010), for example, never publicly came out, although most of his writings and activism were on behalf of civil rights for the LGBT community in Mexico. Monsiváis did not wanted to be pigeonholed as a "gay" writer. When he died in 2010 many activists wanted to have a rainbow flag on his casket, sparking a heated debate between those who defended his right to keep his sexuality private and those who felt he had shirked what they saw as his duty to the gay community by not coming out.

I do not want to say merely that Rosario was Sara García's "companion."[20] I want to describe Rosarito as Sara Garcia's lover or romantic partner. It is not that I think visibility translates into power and that in claiming García as a lesbian, the LGBTQ movement in Mexico will be empowered. No. I want to say that García was lesbian because I want to explore how notions of mexicanidad that have determined who is an ideal woman/mother shift when we consider that García, the grandmother of the nation, was a closeted lesbian. How does our conception of mexicanidad change when we recognize that it is based in part on an idealized version of a woman who decided to not openly own her sexuality? How does our conception of mexicanidad change when we recognize that mothers can be killers, can sell their own daughters, when fathers and father figures can be less macho, not macho at all, but rather nurturing and loving, when fathers are La Virgen de Guadalupe?

What shocked me again—even more—when I shared with colleagues and friends that I had learned García was a lesbian, was to learn of rumors, among those who already knew she was a lesbian, that she was very "macho." I had naively assumed that all lesbians were politically aware of oppression, were feminist, would not reproduce the power structures that oppress them, but instead would want to occupy a position of power to make a change.[21] When I say "macho," I am not identifying lesbians with a masculine gender expression, but rather the total opposite—I am moving away from equating masculinity with machismo. I am equating macho with a position of power, a position that both men and women can occupy independently if there is an embodiment of femininity or masculinity.

Some actors who knew both women referred to Rosarito as the "victim," because García apparently was known for her "machoness." This machoness refers to possessiveness, control, and domination. It is said that García, while filming a telenovela, constantly teased the women actors on the set with double entendres. I imagine that García was a Pedro Infante, a Jorge Negrete, that is, a seducer, a womanizer, the ideal mestizo macho. The ideal Mexican.

Rosarito was the victim of Sara García.

Victims are those victimized by those in macho positions of power, be it a man or a woman, a heterosexual, a homosexual.

How does our conception of mexicanidad change when we recognize that lesbians and homosexuals also reproduced the ideal of toxic masculinity promoted in film and popular culture and equated with machismo?[22]

In earlier work, during my doctorate, I analyzed photographs of *mujercitos*, travestis who were photographed for the front pages of *Alarma!* I looked at all the issues of *Alarma!* from the first, in 1963, to 1986, when the periodical shut down, censored by the government. I wanted to investigate why *mujercitos* were shown posing for the camera of *Alarma!*

while the text condemned them as degenerate and how these photographs circulated. These individuals appeared, posing, while detained in police stations, during a raid of a private party, and, on many occasions, while celebrating a "wedding." I concluded that *mujercitos* were being criminalized not for their homosexuality, which is not illegal, or for wearing makeup, dresses, and wigs. In fact, they were allowed in the photographs the feminine subjectivity that society at large denies them. Their adoption of women's names such as Claudia and Lorena and their appearances in the photographs were encouraged, celebrated; Lorena, for example, was said to be the most gorgeous women the photographer, the police officers, and even sometimes the judge had ever seen—but Alejandro, Lorena's legal name, Alejandro was a degenerate. I suggest that it was the failure of masculinity that was most punished. In the case of *hombrecitas*, it was the embodiment of masculinity that was punished, in the most violent of ways; *hombrecitas* were not allowed any space of masculinity, were always called by their legal names, and no photos of them posing for the camera were shown. For *hombrecitas*, occupying the "privileged" position of masculinity was the worst of crimes.

As I have discussed, the idealized Mexican, through mexicanidad discourses, is the intertwined figure of the mestizo macho, the heterosexual male, embodying a toxic masculinity, one that is controlling, possessive, and territorial to the point of erasing the other. I am interested in seeing the position of macho not as a subject position essentialized through biology and reserved for cis-men, but as another space of privilege, a space in which you are not killed but you kill. Macho as a space of power that grants the privilege of not being killed. It is further interesting to note how paradoxical this position of privilege works, since many men have to prove their machoness by actively having sex with another man, occupying the "active" role, that of the macho probado. Although having sex with mujercitos, for instance, might appear to fulfill this fantasy, since they are travestis and assumed to be in the passive position, it is they who actually tend to play the active role in intimate relations.

Mujercitos were criminalized for their failure of masculinity. Juana Barraza was criminalized for the gender transgression she exercised.

Barraza has a very bad back, the result of a wrestling injury, and she can barely walk. She has been in poor health, and I was not able to meet with her again. During our one meeting, though, I learned a lot. When I tell colleagues and friends that I met with Barraza, I am often asked, Why did she do it?

I did not have a chance to ask Barraza if she actually killed elderly women, if she had killed one, sixteen, or forty-nine of them, or if she had strangled Ana María Reyes Alfaro, the elderly women asphyxiated in the house she was caught fleeing. At the same time, I am not convinced there are satisfying answers to these questions. When we met, Barraza talked a lot, close to two hours, but the conversation centered on her kids; she did mention the killings of elderly women. She told me she had never killed anyone, that she would never dare to take someone's life because "that would be mediocre." As I understood it, she denied over and over "taking someone's life" not because she was not capable of it, but because doing it was not in her character. In excerpts of an interview available on YouTube through Azteca Noticias, published on November 1, 2016,[23] Barraza speaks to the camera in a white office, presumably in police custody, still dressed in red, weeping and saying: "Odiaba a las señoras porque mi mamá me maltrataba. Siempre me maldecía. Me regaló con un señor grande y yo fui abusada" (I hated old women because my mom mistreated me. She always cursed me. She gave me away to an old man and I was abused). The crying intensifies as she says, "Por eso odiaba a las señoras. Se que no es excusa, que no merezco perdón ni de dios, ni de nadie" (That is why I hated older woman. I know it is not an excuse, that I do not deserve forgiveness from God or from anyone). As she talks, people pass back and forth behind her, going about their administrative business.

Barraza's narrative is overwhelmed by incongruities and contradictions, but so are news, criminologists, and police narratives on the investigation, capture, and criminalization of El/La Mataviejitas. According to Renato Sales, El Mataviejitas "had an accomplice."[24] According to Bernardo Bátiz, the killer "acted alone."[25] That belief was shared by neuropsychologist Feggy Ostrosky, who concluded after the "results of laboratory analysis" (it is not clear what kind) that the "serial killer acted alone."[26] The Mexico City Justice Department created a three-dimensional bust of the Mataviejitas accomplice.[27] It was later believed with certainty that El Mataviejitas had committed suicide.[28]

CONCLUSION | 197

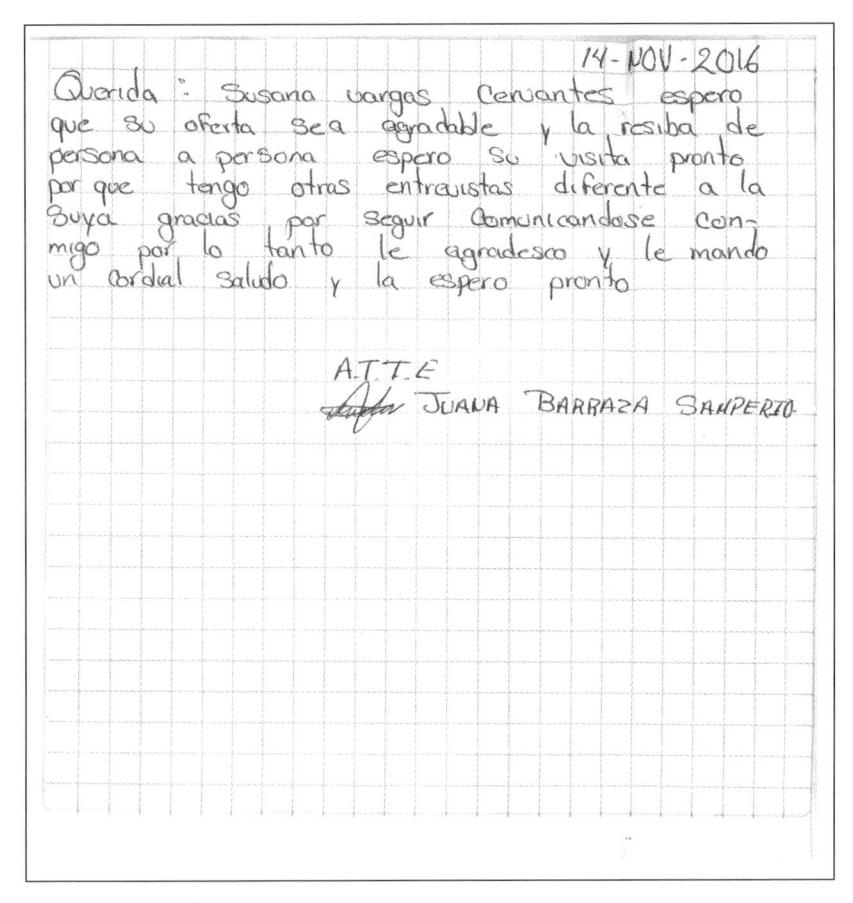

```
14-NOV-2016

Querida: Susana vargas Cervantes espero
que su oferta sea agradable y la resiba de
persona a persona espero su visita pronto
por que tengo otras entrevistas diferente a la
suya gracias por seguir comunicandose con-
migo por lo tanto le agradesco y le mando
un cordial saludo y la espero pronto

                            A.T.T.E
                            JUANA BARRAZA SAMPERIO
```

Figure C.1. Letter from Juana Barraza to the author.

Many reports stated that "luck" had been crucial in the detention of serial killers around the world.[29] Similarly, criminologist Martín Barrón stated that "it might even take twenty years" to arrest El Mataviejitas and the detention was likely to "happen in a fortuitous manner."[30] Less than a year later, though, after the arrest of Juana Barraza, Barrón was convinced that La Mataviejitas had been captured thanks to good police work and investigation.[31] Luis José Hinojosa, president of the National Centre of Criminalistic Research, meanwhile was certain that the detention of Juana Barraza "was a stroke of good luck and not the result of police investigation."[32]

Bátiz stated in October 2005 that "El Mataviejitas was brilliant and didn't leave any fingerprints on the crime scenes."[33] Three months later, when Barraza was arrested, Bátiz confirmed that Juana Barraza was undoubtedly La Mataviejitas because her "10 fingerprints" had been found in eleven homicides and one failed homicide.[34] In the same press conference, held just six hours after Barraza's arrest, Bátiz further stated police had determined that the one fingerprint they got from an X-ray, in the failed homicide, was "very similar" to Barraza's fingerprints.[35] In spite of announcing beforehand that police "had only fragments"[36] of fingerprints as evidence of past homicides, Bátiz declared in the press conference that they had "enough [fragments] to consider that it was the same person."[37] Renato Sales Heredia was certain that "there is a problem in relation to fingerprints. We need in the country a computerized system that allows us to compare fingerprints in a digital manner, given that a manual comparison takes a lot of time."[38] He further stated that "a database with fingerprints is of little use if they cannot establish a relation between the victim and the criminal."[39]

In the search for El Mataviejitas, police were certain that the serial killer was, like any other of his kind, just a "common citizen."[40] When police arrested Juana Barraza, the Justice Department's Margarita Guerra was certain that she not a sociopath.[41] According to academic Isabel Bueno, Barraza is a "sociopath just like Hitler and *El Mochaorejas*, whose strong personality attracts and fascinates."[42]

My intent is to point out how media, police, and criminologists are not *demanding responsibility* from Barraza for the killing of elderly women but are pathologizing her for her class, race, and most of all her nonnormative gender and wrestling practice. It is La Dama del Silencio who is being criminalized and not Juana Barraza. When Barraza was arrested, the Mataviejitas case was closed, suggesting that only one serial killer was responsible for all the killings of elderly women, despite the large number of unresolved cases.

Juana told me she was writing a book of her own. Her manuscript, called "When Women Cry," narrates what happens to women at night while in prison "because when the dark comes, and they are in their bunks, they howl, they cry a lot. It is very hard to be here. It is very hard to be locked up." She started crying and had to take a moment to collect herself. I remained silent and waited, looking at my hands in my lap. She

Ciudad de México a 11-16-2a

SUSANA VARGAS CERVANTES.

De acuerdo a la petición que me hicieron llegar, es menester señalar que estoy de acuerdo en dicha entrevista para su libro. Solo pido una gratificación para mis gastos personales como vera a mi nadien me apoya economicamento yo trabajo para mis gastos no se espante no estamos hablando de cantidades fuertes solo usted decide y espero su contestacion La señorita Karla me hara llegar su contestacion y solo habra verdades ya que quiere saber la verdad y lo que no he podido decir espero pronto su respuesta y disculpeme que tarde en contestar ya que no confio en nadien ya que no he dado entrevistas y me an destrozado por el momento estado y espero su respuesta.

Es todo lo que dice Juana Samperio

Figure C.2. Letter from Juana Barraza to the author.

also insisted that she never gets into trouble, "It's not like me. I like to be good. I never swear or try not to swear." When we exchanged letters, Barraza had asked me for money—living in prison is not cheap and she had a lot of expenses, not least continuing to provide for her children (fig. C.1). I gave her 500 pesos that I had on me.

What felt most important to me about my meeting with Barraza was her emphasis on motherhood. As she put it, Juana Barraza could be anything you or I, or the media, or a criminologist, wanted, but a bad mother? No, that she could not be called. This to me is the highlight of my visit with her and the backbone of this book. Even Barraza, the alleged one and only female serial killer in Mexican history, knows full well how discourses on mexicanidad work, how being a good mother is the single most important cultural and social role for a woman. Again, I am not saying that all Mexican women feel this, or are good mothers, but Mexican women have to negotiate with this ideal, with this interiorized discourse, in which to be a good Mexican woman means being a good mother and the severe consequences of this discourses on mexicanidad. Being a bad mother, being called a bad mother is the worst, it crosses the line, even for an alleged serial killer, and Juana knows it. Being a bad mother would be being like her own mother, like Malinalli's mother.

In this regard, there is nothing I could agree on more with Barraza, and that to me is the most crucial element of her alleged criminality. In discourses of mexicanidad, a bad mother, a woman who does not fulfill her most important and sacred role, is the criminal. A woman who murders those who embody that role is the most horrible of criminals.

ACKNOWLEDGMENTS

This research started in the Esperanza—now Cagibi—café in Montreal. Will and I were having a *cinq à sept* when I told him about the story of a female wrestler who had just been detained that morning in Mexico City, allegedly as La Mataviejitas, the serial killer of elderly women. Will's excitement about this true crime tale could not be contained; he encouraged me to start an M.A at McGill University and get to work on researching the story. I did. And with that I started not only an academic career, but also following Will's advice. This book is the result. Thank you.

For always being a critical and generous, sharp and loving reader and discusser, I am especially thankful to Johanne Sloan. Much of our conversations and her critical engagements are reflected here, from the introduction to the conclusion.

Jeff Ferrell foresaw the beginning of this manuscript in the article "Performing Criminalidad: Mexicanidad and Lucha Libre" for *Crime, Media and Culture*. Without his careful reading, generosity, and help this book would not have been possible. I am also deeply thankful to my editor at NYU Press, Ilene Kalish, who supported this project enthusiastically and provided the most helpful edits. This book also greatly benefited from the careful and engaged readings of my three anonymous reviewers.

I would not have been able to finish this project without the constant support and loving care of Linda Palacios. Her engaged critical perspective not only shaped my arguments, I confess that our conversations are often reproduced verbatim in this text. I am grateful too for her sharing the material necessary for me to understand my own mexicanidad and machismo.

The teaching of Carrie A. Rentschler and the careful readings of Alanna Thain and Leticia Sabsay shaped the beginning of this project, gave it a direction, and provided the encouragement I needed to make it a book. Gretchen Bakke was more than an editor and a coach; she was at the same time patient and extremely persuasive in pushing me to write. The support of Graciela Martínez Zalce and the Centro de Investigaciones Sobre América del Norte have also been key—thank you. And to Amelia Jones and Cuauhtémoc Medina, thank you for your constant support.

My friend Paloma Martínez helped me figure out how get to Santa Martha Acatitla. I am grateful to Lucía Nuñez, who offered to convey correspondence between Juana Barraza and myself during her own visits to Santa Martha, which made it possible for me to talk to Barraza. For helping me navigate Santa Martha with much consideration, care, and awareness, I am deeply thankful to Ana Luisa Sánchez. The help of Lic. Fernando Martínez was also essential to my visit. Thank you to Juana Barraza for agreeing to meet with me. Thank you, as well, to Comandante Victor Hugo Moneda and anthropologist Carlos Serrano for sharing material vital to the research for this book.

Many friends helped me throughout the writing process, offering constant critical listening and encouragement: Damian Hernández, Marisa Herrán, Cristina Paoli, Michele Fiedler, Jan Mot, Héctor Bialostosky, Victor Costales, Adela Rangel, Jessica Berlanga, Dorothee Depuis, Diego del Valle, Devon Van Houten, Lienne Sawatsky, Dan Williams, Lucia Anaya, Raquel Alarcón and La Chicha, Ana Paula Ruiz Galindo, Mecky Reuss, Fernando Mesta, Jess Lee, Kiva Stimac, Mauro Pezzente, Katie Stelmanis, Tania Hernández, Chris Gutiérrez, Erandy Vergara, Sarah Neufeld, and Dean Spade. Thank you to Magali Arriola and the Merida seminar. And thank you, Clara Jusidman.

Despite our geographical distance, Emy Story accompanied me through every step of my research, through the visits to Santa Martha, and through the writing of each page—through text messages and FaceTime, it was always as if we were in the same room. I am deeply thankful for her care and support.

I still cannot believe I have not been too much for Patti Schmidt and Meg Hewings, who have provided so much love and care and support as I worked to finish this book. I am actually writing these lines from their kitchen table.

Thank you to Raul Arriaga for the critical feedback and generosity. Thank you to Mariana Flores for her research help. And to Annia Mayerstein for her help in the third chapter. For her careful edits and suggestions, I am thankful to Alison Jacques, who was involved at the beginning of this project while we both were in a class dealing with female criminality and, many years later, toward its end, with careful reading and editing. I also would like to thank Silvia Nava and María Luisa Espinosa at the Biblioteca Carlos Monsiváis and Carmen Negrete for listening to my stories and preparing delicious tlacoyos outside the Biblioteca México.

Thank you, Nuria Úrculo, for arriving at the end of this project, encouraging and challenging my thinking. Thank you for your love and support. Endlessly.

NOTES

INTRODUCTION

1 Agustín Salgado and Mirna Servín, "Cae mataviejitas tras consumar otro de sus crímenes; es mujer," *La Jornada*, January 26, 2006; Carlos Jiménez, "Atrapan a La mataviejitas: es mujer y es luchadora," *Crónica*, January 26, 2006. Oscar Herrera, Icela Lagunas, and Rubelio Fernández, "Luchadora de 48 años fue detenida luego de estrangular a una mujer. Cae presunta mataviejitas," *El Universal*, January 26, 2006.

2 Renato Sales Heredia, deputy prosecutor with the Mexico City Department of Justice, referred to serial killing as an "unknown phenomenon" in Mexico. Heredia, "Seis visiones en busca de un serial," *Proceso*, February 12, 2006.

3 Los Zetas are notorious for their brutality, for example, torturing victims for hours at a time. George W. Grayson, *The Evolution of Los Zetas in Mexico and Central America: Sadism as an Instrument of Cartel Warfare* (Carlisle Barracks, PA: US Army War College Press, 2014); Samuel Logan, "Preface: Los Zetas and a New Barbarism," *Small Wars and Insurgencies* 22, no. 5 (2011): 718–27. The narcosatánicos were a group of high-profile drug lords and police officers who, at the end of the 1980s, were involved in drug trafficking and satanic rituals (see chapter 1).

4 See Julia Estela Monárrez Fragoso, "La cultura del feminicidio en Ciudad Juárez," *Frontera Norte* 12, no. 23 (2000): 87–117; Julia Estela Monárrez Fragoso, "Feminicidio sexual serial en Ciudad Juárez: 1993–2001," *Debate Feminista* 25, no. 13 (2002): 279–305; Mariclaire Acosta, "The Women of Ciudad Juárez" (policy paper no. 3, Center for Latin American Studies. University of California, Berkeley, 2005).

5 Heredia, "Seis visiones."

6 According to the 2016 United Nations report *La violencia feminicida en México* (Feminicide violence in Mexico), "the crime of feminicide is that which deprives of life a woman for reasons of gender. It is considered that there are gender factors when any of the following circumstances are present: I. The victim shows signs of sexual violence of any kind; II. The victim has been inflicted degrading injuries or mutilations prior to or after the deprivation of life or acts of necrophilia; III. There is a history or data of any kind of violence in the family, work or school setting of the perpetrator against the victim; IV. It has existed between the perpetrator and the victim a sentimental, emotional or relationship of trust; V. Data exists to establish that there were threats related to the

criminal act, harassment or injury from the perpetrator against the victim; VI. The victim was incommunicado, prior to the deprivation of life; VII. The body of the victim is exposed or displayed in a public place." Carlos Javier Echarri Cánovas, *La violencia feminicida en México: Aproximaciones y tendencias 1985–2014* (Mexico Secretaria de Gobernación, Instituto Nacional de las Mujeres, ONU Mujeres, Entidad de las Naciones Unidas para la Igualdad de Género y el Empoderamiento de las Mujeres, April 2016), 20. The term "feminicide" was coined in the 1990s by academic Marcela Lagarde, who adapted the English term "femicide" to the Spanish "*feminicidio*"—not merely to be the feminization of the term "homicide," but also to imply state responsibility (see chapter 4). See Lagarde, "Del femicidio al feminicidio," *Desde el Jardín de Freud. Revista de Psicoanálisis*, no. 6 (2006): 216–25.

7 Julia Estela Monárrez Fragoso, *Trama de una injusticia: feminicidio sexual sistémico en Ciudad Juárez* (Chihuahua: El Colegio de la Frontera Norte, 2012), 8.

8 Humberto Padgett and Eduardo Loza, *Las muertas del estado: feminicidios durante la administración mexiquense de Enrique Peña Nieto* (Mexico City: Grijalbo, 2014), e-book, statistical index, 7.

9 Mauro Cabral and Paula Viturro, "(Trans)Sexual Citizenship in Contemporary Argentina," in *Transgender Rights*, ed. Paisley Currah, Richard M. Juang, and Shannon Minter (Minneapolis: University of Minnesota Press, 2006), 270.

10 Marta Lamas, "De trasvestis y asesinos en serie," *Proceso*, November 6, 2005: 72–73.

11 Miguel Nila, "Ningún trasvesti resultó ser El Mataviejitas: Bátiz," *Noticieros Televisa*, October 24, 2005.

12 The federal government, then under the control of the right-wing Partido de Acción Nacional (PAN) insisted that Mexico City's violence had increased dramatically since López Obrador became Mexico City's mayor and that the homicides of older women spoke to that. According to news reports, El Mataviejitas killed elderly women who were registered in Mexico City's controversial program of public aid for elderly citizens that López Obrador had instituted. López Obrador denied the existence of a serial killer and blamed the El Mataviejitas phenomenon on a conspiracy by the federal oppositional party against his government's social policies. At the time, López Obrador had been threatened with a prison sentence for building a road—one which traversed private property—to a private hospital outside Mexico City's perimeter. This conflict ended with a potential *desafuero*, (a process through which official immunity is removed and criminal prosecution is possible) whose principal promoter was the federal government, under then president Vicente Fox. López Obrador's supporters believed the *desafuero's* only motivation was to impede his campaign for the presidency.

However, López Obrador graduated from popular mayor to social phenomenon in April 2005 when he called for a massive demonstration, called the "March of Silence," against the *desafuero*. Close to one million people showed up at Mexico City's main square to support him. After the march, Vicente Fox pulled out of the *desafuero* (although Mariana Gómez, a local PAN deputy, decided to post "bail" in court to free López Obrador who said he would rather stand trial and go to jail since he "wasn't guilty"). López Obrador further suggested the killings of elderly women were isolated cases and blamed the media for magnifying the news. From the beginning of his term as mayor in 2001 until he left the position in July 2005 to campaign for the presidency, López Obrador denied the existence of a serial killer.

13 Raymundo Sánchez, "No era compló, sí existía, ya confesó," *Crónica*, January 27, 2006.
14 Mirna Servín and Agustín Salgado, "De 1998 a la fecha, 49 asesinatos de ancianos," *La Jornada*, January 26, 2006.
15 Adrián Reyes, "Seguridad-México: ancianas en la mira de la misoginia," *Inter Press Service*, December 16, 2005.
16 Arturo Sierra and Leticia Fernández, "Tienen 64 rostros del 'Mataviejitas,'" *Reforma*, November 29, 2005; Luis Brito and Juan Corona, "Atrapan a Mataviejitas, lleva lista de ancianas," *Reforma*, January 26, 2006.
17 When Felipe Calderón attacked Elena Poniatowska, a López Obrador supporter and highly respected novelist, everyone got involved, including leading Mexican leader cultural critic Carlos Monsiváis and internationally renowned writers like Eduardo Galeano, Doris Summer, and Nobel Prize–winner José Saramago, who all signed an open letter condemning Calderón's attack.
18 Servín and Salgado, "De 1998 a la fecha."
19 Jorge Pérez, "Desoye Bátiz a ALDF," *Reforma*, September 15, 2005; "Atacan panistas al GDF con el tema del 'Mataviejitas' Trejo Pérez," *Agencia Mexicana de Noticias*, December 4, 2005.
20 PAN's local deputy, Mariana Gómez, "called for the resignation of Bernardo Bátiz", chief of Mexico City's Department of Justice, "if in the following 10 days Bátiz didn't give concrete results regarding El Mataviejitas." Members of the PRD denounced this as "clear media exploitation of the El Mataviejitas phenomenon in order to politically harm the local government." Ten days later, deputies Gabriela González and Mariana Gómez stated that Bátiz "had failed in his charge as chief prosecutor" as El Mataviejitas had not been arrested, and called on Bátiz to resign "for the sake of dignity." See "Tiene Bátiz 10 días para atrapar al 'Mataviejitas': diputadas del PAN," *Agencia de Noticias Notimex*, November 30, 2005.;"Atacan panistas al GDF con el tema del 'Mataviejitas': Trejo Pérez."; Pediran Panistas Destituir a Bátiz Por No Atrapar Al "Mataviejitas,"'" *Agencia Mexicana de Noticias*, December 8, 2005.
21 Julio Hernández López, "Teatritos," *La Jornada*, February 13, 2006.
22 Ibid.
23 Carlos Monsiváis, *Mexican Postcards*, trans. John Kraniauskas (London: Verso, 1997); Octavio Paz, *El laberinto de la soledad*, 2nd ed. (Mexico City: Fondo de Cultura Económica, 1998).
24 Paz, *El laberinto*.

25 Roger Bartra, *La jaula de la melancolía: identidad y metamorfosis del mexicano* (Mexico City: Grijalbo, 1996), 206–17.
26 Ibid.
27 Carlos Monsiváis, "¿Tantos millones de hombres no hablaremos inglés? (La cultura Norteamericana y México)," in *Simbiosis de Culturas*, ed. Guillermo Bonfil Batalla (Mexico, D.F.: Fondo de Cultura Económica. Consejo Nacional para la Cultura y las Artes, 1993), 476.
28 Ibid., 478.
29 Ibid.
30 Ibid.
31 Héctor Carrillo, "Cultural Change, Hybridity and Male Homosexuality in Mexico," *Culture, Health & Sexuality* 1, no. 3 (1999): 225 (italics in original).
32 Mathew C. Gutmann, *The Meanings of Macho: Being a Man in Mexico City* (Berkeley: University of California Press, 1996), 224.
33 For instance, in 2016 the #primaveravioleta sprung against the systemic violence against women, specifically against machista violence and machos. At least eight thousand women in twenty-seven different states took to the streets to protest. "Estamos hartas de todos los tipos de violencia machistas" (We are fed up with all types of machista violence) announced the participants of the Feminist Spring march. "Aquí estamos, ya volvimos a salir, somos incómodas, no descansaremos. No volverán a dormir tranquilos los acosadores, corruptos, proxenetas, agresores y machistas" (We are here, we have come out again, we are uncomfortable, we will not rest. The stalkers, the corrupt, the pimps, the aggressors and the machistas will not go back to sleep). During the protests, a further debate sprung around the essentialization of the macho as a cis-gender man. For more, see Blanca Juárez, "Marcha de la primavera feminista: 'hartas de la violencia,'" *La Jornada,* April 24, 2016.
34 For more on the ambiguous and contradictory meanings of being macho, see Gutmann, *Meanings of Macho*.
35 The figure of the macho probado and the deconstruction of the ideal Mexican macho has been shown in films such as Arturo Ripstein's *El lugar sin límites* (1977), Jaime Hermosillo's *Doña Herlinda y su hijo* (1985), Jorge Fons's *El callejon de los milagros* (1993), and more recently in Alfonso Cuaron's *Y tu mamá también* (2001), starring Mexican Hollywood actors Gael García Bernal and Diego Luna. For more information, see Michael K. Shuessler, "Vestidas, locas, mayates y machos. Historia y homosexualidad en el cine," in *México se escribe con J*, ed. Michael K. Shuessler and Miguel Capistrán (Mexico City: Editorial Planeta Mexico, S.A. de C.V., 2010), 150–66; Ben Sifuentes Jauregui, "Gender without Limits: Transvestism and Subjectivity in *El lugar sin limites*," in *Sex and Sexuality in Latin America*, ed. Daniel Balderston and Donna J. Guy (New York: New York University Press, 1997), 44–61; Sergio De la Mora, *Cinemachismo: Masculinities and Sexuality in Mexican Film* (Austin: University of Texas Press, 2006). For the figure of the macho probado in social everyday practices, see, for example, Óscar

David López, "Macho calado: ya probaste y no te gustó, ¿o sí?," *Vice News*, August 10, 2015, www.vice.com. For research on men having sex with other men and not necessarily identifying as gay or homosexual, see Guillermo Nuñez Noriega, *Sexo entre varones. Poder y resistencia en el campo sexual* (Hermosillo and Mexico City: El Colegio de Sonora/Universidad Nacional Autónoma de México, 1999).
36 Carlos Monsiváis, "Tantos millones de hombres," 478.
37 David Robichaux, "Familia, grupo doméstico y grupos localizados de parentesco en el área cultural mesoamericana," in *Familia y tradición: herencias tangibles e intangibles en escenarios cambiantes*, ed. Nora Edith Jímenez Hernández (Zamora: El Colegio de Michoacán, 2010), 86.
38 On the negotiations of the what virginity represents through traditional Catholic prescriptions on sexuality and their transformations through Modern Mexico, and its individual negotiations see the work of Ana Amuchástegui. For instance: Ana Amuchástegui, "Dialogue and the Negotiation of Meaning: Constructions of Virginity in Mexico," in *Culture, Health & Sexuality* 1, no. 1 (1999): 79–93; Ana Amuchástegui, and Peter Aggleton, "I Had a Guilty Conscience Because I Wasn't Going to Marry Her: Ethical Dilemmas for Mexican Men in Their Sexual Relationships with Women," *Sexualities* 10, no. 1 (2016): 61–81.
39 For more on "the pockets of resistance" to the "still prevalent homogenizing tendencies of 'national' culture" to portray Mexican women as either "the passive, abnegated mother (previously virginal), or the impious, voracious, bad (active) woman" on literature and film, see Ilana Dann Luna, *Adapting Gender: Mexican Feminisms from Literature to Film* (Albany: SUNY Press, 2018).
40 Lisa Duggan, *Sapphic Slasher: Sex, Violence, and American Modernity* (Durham, NC: Duke University Press, 2000), 4.
41 Paula Ruth Gilbert, "Discourses of Female Violence and Societal Gender Stereotypes," *Violence against Women* 8, no. 11 (2002): 1271–300; Helen Birch, introduction to *Moving Targets: Women, Murder and Representation*, ed. Helen Birch (Berkeley: University of California Press, 1994); Candice Skrapec, "The Female Serial Killer," in *Moving Targets: Women, Murder and Representation*, ed. Helen Birch (Berkeley: University of California Press, 1994); Deborah S. Reisinger, "Murder and Banality in the Contemporary *fait divers*," *South Central Review* 17, no. 4 (2000): 84–99; Pamela J. Schram and Barbara Koons-Witt, *Gendered (in) Justice: Theory and Practice in Feminist Criminology* (Long Grove, IL: Waveland Press, 2004); Nicole Hahn Rafter and Frances Heidensohn, *International Feminist Perspectives in Criminology: Engendering a Discipline* (Buckingham: Open University Press, 1995).
42 Duggan, *Sapphic Slasher*; Judith R. Walkowitz, *City of Dreadful Delight: Narratives of Sexual Danger in Late-Victorian London* (Chicago: University of Chicago Press, 1992).
43 Robert M. Buffington, *Criminal and Citizen in Modern Mexico* (Lincoln: University of Nebraska Press, 2000), 35–51.
44 Allan Sekula, "The Body and the Archive," *October* 39 (1986): 8.

45 Robichaux, "Familia," 84.
46 See "the Indian problem" in Guillermo Bonfil Batalla, *México Profundo: Reclaiming a Civilization*, trans. Philip Adams Dennis (Austin: University of Texas Press, 1996).
47 Many authors have used different terminology when referring to communities that used to be considered "indian," which are the majority in the rural center and south of Mexico and in Central America. Examples include "*indomestizo*" (Manuel Gamio, "Poblacion indo-mestiza," in *Acculturation in the Americas: Proceedings and Selected Papers of the XXIXth International Congress of Americanists*, ed. Sol Tax, 267–70 [Chicago: University of Chicago Press, 1952]), *indios transnacionales* (Richard N. Adams, "Cultural Components of Central America," *American Anthropologist* 58, no. 5 (1956): 881–907), and *posnahuas* (Hielen Mulhare, "Respetar y confiar: ideología de género versus comportamiento en una sociedad nahua," in *Familia y parentesco en México y Mesoamérica: Unas miradas antropológicas*, ed. David Robichaux, 267–91 [Mexico City: Universidad Iberoamericana, 2003]). On this topic, see Robichaux, "Familia," 85–86. There were, however, other Indigenist thinkers who thought of the process of mestizaje as an ideal both culturally and biosocially that, unless directed by the state, would bring indigenous communities to a desperate situation. See Olivia Gall, "Identidad, exclusión y racismo: reflexiones teóricas y sobre México," *Revista Mexicana de Sociología* 66, no. 2 (2011): 241.
48 Gayle Rubin, "The Traffic in Women: Notes on the 'Political Economy' of Sex," in *Toward an Anthropology of Women*, ed. Rayna Reiter (New York: Monthly Review Press, 1975), 165.
49 Michael Foucault, "The Confession of the Flesh" in *Power/Knowledge Selected Interviews and Other Writings*, ed. Colin Gordon (New York: Pantheon Books: 1980), 194.
50 In chapter 2, I elaborate on this system and analyze why I chose to engage with skin tonalities as opposed to race or ethnicity.
51 Victor Hugo Moneda, interview by the author, August 13, 2007.
52 Stuart Hall et al., *Policing the Crisis: The State, Mugging and Law and Order* (London: Macmillan, 1978), 35, 57–69.
53 Duggan, *Sapphic Slasher*, 4.

CHAPTER 1. FRAMING THE SERIAL KILLER

1 Simpson Phillip L, "Serial Killing and Representation," in *Oxford Research Encyclopedia of Criminology*, ed. Henry N. Pontell (Oxford: Oxford University Press, 2017).
2 Ibid.
3 Ibid.
4 In Mexico, as in the United States, differences exist in how a serial killer is defined (i.e., the qualifying number of victims and temporal proximity of their execution) and therefore criminalized and sentenced. That is, there are different ways

of determining who qualifies as a serial killer. Many criminologists in Mexico subscribe to the FBI definition: "an offender associated with the killing of at least four victims" in a period of "greater than seventy-two hours." Mark Seltzer, *Serial Killers: Death and Life in America's Wound Culture* (New York: Routledge, 1998), 9. In the case of El/La Mataviejitas, it is not so much how a serial killer is defined that is at issue, but more importantly *why* these homicides got more attention from police than, for example, the killings of single women or homosexual men.

5 Alberto Nájar, "La cacería de El Mataviejitas, el costo de negar al asesino," *La Jornada*, October 9, 2005.
6 Ibid.; Juan Arvizu, "Mataba a una viejita cada mes," *Reforma*, January 25, 2007.
7 Nájar, "La cacería."
8 Ibid.
9 Richard Quinney, "Who Is the Victim?," *Criminology* 10, no. 3 (1972): 318.
10 Nichole Sanders, "Mothering Mexico: The Historiography of Mothers and Motherhood in 20th-Century Mexico," *HIC3 History Compass* 7, no. 6 (2009): 1542.
11 Ibid.
12 Ibid., 1545.
13 William E. French, "Prostitutes and Guardian Angels: Women, Work, and the Family in Porfirian Mexico," *Hispanic American Historical Review* 72, no. 4 (1992): 529.
14 Ibid.
15 Ibid., 530.
16 Ibid.
17 Ibid.
18 Sanders, "Mothering Mexico."
19 French, "Prostitutes and Guardian Angels."
20 Patience A. Schell, *Church and State Education in Revolutionary Mexico City* (Tucson: University of Arizona Press, 2003), xxii, 24.
21 Octavio Paz has famously analyzed the colloquial uses of the verb *chingar*, which has been commonly translated as "to fuck." *Hijo de la chingada* is the most common of its uses, meaning sons of the raped women, not having decency, not having a caring ideal mother who instills Mexican decency and moral values. When used in its feminized version—*me llevó la chingada*—it means that a terrible thing happened, it is all ruined and the person saying the sentence has been fucked, or fucked over. When used in is masculinized version—*qué chingón*—it describes something as incredible, amazing, and beyond belief. *Chingón* is amazing while *chingada* is raped, fucked. Paz argues that the uses of the verb *chingar* reveal the character of Mexicans in which "life is the possibility of 'chingar' or to be 'chingado'. Life for Mexicans is either to fuck somebody (raping, taking advantage) or to be fucked (humiliated, punished)." See Paz, *El laberinto*, 27–36.
22 Agustin Palacios, "El problema de La Malintzin como expresión concreta del encuentro," in *El mexicano: educación, historia y personalidad* (Mexico City: Ediciones Oasis, S.A., 1966).

23 Bartra, *La jaula de la melancolía*.
24 Ibid., 216.
25 *Moriscos* were former Muslims coerced into converting to Christianity. See ibid.
26 Roger Bartra, *The Cage of Melancholy: Identity and Metamorphosis in the Mexican Character* (New Brunswick, NJ: Rutgers University Press, 1992), 216; Paz, *El laberinto*.
27 For more on the similarities between Marian apparitions and the Virgin of Guadalupe apparition, see Kristy Nabhan-Warren, *The Virgin of El Barrio: Marian Apparitions, Catholic Evangelizing, and Mexican American Activism* (New York: New York University Press, 2005).
28 Bartra, *La jaula de la melancolía*, 220.
29 In 1916, the first feminist congress in Mexico was held in Yucatan. In 1922, when the government showed sympathy from women's demands for divorce and sexual education for women, conservatives retaliated by institutionalizing (with great success to this day) Mother's Day, on May 10. In particular, the most conservative sectors of society opposed the "denigration of the highest function of women which consists not only in giving birth but also in educating her children." Fernando Muñoz, *Sara García* (Mexico City: Editorial Clio, libros y video, S.A. de C.V., 1998), 34. Bartra also talks about how the cult of the mother runs parallel to that of the Virgin in Mexico; see Bartra, *Cage of Melancholy*, 220.
30 Carlos Monsiváis, "¡Esa no es mi hija!, ¡Ésa es una perdida! El melodrama y la invención de la familia," in *Familia y tradición: herencias tangibles e intangibles en escenarios cambiantes*, ed. Nora Edith Jímenez Hernández (Zamora: El Colegio de Michoacán, 2010), 605.
31 J. Tuñon, *Mujeres de luz y sombra en el cine mexicano: La construcción de una imagen (1939–1952)* (Mexico City: El Colegio de México, 1998), 173, cited in Sanders, "Mothering Mexico," 1548.
32 Ibid.
33 Ileana Baeza Lope, "Sara García: Sapphic Romance in Mexican Golden Age Filmmaking," *Journal of Popular Romance Studies* 4, no. 1 (2014), http://jprstudies.org/.
34 Monsiváis, "¡Esa no es mi hija!," 606.
35 Take, for instance, the titles of the most famous movies: *Así es la mujer* (Such is the woman), *Las mujeres mandan* (Women command), and *Malditas sean las mujeres* (Damn women) (all 1936), *Mi madrecita, ahí esta el detalle* (My dear mother, there is the detail) (1940), *Cuando los hijos se van* (When the children leave) (1942), *Mis hijos* (My children) and *El secreto de la solterona* (The secret of the spinster) (both 1944), and *Mamá Inés* (1945), among others.
36 Monsiváis, "¡Esa no es mi hija!," 607.
37 Ibid.
38 Jesús Padilla, "Es 'serial' prioridad para Bátiz," *Reforma*, September 1, 2005.
39 Pedro Infante, one of the most influential actors in Mexico, was known as "the idol of the people." For Monsiváis, Infante embodied, if not defined, mexicanidad and what it is to be Mexican. Infante immortalized the image of the Mexican

macho. See Carlos Monsiváis, *Pedro Infante: Las leyes del querer* (Mexico City: Ediciones Raya en el agua, S.A. de C.V., 2008); Daniel Gonzáles, "¿Es que no sábes que eres un hombre? Star system y masculinidades en cinco autores del cine mexicano" (paper presented at Cineteca Nacional, July 22, 2015). Most recently, Sergio de la Mora has studied Infante's masculinity in the films of the *Época de Oro* in relation to homosociality, homoeroticism, and homosexuality. De la Mora, *Cinemachismo: Masculinities and Sexuality in Mexican Film* (Austin: University of Texas Press, 2006).

40 Monsiváis, "¡Esa no es mi hija!," 607.
41 Ibid.
42 David Robichaux uses the term "Mesoamerican family." He differentiates the "Mexican family" from the "Mesoamerican family" to include the arrangements of those segments of the population officially classified as "indigenous" because of their use of indigenous languages, as well as of those segments categorized as "mestizos." Robichaux, "Familia," 93. In part, parents, children, and grandparents in Mexico share the same residence for financial reasons. See Larissa Lomnitz and Marisol Pérez Lizaur, "Dynastic Growth and Survival Strategies: The Solidarity of Mexican Grand-Families," in *Kinship Ideology and Practice in Latin America*, ed. Raymond T. Smith (Chapel Hill: University of North Carolina Press, 1984). Also, Rosío Córdoba Plaza's findings on family arrangements after migration flows in Veracruz suggest that after men migrate, women and their children go to live with her in-laws. Córdoba Plaza, "Sexualidad, género y parentesco: dinámicas familiares en un contexto de significados en transformación," in *Familia y tradición: herencias tangibles e intangibles en escenarios cambiantes*, ed. Nora Edith Jímenez Hernández (Zamora: El Colegio de Michoacán, 2010). On the other hand, Robichaux argues that it is not solely because of economic reasons that parents and children share the same home, but rather that is a legacy of pre-Hispanic arrangements. Whether the reasons why the same residence is shared by grandparents, parents, and children is economic or cultural, the important thing to highlight for my argument is that in most of Mexico it is a common practice to live with one's grandparents and to take care of them.
43 Robichaux, "Familia," 93.
44 Ibid.
45 Muñoz, *Sara García*.
46 Ibid.
47 Nora Edith Jiménez Hernández, introduction to *Familia y tradición: herencias tangibles e intangibles en escenarios cambiantes*, ed. Nora Edith Jímenez Hernández (Zamora : El Colegio de Michoacán, 2010), 14.
48 Ibid.
49 Heredia, "Seis visiones."
50 Nájar, "La cacería."
51 Lomnitz and Pérez Lizaur, "Dynastic Growth," 183, 193.
52 Heredia, "Seis visiones."

53 Nájar, "La cacería."
54 Acosta, "Women of Ciudad Juárez." Julia Monárrez, academic and activist working on feminicides in Ciudad Juárez, has noted that while 4,587 women have been registered as disappeared, not all of these women continue to be missing; some of them have been found. See Monárrez, *Trama de una injusticia*, 8.
55 Acosta, "Women of Ciudad Juárez."
56 Ciudad Juárez is not the only city in Mexico with such a high rate of feminicides. Estado de México has an even higher number of feminicides. See chapter 4. In Mexico in the last twenty-five years, more than "35 thousand women have died with the presumption of homicide." ONU Mujeres México, "Eliminación de la violencia contra mujeres y niñas," accessed May 2017, http://mexico.unwomen.org/es/nuestro-trabajo/eliminar-la-violencia-contra-mujeres-y-niñas; Echarri Cánovas, *La violencia feminicida*.
57 Acosta, "Women of Ciudad Juárez."
58 Nájar, "La cacería."
59 Quinney, "Who Is the Victim?," 314.
60 Acosta, "Women of Ciudad Juárez," 3.
61 Katherine Elaine Bliss, *Compromised Positions: Prostitution, Public Health and Gender Politics in Revolutionary Mexico City* (University Park: Pennsylvania State University Press, 2001).
62 Heredia, "Seis visiones," 46–49.
63 Ricardo Ham and Cutberto Enríquez, *Exposición asesinos seriales* (Mexico City: Centro Cultural Policial, 2007), 21.
64 Angel Vargas, "Sara Aldrete Escribe 'Para convertir las remembranzas en historia,'" *La Jornada*, October 11 2003.
65 Monsiváis, *Mexican Postcards*.
66 Ibid., 164.
67 Ibid.
68 Ibid., 165.
69 Seltzer, *Serial Killers*, 1.
70 Ibid.
71 Caroline Picart, "Crime and the Gothic: Sexualizing Serial Killers," *Journal of Criminal Justice and Popular Culture* 13, no. 1 (2006): 1.
72 Caroline Picart and Cecil Greek, "The Compulsion of Real/Reel Serial Killers and Vampires: Toward a Gothic Criminology," *Journal of Criminal Justice and Popular Culture* 10, no. 1 (2003): 39–68.
73 Ibid., 45.
74 Seltzer, *Serial Killers*, 6.
75 Picart and Greek, "Real/Reel Serial Killers and Vampires."
76 Graciela Martínez-Zalce, Laura Carballido, and Victor Manuel Grandos, "Representaciones cinematográficas y cartográficas de la violencia en la Ciudad de México," *El cotidiano: revista de la realidad mexicana actual* 22, no. 145 (2007): 43–47.
77 Ibid.

78 Ibid.
79 Ibid.
80 William Straw, "Nota Roja and Journaux Jaunes: Popular Crime Periodicals in Quebec and Mexico," in *Aprehendiendo al delincuente: crimen y medios en América del Norte*, ed. Graciela Martínez-Zalce, William Straw, and Susana Vargas Cervantes (Mexico City: Universidad Nacional Autónoma de México, Centro Estudios sobre América del Norte, and Media@McGill, 2011), 53.
81 Monsiváis, *Mexican Postcards*, 149.
82 Saydi Cecilia Núñez Cetina, "Delito, género y transgresiones: los discursos sobre la criminalidad femenina en la Ciudad de México, 1877–1910" (MA thesis, Colegio de México, 2005).
83 Ibid.
84 According to Ricardo Ham, El Chalequero killed twenty prostitutes, but according to news reporters, he killed thirteen. See Ham, *México y sus asesinos seriales* (Mexico City: Ediciones Samsara, 2007).
85 See Bliss, *Compromised Positions*.
86 Monsiváis, *Mexican Postcards*, 149.
87 Ibid.
88 Sandra Ávalos Guzmán, *La nota roja: la sangre nuesta de cada día* (Mexico City: Universidad Nacional Autónoma de México, 1988).
89 Ibid.
90 Carlos Monsiváis, *Los mil y un velorios: crónica de la nota roja en México* (1994; Mexico City: Debate/Fondo de Cultura Económica, 2010).
91 Monsiváis, *Mexican Postcards*, 148.
92 Seltzer, *Serial Killers*, 6.
93 Ibid.
94 Piccato, Pablo. "'El Chalequero' or the Mexican Jack the Ripper: The Meanings of Sexual Violence in Turn-of-the-Century Mexico City," *Hispanic American Historical Review* 81, no. 3 (2001): 630.
95 Ibid., 623.
96 Ibid., 631.
97 Ibid., 636.
98 Ibid., 642–43.
99 Ibid., 643.
100 Piccato, "'El Chalequero' or the Mexican Jack the Ripper," 625.
101 Ibid., 628.
102 Ibid., 623.
103 Ibid., 650.
104 Juan Carlos Aguilar García, "La Mataviejitas pertenece al tipo de asesino serial sin plan," *Crónica*, January 28, 2006, 149.
105 Juan de Dios Vázquez, "La fábrica del asesino: El Goyo Cárdenas y las transformaciones identitarias de un asesino serial," *Estudios de historia moderna y contemporánea de México*, no. 42 (2011): 110.

106 Alfonso Quiroz Cuarón, *Un estrangulador de mujeres* (Mexico City s.e., 1952), 19.
107 Ibid., 49.
108 Vázquez, "La fábrica del asesino," 135.
109 Ibid.
110 Nájar, "La cacería."
111 Monsiváis, *Mexican Postcards*, 151.
112 Ibid.
113 Ibid., 150.
114 Ham, *México y sus asesinos seriales*.
115 Ham and Enríquez, *Exposición asesinos seriales*, 20.
116 Fabiola Bailón, "Prostitución, lenocinio y crimen: diferentes miradas en torno al caso de 'Las Poquianchis,'" in *Crimen y justicia en la historia de México. Nuevas Miradas*, ed. Elisa Speckman and Salvador Cárdenas (Mexico City: Suprema Corte de Justicia de la Nación, 2011), 426.
117 Ibid., 429.
118 Ibid., 438.
119 Ham, *México y sus asesinos seriales*.
120 Bailón, "Prostitución, lenocinio y crimen," 440.
121 Silvia Otero, "Presenta AFI a asesino serial de homosexuales," *El Universal*, January 26, 2006.
122 Ibid.
123 El Coqueto was apprehended on February 22, 2012, by Mexico City police after an investigation in response to the report of his first victim, who had survived his attacks. He was not called a serial killer, however, before his apprehension. Police were looking for a feminicide. El Coqueto escaped from police custody the next day, injuring his back and ankles in the process; unable to walk, he was eventually captured again. "¿Qué pasó con? . . . 'El Coqueto,' el feminicida que violaba en un microbus," *El Universal*, June 12, 2017.
124 Israel Yañez and Hilda Escalona, "El caníbal de la guerrero quería ser madre," *Crónica*, October 13, 2007.
125 Israel Yañez, "Encuentran ahorcado a el caníbal en su celda," *Crónica*, December 11 2007.
126 Yañez and Escalona, "El caníbal de la guerrero."
127 This will be analyzed in detail in chapter 4.
128 Fernando Martínez, "Detienen a 'El Coqueto'"; un feminicida serial," *El Universal*, February 27, 2012.
129 Ibid.
130 "Matanovias destrozó la vida de mi hermana en dos meses," *Milenio Digital*, March 15, 2017; "Encuentran fotos de víctima de 'Matanovias,' tomadas horas antes de su muerte," *El Universal*, March 23, 2017.
131 "Matanovias destrozó la vida de mi hermana."
132 Richard Collier, *Masculinities, Crime, and Criminology: Men, Heterosexuality, and the Criminal(ised) Other* (London: Sage, 1998), 178.

133 Heredia, "Seis visiones."
134 Seltzer, *Serial Killers*, 126.
135 Leticia Fernández, "Es 'Mataviejitas' brillante: Bátiz," *Reforma*, October 11, 2005.
136 Jesús Padilla and Jorge Pérez, "Tarda hasta 20 años captura de asesinos," *Reforma*, November 12, 2005.
137 Picart, "Crime and the Gothic," 29.
138 Seltzer, *Serial Killers*.
139 James Alan Fox and Jack Levin, "Multiple Homicide: Patterns of Serial and Mass Murder," *Crime and Justice* 23 (1998): 407.
140 R. Holmes and J. DeBurger, *Serial Murder* (Newbury Park, CA: Sage, 1988), 24 quoted in Seltzer, *Serial Killers*, 42.
141 Heredia, "Seis visiones."
142 Arturo Sierra, Ricardo Zamora, and Antonio Baranda, "Abusan en infancia de asesino en serie," *Reforma*, August 31, 2005.
143 Skrapec, "Female Serial Killer," 242–43.
144 Ibid., 243.
145 Heredia, "Seis visiones."
146 Lamas, "De trasvestis."
147 Ron Rosenbaum, "The FBI's Agent Provocateur," *Vanity Fair*, April 1993, 124, quoted in Seltzer, *Serial Killers*, 13.
148 Carlos Jiménez, "Juana Barraza: Analfabeta, su madre la regaló a los 12 años, fue violada y le mataron un hijo a batazos," *Crónica*, January 27 2006.
149 Nila, "Ningún trasvesti."

CHAPTER 2. THE LOOK OF THE SERIAL KILLER

1 I refer to Lisa Duggan's argument that the "process of narrativization" in which newspapers "found themselves mired in narrative confusions"—reporting on both the defense and the prosecution, with the aim to "enhance the newspaper marketing of sensational news"—works to "narrativize" material from police authorities. See Duggan, *Sapphic Slasher*, 34–49.
2 Brito and Corona, "Atrapan a Mataviejitas"; Sierra and Fernández, "Tienen 64 rostros."
3 Brito and Corona, "Atrapan a Mataviejitas."
4 Antonio Baranda and Ricardo Zamora, "Alista PGJDF retrato de otro mataviejitas," *Reforma*, August 24, 2005.
5 Sandra S. Phillips, "Identifying the Criminal," in *Police Pictures: The Photograph as Evidence* (San Francisco: San Francisco Museum of Modern Art; Chronicle Books, 1997), 11.
6 David Green, "Veins of Resemblance: Photography and Eugenics," *Oxford Art Journal* 7, no. 2 (1984): 8.
7 Phillips, "Identifying the Criminal," 11.
8 Ibid.
9 Sekula, "Body and Archive," 11.

10 Procuraduría General de Justicia del Distrito Federal, "El sistema de retrato hablado más avanzado del país en la PGJDF," news release, June 20, 2004.
11 María Villanueva, Jesús Luy, and Karl F. Link, *La Cara del Mexicano: Sistema de retrato hablado asistido por computadora*, 2nd ed. (Mexico City: Instituto de Investigaciones Antropológicas and Procuraduría General de Justicia del D.F., 2002).
12 Carlos Serrano, interview by the author, April 27, 2007.
13 For the identity of "Indian" invented by Europeans, see Guillermo Bonfil Batalla, *Utopía y revolución: el pensamiento político contemporáneo de los indios en América Latina* (Mexico City: Editorial Nueva Imagen, 1981), 19.
14 Alan Knight, "Racism, Revolution, and Indigenismo: Mexico, 1910–1940," in *The Idea of Race in Latin America, 1870–1940*, ed. Richard Graham et al. (Austin: University of Texas Press, 1990), 73.
15 Peter Wade, "Rethinking 'Mestizaje': Ideology and Lived Experience," *Journal of Latin American Studies* 37, no. 2 (2005): 239.
16 Knight, "Racism, Revolution, and Indigenismo."
17 Marco Antonio Pérez Jiménez, "Nación deseada, nación heredada: la población negra y el imaginario de las élites dirigentes en México: El caso de Guanajuato (1808–1830)" (PhD diss., Universidad Nacional Autónoma de México, 2011), 17.
18 Peter Wade, *Blackness and Race Mixture: The Dynamics of Racial Identity in Colombia* (Baltimore: Johns Hopkins University Press, 1993) p. 9.
19 Carolyn Dean and Dana Leibsohn, "Hybridity and Its Discontents: Considering Visual Culture in Colonial Spanish America," *Colonial Latin American Review* 12, no. 1 (2003): 6–7.
20 Marisol De la Cadena, "Mestizos Are Not Hybrids: Genealogies, Dialogues, and Mestizajes in Peru" (unpublished MS, University of California-Davis, 2001), 4, cited in Alonso, "Conforming Disconformity."
21 Judith Friedlander, *Being Indian in Hueyapan: A Study of Forced Identity in Contemporary Mexico*, rev. ed. (New York: St. Martin's Press, 2006), 77.
22 Núñez, "Delito, género y transgresiones."
23 Ibid.
24 Buffington, *Criminal and Citizen*, 35.
25 Ibid., 50.
26 Francisco Martínez Baca and Manuel Vergara, *Estudios de antropología criminal* (Puebla: Benjamin Lara, 1892), 7.
27 Ibid., 97, cited in Buffington, *Criminal and Citizen*, 51.
28 Ibid.
29 Ibid.
30 Martínez and Vergara, *Estudios de antropología criminal*, 101.
31 Ibid., 2.
32 Ibid.
33 Green, "Veins of Resemblance," 8.
34 Ibid., 12.

35 Ibid.
36 Ibid., 50.
37 Buffington, *Criminal and Citizen*, 51.
38 Ibid., 59.
39 Ibid., 60.
40 Andrés Villarreal, "Stratification by Skin Colour in Contemporary Mexico," *American Sociological Review* 75, no. 5 (2010): 659.
41 Rafael Lemus, "La raza cósmica," *Letras Libres*, March 31, 2010.
42 José Vasconcelos, *La raza cósmica: misión de la raza iboeroamericana* (Madrid: Agencia mundial de la librería, 1925), 95.
43 Alonso, "Conforming Disconformity," 462.
44 Villarreal, "Stratification by Skin Colour," 656.
45 Pierre L. Van den Berghe, *Race and Racism: A Comparative Perspective* (New York: Wiley, 1967), 55.
46 Ibid.
47 Ibid., 671.
48 Moreno Figueroa, "Distributed Intensities," 397.
49 Moreno Figueroa cites, for example, Sara Ahmed, "Declarations of Whiteness: The Non-Performativity of Anti-Racism," *Borderlands* 3, no. 2 (2004), www.borderlands.net.au; Sara Ahmed, "A Phenomenology of Whiteness," *Feminist Theory* 8, no. 2 (2007): 149–68; Abby L. Ferber, "Whiteness Studies and the Erasure of Gender," *Sociology Compass* 1, no. 1 (2007): 265–82; R. Frankenberg, "On Unsteady Ground: Crafting and Engaging in the Critical Study of Whiteness," in *Researching Race and Racism*, ed. M. Bulmer and J. Solomos (London and New York: Routledge, 2004); Anoop Nayak, "Critical Whiteness Studies," *Sociology Compass* 1, no. 2 (2007): 737–55; Vron Ware and Les Back, *Out of Whiteness: Color, Politics, and Culture* (Chicago: University of Chicago Press, 2002).
50 Moreno Figueroa, "Distributed Intensities," 397.
51 Ibid.
52 Ibid., 398. See also Mónica G. Moreno Figueroa, "Historically Rooted Transnationalism: Slightedness and the Experience of Racism in Mexican Families," *Journal of Intercultural Studies* 29, no. 3 (2008): 283–97; Mónica G. Moreno Figueroa, "Looking Emotionally: Photography, Racism and Intimacy in Research," *History of the Human Sciences* 21, no. 4 (2008): 68–85; Mónica G. Moreno Figueroa and Emiko Saldívar Tanaka, "'We Are Not Racists, We Are Mexicans': Privilege, Nationalism and Post-Race Ideology in Mexico," *Critical Sociology* 42, nos. 4–5 (2016): 515–33.
53 Moreno Figueroa, "Distributed Intensities," 397.
54 Villarreal, "Stratification by Skin Colour," 652.
55 Ibid., 671.
56 Carlos Serrano Sánchez, "Un sistema automatizado de identificación de rasgos faciales (retrato hablado) para la población mexicana," in *La bibliotecología y la*

documentación en el contexto de la internacionalización y el acceso abierto (Mexico City: Universidad Nacional Autónoma de México 2013), 3.
57 Ibid., 1.
58 Ibid.
59 Sekula, "Body and Archive," 16.
60 Serrano Sánchez, "Sistema automatizado," 6.
61 Sekula, "Body and Archive," 11.
62 Serrano Sánchez, "Sistema automatizado," 6.
63 Ibid.
64 Sekula, "Body and Archive," 11.
65 Ibid., 9.
66 Serrano Sánchez, "Sistema automatizado," 4.
67 Sekula, "Body and Archive," 33.
68 Carlos Serrano Sánchez et al., "Los rasgos faciales del mexicano y los retratos hablados por computadora," *Revista Universidad de México*, no. 575 (1998): 63.
69 Sekula, "Body and Archive," 40.
70 Sketches obtained by the author in a personal interview with Comandante Victor Hugo Moneda at the Policía Judicial del Distrito Federal, August 13, 2007.
71 Baranda and Zamora, "Alista PGJDF retrato."
72 Reisinger, "Murder and Banality," 83.
73 Lisa E. Hasel and Gary L. Wells, "Catching the Bad Guy: Morphing Composite Faces Helps," *Law and Human Behavior* 31, no. 2 (2007): 193.
74 Donald Christie et al., "Evaluating a New Computer-Based System for Face Recall," *Law and Human Behavior* 5, nos. 2–3 (1981): 209–18.
75 Hasel and Wells, "Catching the Bad Guy." 295–96.
76 Arturo Sierra and Antonio Baranda, "Toman huellas de 46," *Reforma*, October 5, 2005.
77 Ibid.
78 Óscar Herrera, "Hampones comunes copian el estilo del Mataviejitas," *El Universal*, January 24, 2006.
79 Carlos Jiménez and R. Sánchez, "Detiene PGJDF a 49, pero ninguno es El Mataviejitas," *Crónica*, October 5, 2005.
80 Fernández, "Es 'Mataviejitas' brillante."
81 Sierra, Zamora, and Baranda, "Abusan en infancia."
82 Arturo Sierra, "Intenta PGJDF encuadrar perfil de asesina serial," *Reforma*, February 16, 2006.
83 Ibid.
84 Fernández, "Es 'Mataviejitas' brillante."
85 Arturo Sierra, "Analizan a seriales de Europa," *Reforma*, October 24, 2005.
86 Arturo Sierra, "Usan estilo francés con asesinos seriales," *Reforma*, January 10, 2006.
87 Ibid.
88 Ibid.

89 Cabral and Viturro, "(Trans)Sexual Citizenship," 270.
90 Flavio Rapisardi, "Regulaciones políticas: identidad, diferencia y desigualdad. Una crítica al debate contemporáneo," in *Sexualidades migrantes: género y transgénero*, ed. Diana Maffía (Buenos Aires: Librería de Mujeres Editoras, 2009), 106–7.
91 Lohanna Berkins, *Cumbia, copeteo y lágrimas* (Buenos Aires: ALITT, 2007), 157.
92 Vek Lewis, *Crossing Sex and Gender in Latin America* (New York: Palgrave Macmillan, 2010), 7.
93 Agustín Salgado and Mirna Servín, "A Juana Barraza Zamperio le gusta el rojo y prefería los martes y miércoles para matar," *La Jornada*, January 26, 2006.
94 Jiménez, "Juana Barraza."
95 Claudia Bolaños, "Buscan 'mataviejitas' entre-sexoservidores," *El Universal*, October 18, 2005; Lamas, "De trasvestis"; Claudia Bolaños and Fabiola Cancino, "Saldrá libre con fianza ex amiga de La Mataviejitas," *El Gráfico*, February 9, 2006.
96 Claudia Schaefer, *Danger Zones: Homosexuality, National Identity, and Mexican Culture* (Tucson: University of Arizona Press, 1996), 81–96.
97 Luis Zapata, "Prólogo. *Highlight* de mi vida como gay," in *México Se Escribe Con J*, ed. Michael K. Shuessler and Miguel Capistrán (Mexico City: Editorial Planeta Mexico, S.A. de C.V., 2010), 12.
98 For more on homonationalism, see Jasbir K. Puar, *Terrorist Assemblages: Homonationalism in Queer Times*, tenth-anniv. expanded ed. (Durham, NC: Duke University Press, 2017), and Tim McCaskell, *Queer Progress: From Homophobia to Homonationalism* (Toronto: Between the Lines, 2016). For more on a legal critical view on gay marriage, see the work of Dean Spade.
99 See Dean Spade, *Normal Life: Administrative Violence, Critical Trans Politics and the Limits of Law*, revised and expanded ed. (Durham, NC: Duke University Press, 2015).
100 Dirección General de Comunicación por los Derechos Humanos, "CHDF se pronuncia en contra de cualquier acto de violencia y discriminación hacia la comunidad LGBTTI," news release, June 25, 2015, http://cdhdf.org.mx.
101 Sara Pantoja, "México, segundo lugar mundial en crímenes por homofobia," *Proceso*, May 11, 2015.
102 Rodrigo Parrini Rosas and Alejandro Brito Lemus, *Crímenes de odio por homofobia: un concepto en construcción* (Mexico City: Letra S and Sida, Cultura, y Vida Cotidiana, A.C., 2012), 69.
103 Carrie Kahn, "How Mexico Quietly Legalized Same-Sex Marriage," *Parallels*, NPR, June 16, 2015, www.npr.org.
104 "¿Qué dice el frente nacional por la familia?," *Excélsior*, August 23, 2016.
105 Álvaro Delgado, "El Yunque, la mano que mece al frente nacional por la familia," *Proceso*, September 9, 2016.
106 Nila, "Ningún trasvesti."
107 Sekula, "Body and Archive," 17.
108 For other examples, see Caleb Crain, "Lovers of Human Flesh: Homosexuality and Cannibalism in Melville's Novels," *American Literature* 66, no. 1 (1994): 25–53; Reisinger, "Murder and Banality"; Christopher Gittings, "*Zero Patience*, Genre,

Difference, and Ideology: Singing and Dancing Queer Nation," *Cinema Journal* 41, no. 1 (2001): 28–39.
109 Picart and Greek, "Real/Reel Serial Killers and Vampires," 39–40.
110 Seltzer, *Serial Killers*, 4.
111 Ibid., 7.
112 Mirna Servín, "Asesiné por las 'malas compañías': La Mataviejitas," *La Jornada*, January 27, 2006.
113 Ibid.
114 Salgado and Servín, "Cae Mataviejitas."
115 Servín, "Asesiné por las 'malas compañías.'"
116 Herrera, "Hampones comunes."
117 Carlos Jiménez, "Mataviejitas fue a PGJDF a entregarse y no la atendieron," *Crónica*, February 8, 2006.
118 Pérez, "Nación deseada, nación heredada."
119 Mirna Servín, "La Dama del Silencio," *Reforma*, March 23, 2008; Claudia Bolaños, Óscar Herrera, and Ángeles Velazco, "'Las maté por rencor y rabia,'" *Reforma*, January 26, 2006.
120 Salgado and Servín, "Cae Mataviejitas."
121 Ibid.
122 Picart, "Crime and the Gothic," 29.
123 Birch, introduction to *Moving Targets*, 5.
124 Gilbert, "Discourses of Female Violence," 1282.
125 Alma Muñoz, "Mueren siete mujeres al dia en promedio presuntamente víctimas de homicidio," *La Jornada*, November 13, 2014.
126 Gilbert, "Discourses of Female Violence," 1282.
127 Susan Edwards, *Women on Trial* (Manchester: Manchester University Press, 1984), cited in Ruth Ford, "'The Man-Woman Murderer': Sex Fraud, Sexual Inversion and the Unmentionable 'Article' in 1920s Australia," *Gender and History* 12, no. 1 (2000): 170.
128 Dana Crowley Jack, *Behind the Mask: Destruction and Creativity in Women's Aggression* (Cambridge, MA: Harvard University Press, 2001), 30.
129 Ibid.
130 Picart, "Crime and the Gothic," 3.
131 Gilbert, "Discourses of Female Violence," 1283.
132 Salgado and Servín, "Cae Mataviejitas."
133 Arturo Sierra et al., "Asesina Juana por coraje," *Reforma*, January 26, 2006.
134 Bolaños, Herrera, and Velazco, "Las maté por rencor y rabia."
135 Campbell, *Men, Women and Aggression*, 1.
136 Ann Jones, *Women Who Kill*, 2nd ed. (New York: Feminist Press, 2009), 322.
137 Ibid., 78.
138 Grindstaff and McCaughey, "Re-Membering John Bobbitt," 150.
139 Martín Barrón Cruz, *El nudo del silencio: Tras la pista de una asesina en serie, La Mataviejitas* (Mexico City: Editorial Océano de México, 2006), 35.
140 Ibid.

141 Gilbert, "Discourses of Female Violence," 1284.
142 Carlos Jiménez, "La Mataviejitas coleccionaba recortes de periodicos con las historias de sus homicidios," *Crónica*, January 30, 2006.
143 Agustín Salgado, Angel Bolaños, and Rene Ramón, "Tras las rejas, *La Mataviejitas*; el lunes se define su situación legal," *La Jornada*, January 28, 2006.
144 Claudia Bolaños, "Muestra 'Mataviejitas' indiferencia por víctimas," *El Universal*, August 3, 2006.
145 Barrón, *El nudo del silencio*, 102.
146 Adrian Raine, "Psychopathy, Violence and Brain Imaging," in *Violence and Psychopathy*, ed. Adrian Raine and José Sanmartín (New York: Kluwer Academic/Plenum Centro Reina Sofia, 2001), 35.
147 Ibid., 35–36.
148 Ibid., 37.
149 Ibid.
150 Seltzer, *Serial Killers*, 125.
151 Bolaños, "Muestra 'Mataviejitas' indiferencia."
152 Phillips, "Identifying the Criminal," 11.
153 Dirección de Comunicación Institucional, "La Mataviejitas: 'una sociópata,' asegura académica de la UIA," news release, January 26, 2006.
154 Buffington, *Criminal and Citizen*, 51.
155 French, "Prostitutes and Guardian Angels," 550.
156 Feggy Ostrosky, *Mentes asesinas: la violencia en tu cerebro* (Mexico City: Hachette Filipacchi Expansión de R.L. de C.V., 2008), 218.
157 Ibid.
158 Richard Rushton, "What Can a Face Do? On Deleuze and Faces," *Cultural Critique*, no. 51 (2002), 221–22.
159 Ibid., 234.
160 Miriam Basilio, "Corporal Evidence: Representations of Aileen Wuornos," *Art Journal* 55, no. 4 (1996): 57.
161 Claudia Bolaños, "Las maté por rencor y odio," *El Universal*, January 27, 2006; Jiménez, "Juana Barraza"; Sierra et al., "Asesina Juana por coraje."
162 Aguilar García, "La Mataviejitas pertenece."
163 Seltzer, *Serial Killers*, 9.
164 Agustín Salgado, "Del Mataviejitas, 24 de 32 asesinatos: Renato Sales," *La Jornada*, November 17, 2005.
165 Mirna Servín, "Dan 759 años de prisión a *La Mataviejitas*," *La Jornada*, April 1, 2008.
166 Quinney, "Who Is the Victim?" 318.
167 Barrón, *El nudo del silencio*.
168 Phillips, "Identifying the Criminal," 13.
169 Green, "Veins of Resemblance," 4.
170 Robert Hare, "This Charming Psychopath," *Psychology Today*, January 1, 1994, www.psychologytoday.com.

171 Green, "Veins of Resemblance," 14 (italics in original).
172 Robert D. Hare, *Without Conscience: The Disturbing World of the Psychopaths among Us* (New York: Guilford Press, 1999), 209–11.
173 Ibid.
174 Martínez and Vergara, *Estudios de antropología criminal*, 101.
175 Buffington, *Criminal and Citizen*, 62.
176 Ibid., 211.
177 Phillips, "Identifying the Criminal," 13.

CHAPTER 3. PERFORMING MEXICANIDAD I

1 Contradictory accounts of serial killers in Mexico exist, because contradictory accounts of "who counts" as a serial killer—in terms of the number of victims and the time frame of the homicides—also exist. Ricardo Ham, in his self-published book *Mexico y sus asesinos seriales* (2007), considers Las Poquianchis to be serial killers, for instance, while the Department of Justice of Mexico City does not (see chapter 2).
2 Claudia Bolaños, "Otros cuatro, sentenciados por muerte de ancianas," *El Universal*, January 26, 2006. In his book on La Mataviejitas, criminologist Martín Barrón Cruz cites an interview with Araceli Tapia, in which she states she helped Barraza rob elderly women. See Barrón, *El nudo del silencio*, 122–23.
3 Bolaños, "Otros cuatro."
4 Ibid.
5 Fabrizio Mejía, "Mi mente radiante," *Proceso*, December 5, 2004.
6 Two other people were also suspected of killing elderly women in Mexico City during this period. In July 2004, an unnamed homeless man, also described as a drug addict in news reports, was accused of the homicide and rape of a sixty-three-year-old woman. He was sentenced to the Reclusorio Oriente. On January 17, 2006, Oliver Guzmán López was put under house arrest in his mother's house in Iztapalapa, a suburb of Mexico City, suspected of being the former man's accomplice. However, neither has been identified by police as El Mataviejitas. See Bolaños, "Otros cuatro."
7 Salgado and Servín, "Cae Mataviejitas."
8 Ibid.
9 Arvizu, "Mataba a una viejita."
10 Sánchez, "No era compló."
11 Luis Brito García, "Puede Barraza tener 27 víctimas," *Reforma*, February 19, 2006.
12 Monsiváis, *Mexican Postcards*; Paz, *El laberinto*.
13 Bartra, *La jaula de la melancolía*.
14 See the following works by Judith Butler: *Gender Trouble: Feminism and the Subversion of Identity* (New York: Routledge, 1990); *Bodies That Matter: On the Discursive Limits of "Sex"* (London: Routledge, 1993); "Critically Queer," *GLQ: A Journal of Lesbian and Gay Studies* 1, no. 1 (1993): 17–32; *Excitable Speech: A Politics of the Performative* (New York: Routledge, 1997). For more on gender

performativity as a method, see Elena Loizidou, *Judith Butler: Ethics, Law, Politics* (New York: Routledge-Cavendish, 2007), 17–44.
15 Butler, *Bodies That Matter*, 2.
16 Ibid., 3.
17 Ibid.
18 Eve Sedgwick, "Queer Performativity: Henry James's *The Art of the Novel*," *GLQ: A Journal of Lesbian and Gay Studies* 1, no. 1 (1993): 1–16.
19 Ostrosky, *Mentes asesinas*, 180.
20 Ibid.
21 Ibid.
22 Michel Foucault, "The Dangerous Individual," in *Politics, Philosophy, Culture: Interviews and Other Writings 1977–1984*, ed. Lawrence Kritzman (London: Routledge, 1988), 161.
23 Ostrosky, *Mentes asesinas*, 180.
24 Ibid., 204.
25 Ibid.
26 Foucault, "Dangerous Individual."
27 Barrón, *El nudo del silencio*, 102, 105, 130–34, 135–42.
28 Ibid., 105–21.
29 Hare, *Without Conscience*, 61.
30 Ibid.
31 Ibid.
32 Ibid.
33 Barrón, *El nudo del silencio*, 105, 21.
34 Ibid., 121.
35 Ibid., 166.
36 Martínez and Vergara, *Estudios de antropología criminal*, 101.
37 Ibid., 48.
38 Foucault, "Dangerous Individual," 161.
39 Phillip Jenkins, *Using Murder: The Social Construction of Serial Homicide* (New Brunswick, NJ: Transaction Publishers, 1994), 228, quoted in Seltzer, *Serial Killers*, 125.
40 Buffington, *Criminal and Citizen*, 81–86.
41 Ibid.
42 Barrón, *El nudo del silencio*, 162.
43 Katja Gaskell, "Lucha Libre—an Introduction to Mexican Wrestling," *Lonely Planet*, February 2017.
44 Carlos Monsiváis, *Lourdes Grobet: Lucha Libre, Masked Superstars of Mexican Wrestling*, ed. Alfonso Morales (Mexico City: DAP/Trilce, 2008).
45 Heather Levi, "Lean Mean Fighting Queens: Drag in the World of Mexican Professional Wrestling," *Sexualities* 1, no. 3 (1998): 277.
46 Lucha libre—specifically, exótico wrestling—has been read as "queer" in an effort to argue how lucha libre destabilizes notions of gender, sexuality, race, and class

and opens up spaces of resistance. Having grown up in Mexico City, watching Sunday wrestling matches, it is difficult for me to read lucha libre as only a "queer" performance; to me, it is more a performance of mexicanidad, as I argue in this chapter. I cannot remember the first time I saw a wrestling match—it was simply part of growing up in Mexico and watching matches spoke to me more about mexicanidad than queerness. The term "queer," which can work as methodology, theory, practice, and speech act, has much potential in its translation and adaptation to a Latin American context. However, I leave that to other authors and focus on defining mexicanidad and its relationship to lucha libre following my own phenomenological experience. Moreover, I believe that reading mexicanidad into lucha libre does not preclude a reading of queerness in lucha libre. On the contrary, both readings are possible at the same time. For a queer reading of lucha libre as a liminal space, see Nina Hoechtl, "Lucha libre: un espacio liminal. Lis Exótiquis "Juntopuestas" a las categorías clasificadoras, unívocas y fijas," in *La Memoria y el deseo. Estudios gay y queer en México,* ed. Rodrigo Parrini Rosas and Alejandro Brito (Mexico City: México Centro de Investigaciones y Estudios de Género/Universidad Nacional Autónoma de México, 2014), 223–51.

47 Michael Ramos-Araizaga, dir., *Los Exóticos: luchadores completos, pero con diversidad arriba del cuadrilátero,* 2013.
48 Mary-Lee Mulholland, "Mariachi, Myths and Mestizaje: Popular Culture and Mexican National Identity," *National Identities* 9, no. 3 (2007): 251 (italics in original).
49 Ibid. (italics in original).
50 Ibid. (italics in original).
51 Although professional wrestling in Mexico, as will be discussed throughout this chapter, started in the 1930s in Mexico City with wrestlers brought from Texas by promoter Salvador Lutteroth and partner Francisco Ahumada, the manner in which lucha libre is performed in Mexico constitutes a performance of Mexican identity—through the nicknames, masks, beliefs, etc.
52 Mulholland, "Mariachi, Myths and Mestizaje."
53 Lola Miranda Fascinetto, *Sin máscara ni cabellera: lucha libre en México hoy* (Mexico City: Marc Ediciones, S.A. de C.V., 1992), 14.
54 Ibid.
55 Ibid., 26.
56 Levi, "Lean Mean Fighting Queens."
57 By law, the term "puto" constitutes discrimination and hate speech. "Puto" was also frequently shouted during soccer matches, but in 2013 La Federación Mexicana de Futbol (Femexfut—the Mexican Federation of Football) was warned by the Fédération Internationale de Football Association (FIFA), the world governing organization for the sport, that when fans used the term "puto" they would be sanctioned and forced to pay a fine. Fans argued that this infringed on their free speech and that the term "puto" is used in a myriad of ways. For instance, when you're badly hurt or when a car crashes, you might say, "¡Qué

putazo!," adding a superlative to the noun (What a terrible, horrible crash!). However, since 2103, the National Supreme Court of Mexico has similarly stated that terms like "puto," "maricón," and "puñal" are "homophobic manifestations," which are "part of hate speech." "Puto" in particular is a derogatory term due to is association with the "passive role" in the sexual act enacted by a male in a same-sex relation. This association can be dated to before colonization when the *nahua* term "cuiloni" (passive) was used to insult the Spanish conquistadores. For more information on the use of "puto" in wrestling matches, see Ramos-Araizaga, "Los exóticos." For more on the debate around the use of "puto" during soccer matches, see Mónica Cruz, "Por qué no se puede gritar 'puto' en los estadios sin ofender," *El País*, June 21, 2017; "En México la homofobia se paga con multa," *BBC*, March 8, 2013. For the *nahua* use of cuiloni, see Shuessler, "Vestidas, locas," and for more on the relationship between machos, machismo, and homosexuality, see Juan Carlos Bautista, "La noche al margen. Brevísima relación de la vida nocturna gay," in *Mexico se escribe con J*, ed. Michael K. Shuessler and Miguel Capistrán Miguel (Mexico City: Editorial Planeta Mexico, 2010).

58 Paz, *El laberinto*, 31.
59 Debra A. Castillo, "Violencia y trabajadores sexuales travestis y transgéneros en Tijuana," *Debate feminista fronteras norte/sur* 33 (2006): 11.
60 Ibid., 282.
61 Lola Miranda Fascinetto, *Sin máscara ni cabellera: lucha libre en México hoy* (Mexico City: Marc Ediciones, S.A. de C.V., 1992), 184.
62 Ibid., 189.
63 Ibid., 195.
64 Rodrigo Parrini Rosas, *Panópticos y laberintos: subjetivación, deseo, y corporalidad en una cárcel de hombres,* (Mexico City: El Colegio de México, 2007), 223.
65 Ibid., 19.
66 Carrillo, "Cultural Change, Hybridity and Male Homosexuality in Mexico," 225.
67 Ibid.
68 Ibid., 227.
69 Ibid.
70 Ibid., 235.
71 Ibid.
72 Fernando del Rincón, "La verdad de Juan Gabriel," *Primer Impacto*. 2002.
73 Annick Prieur, *Mema's House, Mexico City: On Transvestites, Queens, and Machos* (Chicago: University of Chicago Press, 1998), 29.
74 Martin Nesving, "The Complicated Terrain of Latin American Homosexuality," *Hispanic American Historical Review*, no. 81 (2001): 724.
75 Lola Miranda Fascinetto, *Sin máscara ni cabellera: lucha libre en México hoy* (Mexico City: Marc Ediciones, S.A. de C.V., 1992), 184.
76 "Los momentos importantes de la lucha libre femenil en México," *Excélsior*, July 19, 2017.

77 Jarcoreradiotj, "La lucha libre femenil en México, grandes mujeres que forjaron una trayectoria en tiempos difíciles," *Superluchas*, March 26, 2013, https://superluchas.com; Angelita Dark, "La lucha libre presente en las jornadas universitarias de la UAM Cuajimalpa," *Superluchas*, October 26, 2016, https://superluchas.com.
78 "La múltiple lucha. Mesa de diálogo y proyección de cine." Museo Universitario de Arte Contemporáneo, October 21, 2017.
79 There are arenas that feature matches specifically devoted to mixed combat in which women can fight men, if the latter are exóticos.
80 Nina Hoechtl, "Wrestling Luchadoras and Female Masculinities: La Comandante and Martha Villalobos," *Frauen*solidarität*, no. 127 (2014), www.frauensolidaritaet.org.
81 Ibid.
82 "Deja Martha Villalobos legado en la lucha libre." *Hoy. Estado de México*. October 1, 2012.
83 Elena Poniatowska, "'El Santo' a dos de tres caídas," in *Todo México* (Mexico City: Editoriales Diana, 1990), 259.
84 Ibid., 258.
85 Walkowitz, *City of Dreadful Delight*, 191.
86 Ian Hacking, "Making Up People," in *The Science Studies Reader*, ed. Mario Biagioli (New York: Routledge, 1999), 165.
87 Silvia Otero, "Reconoce crímenes contra gays 'sin remordimientos,'" *El Universal*, January 27, 2006.
88 Hacking, "Making Up People," 165.
89 Ricardo Ham, "Historia 'El Sádico' que atemorizó a la comunidad gay," *El Universal*, June 1, 2014.
90 Fernando Martínez, "Dan 280 de cárcel a asesino de homosexuales," *El Universal*, February 7, 2010.
91 Luis Brito, "Ven en 'poeta caníbal' perfil de asesino serial," *Reforma*, October 11, 2007.
92 Arturo Sierra, "Es 'poeta caníbal' tercer serial en D.F.," *Reforma*, October 15, 2007.
93 Salgado, Bolaños, and Ramón, "Tras las rejas."
94 Anne Marie Balsamo, *Technologies of the Gendered Body: Reading Cyborg Women* (Durham, NC: Duke University Press, 1996), 44.
95 Levi, "Lean Mean Fighting Queens," 278.
96 Servín, "La Dama del Silencio."
97 Lynda Birke and Gail Vines, "A Sporting Chance: The Anatomy of Destiny?," *Women's Studies International Forum* 10, no. 4 (1987): 338.
98 Salgado and Servín, "Cae Mataviejitas."
99 Dirección de Comunicación Institucional, "La Mataviejitas: 'Una sociópata'"; Salgado and Servín, "Cae Mataviejitas"; Ostrosky, *Mentes asesinas*, 189.
100 Barrón, *El nudo del silencio*, 75.
101 Ibid., 164.
102 Jiménez, "La Mataviejitas coleccionaba recortes de periódicos."

103 Ostrosky, *Mentes asesinas*, 185.
104 Ibid.
105 Seltzer, *Serial Killers*, 44.
106 Lamas, "De trasvestis."
107 On serial killers as big business in popular culture, see Brian Jarvis, "Monsters Inc.: Serial Killers and Consumer Culture," *Crime, Media, Culture* 3, no. 3 (2007): 326–44.
108 Jiménez, "Juana Barraza."
109 Levi, "Lean Mean Fighting Queens," 278.
110 Paz, *El laberinto*, 39.
111 Luis Brito, "Nadie estaba listo para Juana Barraza," *Reforma*, January 27, 2007.
112 The video uploaded in September 2007 is no longer online; however, the same video has been posted again: "Amandititita—La Mataviejitas (original)," YouTube video, 3:31, posted by "Pgoste," April 26, 2008, https://www.youtube.com/watch?v=HUhejVTjIE8.
113 Levi, "Lean Mean Fighting Queens," 278.
114 Monsiváis, *Mexican Postcards*, 15.
115 Víctor Ronquillo, *Ruda de corazón: el blues de La Mataviejitas* (Mexico City: Ediciones B, S.A. de C.V, 2006), 49.
116 César Díaz and Arturo Sierra, "Paga Mataviejitas protección a judiciales," *Reforma*, February 2, 2006.
117 Arturo García Hernández, "El caso de La Mataviejitas, retrato de la degradación social que vivimos," *La Jornada*, July 16, 2006.
118 Ibid.
119 Ibid.
120 Robert Ressler with Tom Shachtman, *Whoever Fights Monsters: My Twenty Years Tracking Serial Killers for the FBI* (New York: St. Martin's Press, 1992), 29–30.
121 Ibid.
122 Seltzer, *Serial Killers*, 64.
123 Ibid., 65.
124 Ibid., 129.
125 Reisinger, "Murder and Banality," 86.

CHAPTER 4. PERFORMING MEXICANIDAD II

1 Noel Alvarado, "Practicaba 'La Mataviejitas' magia negra para evitar ser descubierta," *La Prensa*, January 31, 2006.
2 Luis Brito, "Fallan sus amuletos," *Reforma*, February 1, 2006, 7.
3 Forbes Staff, "Los 10 estados con más pobres en México," *Forbes México*, August 27, 2015, www.forbes.com.mx.
4 Alejandra Zuñiga, "Ecatepec es el lugar con peor calidad de vida en México," *Vice News*, October 6, 2016, www.vice.com/es_mx; Gerardo Villafranco, "Ecatepec y naucalpan, los peores lugares para vivir en México," *Forbes México*, February 16, 2017, www.forbes.com.mx; Padgett and Loza, *Las muertas del estado*, 2.

5   Padgett and Loza, *Las muertas del estado*.
6   Jill Radford and Diana Russell, *Femicide: The Politics of Woman Killing* (New York: Twayne, 1992), 3.
7   Lagarde, "Del femicidio al feminicidio," 221.
8   Jacobo García, "Estado de México, capital del feminicidio," *El País*, May 18, 2017, http://internacional.elpais.com; Elena Reina, "Ecaptec despierta los deminios de Ciudad Juárez," *El País*, April 22, 2016, https://internacional.elpais.com.
9   Padgett and Loza cross-reference two different sets of death certificates—those produced by the Secretaría Federal de Salud (Federal Health Secretary) and those prepared by doctors—to produce their own statistics. Padgett and Loza, *Las muertas del estado*, statistical index, Los números de odio, 1.
10 Monárrez, *Trama de una injusticia*, 8.
11 Ibid., 56.
12 Ibid., 13.
13 For example, there are news reports of women missing in 1991 and 1992 following similar patterns. See ibid., 11. However, it was not until 1993 that Chávez started rigorously tracking the young women who disappeared. See Davison, "Esther Chávez."
14 These organizations included Mujeres por Juárez, Centro de Investigación y Solidaridad Obrera A.C, Grupo 8 de Marzo, and Casa Amiga, among others. See Monárrez, *Trama de una injusticia*, 16. Also, in 1999, Casa Amiga Centro de Crisis was founded by Esther Chávez with the international support of CNN TV reporter Brian Barger, *Vagina Monologues* playwright Eve Ensler, and others. See Phil Davison, "Esther Chávez: Prominent Women's Rights Activist," *Independent*, January 15, 2010, www.independent.co.uk.
15 Monárrez, *Trama de una injusticia*, 8–9.
16 Clara Eugenia Rojas, "(Re)inventando una praxis política desde un imaginario feminista," in *Primer encuentro de estudios de la mujer en la región "Paso Norte": Retos frente al siglo XXI* (Ciudad Juárez, Chihuahua: El Colegio de la Frontera Norte, 2003), 18, cited in Monárrez, *Trama de una injusticia*, 78.
17 María del Socorro Tabuenca, "Baile de fantasmas en la Ciudad Juárez al final/principio del mileno," in *Más alla de la ciudad letrada: crónicas y espacios urbanos*, ed. Boris Muñoz and Silvia Spitta (Pittsburg, PA: Biblioteca de América, 2003), 420.
18 Monárrez, *Trama de una injusticia*, 18–19; Rafael Castillo, "Asesinadas en el Estado de México: una silenciosa epidemia," *Vice News*, November 24, 2016, www.vice.com/es_mx.
19 Berlanga Gayón, Mariana. *Una mirada al feminicidio*. Mexico, D.F.: Universidad de la Ciudad de México, 2018.
20 Berlanga Gayón, Mariana. "El espectáculo de la violencia en el México actual: del feminicidio al juvenicidio," *Athenea Digital* 15, no. 4 (December 2015): 105–28.
21 Amnistía Internacional, "México: Muertes intolerables—10 años de desapariciones y asesinatos de mujeres en Ciudad Juárez y Chihuahua" (Mexico: Amnistía

Internacional, 2003); Monárrez, *Trama de una injusticia*, 105–7; Diana Washington Valdez, *The Killing Fields: Harvest of Women: The Truth about Mexico's Bloody Border Legacy* (Burbank, CA: Peace at the Border, 2006), 1.
22 Julia Monárrez notes that some of the 4,587 women registered as missing have been located. See Monárrez, *Trama de una injusticia*, 8.
23 Monárrez collected information from the activist Esther Chávez and had previously undertook hemerographic research of nongovernmental organizations, as well as the press report given by the "Subprocuraduría de Justicia del Estado, Zona Norte, and the reports of the Procuraduría General de Justicia del Estado." See Monárrez, "La cultura del feminicidio," 99.
24 Monárrez, "La cultura del feminicidio"; Monárrez, "Feminicidio sexual serial."
25 Jane Caputi, *The Age of Sex Crime* (Bowling Green, OH: Bowling Green State University Popular Press, 1987); Elizabeth Frazer and Deborah Cameron, *The Lust to Kill: A Feminist Investigation of Sexual Murder* (New York: New York University Press, 1987).
26 Monárrez, "Feminicidio sexual serial," 283–86.
27 Ibid., 100.
28 Monárrez, *Trama de una injusticia*, 26–27.
29 Ibid., 110–12.
30 Ibid.
31 Ibid., 112.
32 Ibid., 330. Robert K. Ressler, the ex-FBI agent credited with coining the term "serial killer," visited Ciudad Juárez several times during this period. Ibid., 56. The FBI itself was invited to the city to look into the feminicides, but it is not clear that representatives of the Bureau ever did. Ibid., 331.
33 Padgett and Loza, *Las muertas del estado*, chap. 4, p. 37.
34 "Capturan a presunto feminicida de Chimalhuacán," *El Universal*, October 18, 2006; Rene Ramón, "Sospechan de asesino serial en Edomex," *La Jornada*, April 24, 2006.
35 Gladys Ferrer, "Indaga Edomex ADN del 'asesino del bordo,'" *Reforma*, April 14, 2006.
36 Padgett and Loza, *Las muertas del estado*, chap. 4, p. 37.
37 William Paul Simmons, "Remedies for Women of Ciudad Juárez through the Inter-American Court of Human Rights," *Northwestern Journal of International Human Rights* 4, no. 3 (2006): 492.
38 Carlos Coria Rivas, "Sentencian en Juárez a asesinos de 15 mujeres," *El Universal*, January 7, 2005.
39 Ibid.
40 "Liberan a el cerillo, inculpado en asesinatos de mujeres en Cd Juárez," *Proceso*, July 15, 2005.
41 Ricardo Raphael de la Madrid, "La muerte tuvo permiso," *Nexos*, July 1, 1999.
42 "Liberan a el cerillo."
43 Monárrez, "Feminicidio sexual serial," 298.

44 Monárrez, *Trama de una injusticia*, 28, 33–34.
45 Ibid., 98.
46 Monárrez, "Feminicidio sexual serial," 299.
47 Monárrez, *Trama de una injusticia*, 108.
48 Julia Monárrez Fragoso and César Fuentes, "Feminicidio y marginalidad urbana en Ciudad Juárez en la década de los noventa," in *Violencia contra las mujeres en contextos urbanos y rurales*, ed. Marta Torres Falcón (Mexico City: Colegio de México, 2004), 58–66. Ciudad Juárez has been a destination for immigrants. With the industrialization of the city, many women from other parts of Mexico migrated there to work in maquiladoras. Similarly, Ciudad Juárez became the bridge to the United States for migrants from countries such as El Salvador, Guatemala, and Nicaragua.
49 Monárrez, *Trama de una injusticia*, 292.
50 Padgett and Loza, *Las muertas del estado*, 9, 15.
51 Castillo, "Asesinadas en el Estado de México."
52 Lucía Nuñez has in fact argued that the term "feminicide" has worked many times *against* bringing justice, since many women who have killed other women (not as a sexual crime, but because of other factors) have been charged with the crime of feminicide and in turn served longer sentences than if they had been convicted of homicide. Nuñez also notes that the criminalization of "feminicide" has not deterred the actual misogynist killing of women. See Lucía Nuñez, "Contribución a la crítica de feminismo punitivo," in *La bifurcación del caos: reflexiones interdisciplinarias sobre violencia falocetrica*, ed. María Guadalupe Huacuz Elias (Mexico City: ITACA-UAM Xochimilco, 2012), 173–95. Also, for a critique of the utility and limits of the term *feminicidio* through a case comparison with Mexico and Perú and Guatemala, see Pascha Bueno-Hansen, "*Feminicidio*: Making the Most of an 'Empowered Term,'" in *Terrorizing Women: Feminicide in the Américas*, ed. Rosa Linda Fregoso and Cynthia L. Bejarano (Durham, NC: Duke University Press, 2010), 290–311.
53 Rohry Benítez, Adriana Candia, Patricia Cabrera, Guadalupe de la Mora, Josefina Martínez, Isabel Velázquez, and Ramona Ortiz, *El silencio que la voz de todas quiebra: mujeres y víctimas de Ciudad Juárez* (Chihuahua: Ediciones del AZAR, 1999), 50.
54 Comisión Nacional de los Derechos Humanos, *Informe especial de la CNDH sobre los casos de homicidios y desapariciones de mujeres en el Municipio de Juárez, Chihuahua* (Mexico, 2003), 5, cited in Monárrez, *Trama de una injusticia*, 15.
55 Benítez et al., *El silencio*, 50.
56 Martín Orquiz, "Asesinatos de mujeres: como dejar un dulce en un colegio," *Diario de Juárez*, Ciudad Juárez, August 2, 1998, cited in Monárrez, *Trama de una injusticia*, 302.
57 Ibid.
58 Benítez et al. have actually studied the police reports of the young women missing to determine what were they wearing, concluding that "10 of 137 victims were

wearing shorts or miniskirts, 6 were wearing dresses and 2 leggings." See Benítez et al., *El silencio*, 9.
59 Notimez, "Magnifican ONG's crímenes," *Norte de Juárez*, Ciudad Juárez, June 9, 2002, 5; Manuel E. Aguirre, "Descarta Procurador que se trata de un solo asesino," *Norte de Juárez*, Ciudad Juárez, March 9, 1999, 4B; Rosa Isela Pérez, "Decepcionan a ONG's senadores," *Norte de Juárez*, Ciudad Juárez, February 17, 2001, 2A, all cited in Monárrez, *Trama de una injusticia*, 250–55.
60 Monárrez, *Trama de una injusticia*, 244–45.
61 Ibid., 118.
62 Ibid., 15.
63 Armando Rodríguez, "Son situacionales' los crímenes, dice procurador estatal," *Diario de Juárez*, Ciudad Juárez, February 24, 1999, 9C, cited in ibid., 42.
64 Monárrez, *Trama de una injusticia*, 93.
65 Tabuenca, "Baile de fantasmas," 420.
66 Ibid., 420–27.
67 UN Commission on Human Rights, *Civil and Political Rights, Including the Question of Disappearances and Summary Executions/Report of the Special Rapporteur on Extrajudicial, Summary or Arbitrary Executions, submitted pursuant to Commission on Human Rights resolution 1999/35*, Addendum, Visit to México, 2000.
68 Ibid.
69 Jorge Camargo, en *Norte*, June 4, 1998, 3, cited in Monárrez, "La cultura del feminicidio," 92.
70 Rodríguez, "Son situacionales' los crímenes," cited in Monárrez, "La cultura del feminicidio," 92.
71 Monárrez Fragoso, *Trama de una injusticia*, 207.
72 Horacio Soto Carrasco, "Normal, el porcentaje de homicidios respecto a otras partes del país: Barrio," *Diario de Juárez*, Ciudad Juárez, December 2, 1997, 1B, cited in Monárrez, *Trama de una injusticia*, 249–50.
73 Monárrez, *Trama de una injusticia*, 284–85.
74 Ibid., 161–71.
75 Ibid., 18.
76 Ramos Roberto, "Secundan abogados declaraciones de Ressler," *El Diario Digital*, December 5, 2002, 2A, cited in Monárrez, *Trama de una injusticia*, 259.
77 "Facing Mexico's Murders," *Washington Post*, November 13, 2003, 30A, cited in Monárrez, *Trama de una injusticia*, 283.
78 Padgett and Loza, *Las muertas del estado*.
79 Ibid., 63; Lydia Cacho, "El Estado de México: feminicidios ignorados," *Lydia Cacho* (blog), January 12, 2011, www.lydiacacho.com.
80 "SEGOB emite alerta de género para el Estado de México," *Excélsior*, July 31, 2015.
81 Padgett and Loza, *Las muertas del estado*, 2.
82 Ibid., 4.
83 Ibid., 3, 17.

84 Jo Tuckman, "Computer Files Link TV Dirty Tricks to Favourite for Mexico Presidency," *Guardian*, June 7, 2012, www.theguardian.com; Jo Tuckman, "Pressure on Mexican Presidential Candidate in Televisa Media Row," *Guardian*, June 8, 2012, www.theguardian.com.
85 Padgett and Loza, *Las muertas del estado*, 60.
86 Padgett interviewed Columbia law professor Edgardo Buscaglia, who notes how the high rates of feminicides and organized crime were maintained as a subject of local jurisdiction and did not enter the federal purview. See ibid., chap. 2, 37.
87 Mexico, Ministry of Foreign Affairs, "Gender Alert Declared for the State of Mexico," news release, August 3, 2015, https://embamex.sre.gob.mx.
88 "SEGOB emite alerta de género," 2015.
89 Padgett and Loza, *Las muertas del estado*, 36, 63.
90 Mexico City, Comisión Nacional de Derechos Humanos, "Recomendación Atenco" (Mexico, 2006).
91 Amnesty International, "Mexico: Torture and Sexual Violence against Women Detained in San Salvador Atenco—Two Years of Injustice and Impunity" (United States: Amnesty International, April 29, 2008). Most of the people in these communities have been called "peasants" or "indigenous" in the press. Most of the rural places in Mexico that used to be *repúblicas indias* have transformed into peasant communities. See Bonfil, *México Profundo*.
92 Amnesty International, "Mexico: Violence against Women and Justice Denied in Mexico State" (London: Amnesty International, October 2006).
93 "5th Anniversary of Police Assaults on Women in Mexico," *Amnesty International*, n.d. (2011), www.amnestyusa.org.
94 Padgett and Loza, *Las muertas del estado*, statistical annex.
95 Many authors have worked on this. See Lourdes Arizpe, *Indígenas en la Ciudad de México: el caso de las Marías* (México: Secretaría de Educación Pública, 1980); Lourdes Arizpe, *La mujer en el desarrollo de México y América Latina* (Cuernavaca, Morelos: Universidad Nacional Autónoma de México–Centro Regional de Investigaciones Multidisciplinarias, 1989); Rosalva Aída and Hernández Castillo, eds., *La otra palabra: mujeres y violencia en Chiapas antes y después de Acteal* (Mexico City: Centro de Investigaciones y Estudios Superiores en Antropología Social, 1998); Van den Berghe, *Race and Racism*; Henri Favre, *Cambio y continuidad entre los mayas de México* (Mexico City: Instituto Nacional Indigenista, 1992); Diana Guillén, "Estructuras tradicionales de poder y modernización en América Latina: el caso Chiapaneco" (PhD diss., Universidad Nacional Autónoma de México, 1994), all cited in Gall, "Identidad, exclusión y racismo," 249.
96 Ibid.
97 Claudia Ruiz, "Historia y actualidad del culto a La Santa Muerte," *El Cotidiano. Revista de la Realidad Mexina*, no. 169 (2011): 8.
98 On syncretism, see Perla Fragoso, "De la 'calavera domada' a la subversión santificada: La Santa Muerte, un nuevo imaginario religioso en México," *El Cotidiano. Revista de la realidad mexicana*, no. 169 (2011): 5–16; on pastiche, see Jorge

Degetau, "Malverde y La Santísima: Cultos y credos en el México Posmoderno," *Metapolítica* 12, no. 67 (2009): 20–24; Estela Bravo Lara, "Bajo tu manto nos acogemos: Devotos a La Santa Muerte en la Zona Metropolitana de Guadalajara," *Nueva Antropología A.C.* 26, no. 79 (2013): 11–28; on bricolage see Katia Perdigón Castañeda, *La Santa Muerte, protectora de los hombres*, México, Instituto Nacional de Antropología e Historia, 2008.

99 María C. Lara Mireles, "El culto a La Santa Muerte en el entramado simbólico de la sociedad del riesgo," *Anuario CONEICC de Investigación de la Comunicación*, no. 15 (2008): 285–98.

100 Ruiz, "Historia y actualidad," 54. This term is not a proper Spanish word, but a made-up verb that signifies "throwing smoke" from a cigar.

101 Fragoso, "De la 'calavera domada,'" 13.

102 Anne Huffschmid, "Devoción satanizada: la muerte como nuevo culto callejero en la Ciudad de México," *iMex Revista Mexico Interdisciplinario* 2, no. 3 (2012): 105–7.

103 Laura Roush, "Santa Muerte, Protection, and Desamparo: A View from a Mexico City Altar," *Latin America Research Review* 49 (2014): 129.

104 Juan A. Flores Martos, "Iconografías emergentes y muerte patrimonializadas en América Latina: Santa Muerte, muertos milagrosos y muertos adoptados," *Revista de Antropología Iberoamericana* 9 (2014); Ruiz, "Historia y actualidad."

105 Fragoso, "De la 'calavera domada,'" 11.

106 Ibid.

107 Ibid., 13.

108 Ibid., 49.

109 Flores Martos, "Iconografías emergentes," 122.

110 Ruiz, "Historia y actualidad," 54.

111 Degetau, "Malverde y la santísima," 21.

112 Pilar Castells, "La Santa Muerte y la cultura de los derechos humanos," *LiminaR. Estudios sociales y humanísticos* 6 (2008): 19.

113 Margarita Zires, "Los mitos de la Virgen de Guadalupe: Su proceso de construccion y reinterpretación en el México pasado y contemporaneo," *Mexican Studies/Estudios Mexicanos* 10, no. 2 (1994): 281–313.

114 Bernardino de Sahagún, *1570–1582. Historia general de las cosas de la Nueva España* (Mexico City: Editorial Porrúa, 1989), 33 cited in ibid., 283.

115 Ibid.

116 Ibid.

117 Linda Hall, *Mary, Mother and Warrior: The Virgin in Spain and the Americas* (Austin: University of Texas Press, 2004), 192.

118 Wade, *Blackness and Race Mixture*, 48.

119 Ibid., 22.

120 Ibid.

121 "Plan de la Independencia de México," AGN, Ramo: Gobierno Virreinal, Impresos Oficiales (056), contenedor 25, vol. 60, cited in ibid., 132.

122 Homero Aridjis, *La santa muerte: sexteto del amor las mujeres, los perros y la muerte* (Mexico City: Alfaguara/Consejo Nacional para la Cultural y las Artes, 2004).
123 Claudio Lomnitz, *Death and the Idea of Mexico* (Brooklyn, NY: Zone Books, 2005), 55.
124 Other authors view the Día de los Muertos differently, regarding it as syncretic in origin and elements of it as indigenous. For more views on the Day of the Death, see Regina Marchi, "Hybridity and Authenticity in US Day of the Dead Celebrations," *Journal of American Folklore* 126, no. 501 (2013): 272–30; Shawn D. Haley and Curt Fukuda, *Day of the Dead: When Two Worlds Meet in Oaxaca* (New York and Oxford: Berghahn Books, 2004); Stanley H. Brandes, "Is There a Mexican View of Death?," *Ethos* 31 (2003): 127–44.
125 Lomnitz, *Death and the Idea of Mexico*, 166.
126 Ibid., 463.
127 Ibid., 54.
128 Ibid., 483.
129 Fragoso, "De la 'calavera domada,'" 6.
130 Moctezuma Matos, *Muerte a filo de obsidiana* (Mexico City: Secretaría de Educación Pública, 1974), 105, cited in ibid.
131 Fragoso, "De la 'calavera domada,'" 10.
132 Ibid., 5.
133 Lomnitz, *Death and the Idea of Mexico*, 24.
134 Fragoso, "De la 'calavera domada,'" 6.
135 Ibid., 11.
136 Ibid.
137 Ibid., 13.
138 Carlos Monsiváis, "Un mal día en la vida de Daniel Arizmendi," *Proceso*, August 28, 1998.
139 Ibid.
140 Felipe Gaytán, "Santa entre los malditos: culto a La Santa Muerte en el México del siglo XXI," *LiminaR. Estudios sociales y humanísticos* 6 (2008): 40–51.
141 Sergio González, "Bajo la protección de la santísima," *Reforma*, October 28, 2001.
142 Desirée A. Martín, *Borderlands Saints: Secular Sanctity in Chicano/a and Mexican Culture* (New Brunswick, NJ: Rutgers University Press, 2013), 182–209.
143 Alejandro Almazán, "Su devoción por La Santa Muerte," *El Universal*, April 19, 2001.
144 "Invade Santa Muerte a Tijuana," *Diario el Norte*, September 18, 2006, cited in Gaytán, "Santa entre los malditos," 44.
145 Almazán, "Su devoción."
146 Jaime Whaley, "En aumento, la adoración a la Santísima Muerte," *La Jornada*, November 2, 2003.
147 Daniel Sada, "Cada piedra es un deseo," *Letras Libres*, March 2000.
148 Ibid.

149 See Patricia Price, "Of Bandits and Saints: Jesús Malverde and the Struggle for Place in Sinaloa, México," *Cultural Geographies* 12, no. 2 (2005): 175–97; Kristín Guðrún Jónsdóttir, "De bandolero a ejemplo moral: los corridos sobre Jesús Malverde, el santo amante de la música," *Studies in Latin American Popular Culture* 25 (2006): 25–48; Enrique Flores and Raúl Eduardo González, "Malverde: Exvotos y corridos (en las voces de cantores sinaloenses)," *Caravelle*, no. 88 (January 2007): 111–38; Michel Gerardo Gómez and Jungwon Park, "The Cult of Jesús Malverde: Crime and Sanctity as Elements of a Heterogeneous Modernity," *Latin American Perspectives* 41, no. 2 (2014): 202–14.
150 Robert J. Botsch, "Jesus Malverde's Significance to Mexican Drug Traffickers," *FBI Law Enforcement Bulletin* 77 (2008): 20.
151 Price, "Of Bandits and Saints," 176.
152 Botsch, "Jesus Malverde's Significance," 20; Price, "Of Bandits and Saints," 176.
153 Price, "Of Bandits and Saints," 176.
154 A. L. Hernández, "Jesús Malverde: ángel de los pobres," n.d., cited in Price, "Of Bandits and Saints," 179.
155 Degetau, "Malverde y la santísima," 22.
156 Botsch, "Jesus Malverde's Significance," 20.
157 Ibid., 19.
158 Ibid.
159 Ibid., 21.
160 Ibid.
161 Ibid.
162 Barrón, *El nudo del silencio*, 121.
163 Ibid.
164 Ibid., 124–25.
165 Ibid., 125–26.
166 Ibid., 127.
167 Ibid., 185.
168 Ibid., 130.
169 Ibid., 127.

CONCLUSION

1 According to criminologist Carlos Manuel Cruz Meza, autor of the blog *Escritos con Sangre. El website de los Asesinos* (https://escritoconsangre1.blogspot.com), it wasn't until Lugo died of alchoholism that Barraza came back to her mother's house and developed a relationship with her stepfather, who showed her love and compassion. "Juana Barraza Samperio, 'La Mataviejitas' (entrevista completa)," YouTube video, 40:38, posted by "Carlos Manuel Cruz Meza," July 3, 2013, https://www.youtube.com/watch?v=bZM5xBEl-RA.
2 I thank Linda Palacios very much for bringing Malinalli's life story to my attention. For the devastating stories of young women sexually trafficked from Tlaxcala to New York, see María Luisa Vivas, "Es Tenancingo, Tlaxcala la capital de la trata

de personas," *Proceso*, May 6, 2013; Nathaniel Janowitz, "Así es como los padrotes de Tlaxcala atraen niñas al mundo de la trata," *Vice News*, July 9, 2015. www.vice.com/es_mx. For an excellent historical analysis of the trafficking of young women in Oaxaca during the legalization of prostitution in Mexico, see Fabiola Bailón Vásquez, *Mujeres en el servicio doméstico y la prostitución: sobrevivencia, control y vida cotidiana en la Oaxaca Porfiriana* (Mexico, D.F.: El Colegio de México), 2014.

3 Palacios, "El problema de La Malintzin," 55.
4 Ibid., 60.
5 Ibid.
6 For more on the figure of mandilón, a man who is dominated by his wife or other women, and how men have navigated their identities between these two main spaces for masculinities—macho and mandilón—see Gutmann, *Meanings of Macho*.
7 José Limón, "La Llorona, the Third Legend of Greater Mexico: Cultural Symbols, Women, and the Political Unconscious," in *Between Borders: Essays on Mexicana/Chicana History*, ed. Adelaida del Castillo (Encino, CA: Floricanto Press, 2005), 399–432.
8 Ibid., 408.
9 Fray Bernardino de Saghún, Historia General de las cosas de la Nueva España, Vol. 3 (Mexico, D.F.: Nueva España), 25, cited in Limón, "La Llorona," 408.
10 Robert A. Barakat, "Aztec Motifs in La Llorona," *Southern Folklore Quarterly* 29 (1965): 288–96, cited in Limón, "La Llorona," 408.
11 Rosan A. Jordan, "The Vaginal Serpent and Other Themes from Mexican-American Women's Role," in *Women's Folklore, Women's Culture*, ed. Rosan A. Jordan and Susan J. Kalcik (Philadelphia: University of Pennsylvania Press, 1985), 26–44, cited in Limón, "La Llorona," 410.
12 Limón, "La Llorona," 416.
13 Ibid.
14 Mark Cartwright, "Tenochtitlán," in *Ancient History Encyclopedia*, September 25, 2013, www.ancient.eu.
15 Castillo, "Asesinadas en el Estado de México."
16 Ibid.
17 "#SiMeMatan, la reacción de mujeres ante criminalización de una joven y que llevó a la PGJ a rectificar," *Animal Político*, May 5, 2017, www.animalpolitico.com.
18 Joel de Fandiño Salazar, personal communication, Mexico City, June 23, 2017.
19 Sedgwick considers that the most intimate violence possible, central to the modern history of homophobic oppression, is to "alienate conclusively, definitionally, from anyone on any theoretical ground the authority to describe and name their own sexual desire." Eve Kosofsky Sedgwick, *Epistemology of the Closet* (Berkeley and Los Angeles: University of California Press, 1990), 26.
20 Susana Vargas, "The *Crónica* We Will Never Read," *Macha Mexico* (blog), June 23, 2013, https://machamexico.wordpress.com. (Unfortunately, this blog is no longer online.) In this post, I argued that there was really no way of measuring the power

of saying or not saying when it comes to public figures coming out of the closet and I side with Monsiváis's right to never openly come out.

21 For a history of lesbian and feminist organization in Mexico and Latin America, see Norma Mongrovejo, *Un amor que se atrevió a decir su nombre: la lucha de las lesbianas y su relación con los movimientos homosexual y feminista en América Latina* (Mexico City: Plaza y Valdes, 2000).

22 For more on the "culturally institutionalized machismo" visible among "lesbians who imitate the masculinist ideal produced in film," see Shuessler, "Vestidas, locas."

23 "Juana Barraza, la mataviejitas—Asesinos Seriales." YouTube video, 2:30, posted by "Azteca Noticias," November 1, 2006, www.youtube.com/watch?v=nQQIw5PiL_U.

24 Agustín Salgado, "Del Mataviejitas, 24 de 32 asesinatos: Renato Sales," *La Jornada*, November 17, 2005.

25 Fernández, "Es 'mataviejitas' brillante."

26 Ostrosky, *Mentes asesinas: la violencia en tu cerebro*, 186.

27 Leticia Fernández and Manuel Durán, "Avala encinas a Bátiz en el caso 'mataviejitas,'" *Reforma*, December 20, 2005.

28 Brito and Corona, "Atrapan a mataviejitas, lleva lista de ancianas."

29 Sierra, "Analizan a seriales de Europa."

30 Padilla and Pérez, "Tarda hasta 20 años captura."

31 Barrón, *El nudo del silencio*.

32 Francisco Reséndiz, "La detención por suerte y no por investigación," *Crónica*, January 26, 2006.

33 Fernández, "Es 'mataviejitas' brillante."

34 Salgado and Servín, "Cae mataviejitas."

35 Ibid.

36 Hector Maudeleón, "En el 2003 iniciaron los asesinatos del 'mataviejitas,'" *El Universal*, November 8, 2005.

37 Salgado and Servín, "Cae mataviejitas."

38 Salgado, "Del mataviejitas."

39 Heredia, "Seis visiones en busca de un serial."

40 Padilla and Pérez, "Tarda hasta 20 años captura de asesinos."

41 Arturo Sierra, "Ligan a luchadores con 'mataviejitas,'" *Reforma*, January 31, 2006.

42 Dirección de Comunicación Institucional, "La Mataviejitas: 'una sociópata,' asegura académica de la UIA," news release, January 26, 2006.

BIBLIOGRAPHY

Acosta, Mariclaire. "The Women of Ciudad Juárez." Policy Paper No. 3, Center for Latin American Studies. University of California, Berkeley, 2005.
Adams, Richard N. "Cultural Components of Central America." *American Anthropologist* 58, no. 5 (1956): 881–907.
Aguilar García, Juan Carlos. "La Mataviejitas pertenece al tipo de asesino serial sin plan." *Crónica*, January 28, 2006.
Almazán, Alejandro. "Su devoción por La Santa Muerte." *El Universal*, April 19, 2001.
Alonso, Ana María. "Conforming Disconformity: Mestizaje, Hybridity, and the Aesthetics of Mexican Nationalism." *CUAN Cultural Anthropology* 19, no. 4 (2004): 459–90.
Alvarado, Noel. "Practicaba 'La Mataviejitas' magia negra para evitar ser descubierta." *La Prensa*, January 31, 2006.
Amnesty International. "Mexico: Torture and Sexual Violence against Women Detained in San Salvador Atenco—Two Years of Injustice and Impunity." United States: Amnesty International, April 29, 2008.
Amnesty International. "Mexico: Violence against Women and Justice Denied in Mexico State." London: Amnesty International, October 2006.
Amnistía Internacional. "México: Muertes intolerables—10 años de desapariciones y asesinatos de mujeres en Ciudad Juárez y Chihuahua." Mexico: Amnistía Internacional, 2003.
Amuchástegui, Ana. "Dialogue and the Negotiation of Meaning: Constructions of Virginity in Mexico." *Culture, Health & Sexuality* 1, no. 1 (1999): 79–93.
Amuchástegui, Ana, and Peter Aggleton. "I Had a Guilty Conscience Because I Wasn't Going to Marry Her: Ethical Dilemmas for Mexican Men in Their Sexual Relationships with Women." *Sexualities* 10, no. 1 (2016): 61–81.
Aridjis, Homero. *La Santa Muerte: sexteto del amor las mujeres, los perros y la muerte*. Mexico City: Alfaguara/Consejo Nacional para la Cultural y las Artes, 2004.
Arvizu, Juan. "Mataba a una viejita cada mes." *Reforma*, January 25, 2007.
"Atacan panistas al GDF con el tema del 'Mataviejitas': Trejo Pérez." *Agencia Mexicana de Noticias*, December 4, 2005.
Ávalos Guzmán, Sandra. *La nota roja: la sangre nuesta de cada dia*. Mexico City: Universidad Nacional Autónoma de México, 1988.
Baeza Lope, Ileana. "Sara García: Sapphic Romance in Mexican Golden Age Filmmaking." *Journal of Popular Romance Studies* 4, no. 1 (2014). http://jprstudies.org.

Bailón, Fabiola. "Prostitución, lenocinio y crimen: diferentes miradas en torno al caso de 'Las Poquianchis.'" In *Crimen y justicia en la historia de México. Nuevas Miradas*, edited by Elisa Speckman and Salvador Cárdenas, 409–54. Mexico City: Suprema Corte de Justicia de la Nación, 2011.

———. *Mujeres en el servicio doméstico y la prostitución: sobrevivencia, control y vida cotidiana en la Oaxaca Porfiriana*. Mexico, D.F.: El Colegio de México, 2014.

Balsamo, Anne Marie. *Technologies of the Gendered Body: Reading Cyborg Women*. Durham, NC: Duke University Press, 1996.

Baranda, Antonio, and Ricardo Zamora. "Alista PGJDF retrato de otro mataviejitas." *Reforma*, August 24, 2005.

Barrón Cruz, Martín Gabriel. *El nudo del silencio: tras la pista de una asesina en serie, La Mataviejitas*. Mexico City: Editorial Océano de México, 2006.

Bartra, Roger. *The Cage of Melancholy: Identity and Metamorphosis in the Mexican Character*. New Brunswick, NJ: Rutgers University Press, 1992.

———. *La jaula de la melancolía: identidad y metamorfosis del mexicano*. Mexico City: Grijalbo, 1996.

Basilio, Miriam. "Corporal Evidence: Representations of Aileen Wuornos." *Art Journal* 55, no. 4 (1996): 56–61.

Benítez, Rohry, Adriana Candia, Patricia Cabrera, Guadalupe de la Mora, Josefina Martínez, Isabel Velázquez, and Ramona Ortiz. *El silencio que la voz de todas quiebra: mujeres y víctimas de Ciudad Juárez*. Chihuahua: Ediciones del AZAR, 1999.

Berkins, Lohanna. *Cumbia, copeteo y lágrimas*. Buenos Aires: ALITT, 2007.

Berlanga Gayón, Mariana. "El espectáculo de la violencia en el México actual: del feminicidio al juvenicidio." *Athenea Digital* 15, no. 4 (December 2015): 105–28.

———. *Una mirada al feminicidio*. Mexico, D.F.: Universidad de la Ciudad de México, 2018.

Birch, Helen. Introduction to *Moving Targets: Women, Murder and Representation*, edited by Helen Birch, 1–6. Berkeley: University of California Press, 1994.

Birke, Lynda, and Gail Vines. "A Sporting Chance: The Anatomy of Destiny?" *Women's Studies International Forum* 10, no. 4 (1987): 337–47.

Bliss, Katherine Elaine. *Compromised Positions: Prostitution, Public Health, and Gender Politics in Revolutionary Mexico City*. University Park: Pennsylvania State University Press, 2001.

Bolaños, Claudia. "Buscan 'mataviejitas' entre-sexoservidores." *El Universal*, October 18, 2005.

———. "Otros cuatro, sentenciados por muerte de ancianas." *El Universal*, January 26, 2006.

———. "Las maté por rencor y odio." *El Universal*, January 27, 2006.

———. "Muestra 'Mataviejitas' indiferencia por víctimas." *El Universal*, August 3, 2006.

Bolaños, Claudia, and Fabiola Cancino. "Saldrá libre con fianza ex amiga de La Mataviejitas." *El Gráfico*, February 9, 2006.

Bolaños, Claudia, Óscar Herrera, and Ángeles Velazco. "'Las maté por rencor y rabia.'" *Reforma*, January 26, 2006.

Bonfil Batalla, Guillermo. *Utopía y revolución: el pensamiento político contemporáneo de los indios en América Latina*. Mexico City: Editorial Nueva Imagen, 1981.
———. *México Profundo: Reclaiming a Civilization*. Translated by Philip Adams Dennis. Austin: University of Texas Press, 1996.
Botsch, Robert J. "Jesus Malverde's Significance to Mexican Drug Traffickers." *FBI Law Enforcement Bulletin* 77 (2008): 19–22.
Brandes, Stanley H. "Is There a Mexican View of Death?" *Ethos* 31 (2003): 127–44.
Brito, Luis. "Fallan sus amuletos." *Reforma*, February 1, 2006.
———. "Puede Barraza tener 27 víctimas." *Reforma*, February 19, 2006.
———. "Nadie estaba listo para Juana Barraza." *Reforma*, January 27, 2007.
———. "Ven en 'poeta caníbal' perfil de asesino serial." *Reforma*, October 11, 2007.
Brito, Luis, and Juan Corona. "Atrapan a mataviejitas, lleva lista de ancianas." *Reforma*, January 26, 2006.
Bueno-Hansen, Pascha. "Feminicidio: Making the Most of an 'Empowered Term.'" In *Terrorizing Women: Feminicide in the Américas*, edited by Rosa Linda Fregoso and Cynthia L. Bejarano, 290–311. Durham, NC: Duke University Press, 2010.
Buffington, Robert M. *Criminal and Citizen in Modern Mexico*. Lincoln: University of Nebraska Press, 2000.
Butler, Judith. *Gender Trouble: Feminism and the Subversion of Identity*. New York: Routledge, 1990.
———. *Bodies That Matter: On the Discursive Limits of "Sex."* London and New York: Routledge, 1993.
———. "Critically Queer." *GLQ: A Journal of Lesbian and Gay Studies* 1, no. 1 (1993): 17–32.
———. *Excitable Speech: A Politics of the Performative*. New York: Routledge, 1997.
Cabral, Mauro, and Paula Viturro. "(Trans)Sexual Citizenship in Contemporary Argentina." In *Transgender Rights*, edited by Paisley Currah, Richard M. Juang, and Shannon Minter, 262–73. Minneapolis: University of Minnesota Press, 2006.
Cacho, Lydia. "El Estado de México: feminicidios ignorados." *Lydia Cacho* (blog), January 12, 2011. www.lydiacacho.com.
Campbell, Anne. *Men, Women and Aggression*. New York: Basic Books, 1993.
"Capturan a presunto feminicida de Chimalhuacán." *El Universal*, October 18, 2006.
Caputi, Jane. *The Age of Sex Crime*. Bowling Green, OH: Bowling Green State University Popular Press, 1987.
Castells, Pilar. "La Santa Muerte y la cultura de los derechos humanos." *LiminaR. Estudios sociales y humanísticos* 6 (2008): 13.
Castillo, Rafael. "Asesinadas en el Estado de México: una silenciosa epidemia." *Vice News*, November 24, 2016. www.vice.com.
Chesnut, R. Andrew. *Devoted to Death: Santa Muerte, the Skeleton Saint*. New York: Oxford University Press, 2012.
———. "Devoted to Death: Santa Muerte, the Skeleton Saint." *Contemporary Sociology* 42, no. 4 (2013): 635.

Christie, Donald, Graham Davies, John Shepherd, and Ellis Haydyn. "Evaluating a New Computer-Based System for Face Recall." *Law and Human Behavior* 5, nos. 2–3 (1981): 209–18.

Collier, Richard. *Masculinities, Crime, and Criminology: Men, Heterosexuality, and the Criminal(ised) Other*. London: Sage, 1998.

Córdoba Plaza, Rosío. "Sexualidad, género y parentesco: dinámicas familiares en un contexto de significados en transformación." In *Familia y tradición: herencias tangibles e intangibles en escenarios cambiantes*, edited by Nora Edith Jímenez Hernández, 361–78. Zamora: El Colegio de Michoacán, 2010.

Crain, Caleb. "Lovers of Human Flesh: Homosexuality and Cannibalism in Melville's Novels." *American Literature* 66, no. 1 (1994): 25–53.

Cruz, Mónica. "Por qué no se puede gritar 'puto' en los estadios sin ofender." *El País*, June 21, 2017.

Dark, Angelita. "La lucha libre presente en las jornadas universitarias de la UAM Cuajimalpa." *Superluchas*, October 26, 2016. https://superluchas.com.

Davison, Phil. "Esther Chávez: Prominent Women's Rights Activist." *Independent*, January 15, 2010. www.independent.co.uk.

Dean, Carolyn, and Dana Leibsohn. "Hybridity and Its Discontents: Considering Visual Culture in Colonial Spanish America." *Colonial Latin American Review* 12, no. 1 (2003): 5–35.

Degetau, Jorge. "Malverde y la santísima: cultos y credos en el México Posmoderno." *Metapolítica* 12, no. 67 (2009): 20–24.

"Deja Martha Villalobos legado en la lucha libre." *Hoy. Estado de México,* October 1, 2012.

De la Madrid, Ricardo Raphael. "La muerte tuvo permiso." *Nexos*, July 1, 1999.

De la Mora, Sergio. *Cinemachismo: Masculinities and Sexuality in Mexican Film*. Austin: University of Texas Press, 2006.

Delgado, Álvaro. "El Yunque, la mano que mece al Frente Nacional por la familia." *Proceso*, September 9, 2016.

Díaz, César, and Arturo Sierra. "Paga mataviejitas protección a judiciales." *Reforma*, February 2, 2006.

Diez, Jordi. "La trayectoria política del movimiento lésbico-gay en México." *Estudios Sociológicos* 29, no. 86 (2011): 687–712.

Dirección de Comunicación Institucional. "La Mataviejitas: 'una sociópata,' asegura académica de la UIA." News release, 2006.

Duggan, Lisa. *Sapphic Slasher: Sex, Violence, and American Modernity*. Durham, NC: Duke University Press, 2000. doi: 0-8223-2609-4.

Echarri Cánovas, Carlos Javier. *La violencia feminicida en México: aproximaciones y tendencias 1985–2014*. México Secretaria de Gobernación, Instituto Nacional de las Mujeres, ONU Mujeres, Entidad de las Naciones Unidas para la Igualdad de Género y el Empoderamiento de las Mujeres, April 2016.

"Encuentran fotos de víctima de 'Matanovias,' tomadas horas antes de su muerte." *El Universal*, March 23, 2017.

"En México la homofobia se paga con multa." *BBC*, March 8, 2013.
Fascinetto, Lola Miranda. *Sin máscara ni cabellera: lucha libre en México hoy*. Mexico City: Marc Ediciones, S.A. de C.V., 1992.
Fernández, Leticia. "Es 'mataviejitas' brillante: Bátiz." *Reforma*, October 11, 2005.
Fernández, Leticia, and Manuel Durán. "Avala Encinas a Bátiz en el caso 'mataviejitas.'" *Reforma*, December 20, 2005.
Ferrer, Gladys. "Indaga Edomex ADN del 'asesino del bordo.'" *Reforma*, April 14, 2006.
Flores, Enrique, and Raúl Eduardo González. "Malverde: exvotos y corridos (en las voces de cantores sinaloenses)." *Caravelle*, no. 88 (January 2007): 29.
Flores Martos, Juan A. "Iconografías emergentes y muerte patrimonializadas en América Latina: Santa Muerte, muertos milagrosos y muertos adoptados." *Revista de Antropología Iberoamericana* 9 (2014): 115–40.
Forbes Staff. "Los 10 estados con más pobres en México." *Forbes México*, August 27, 2015. www.forbes.com.mx.
Ford, Ruth. "'The Man-Woman Murderer': Sex Fraud, Sexual Inversion and the Unmentionable 'Article' in 1920s Australia." *Gender and History* 12, no. 1 (2000): 158–96.
Foucault, Michel. "The Confession of the Flesh." In *Power/Knowledge: Selected Interviews and Other Writings*, edited by Colin Gordon. New York: Pantheon Books, 1980.
———. "The Dangerous Individual." In *Politics, Philosophy, Culture: Interviews and Other Writings 1977–1984*, edited by Lawrence Kritzman. London: Routledge, 1988.
Fox, James Alan, and Jack Levin. "Multiple Homicide: Patterns of Serial and Mass Murder." *Crime and Justice* 23 (1998): 407–55.
Fragoso, Perla. "De la 'calavera domada' a la subversión santificada: La Santa Muerte, un nuevo imaginario religioso en México." *El Cotidiano: Revista de la realidad mexicana*, no. 169 (2011): 5–16.
Frazer, Elizabeth, and Deborah Cameron. *The Lust to Kill: A Feminist Investigation of Sexual Murder*. New York: New York University Press, 1987.
French, William E. "Prostitutes and Guardian Angels: Women, Work, and the Family in Porfirian Mexico." *Hispanic American Historical Review* 72, no. 4 (1992): 529–53.
Friedlander, Judith. *Being Indian in Hueyapan: A Study of Forced Identity in Contemporary Mexico*. Revised and updated ed. New York: St. Martin's Press, 2006.
Gall, Olivia. "Identidad, exclusión y racismo: reflexiones teóricas y sobre México." *Revista Mexicana de Sociología* 66, no. 2 (2004): 221–59.
Gamio, Manuel. "Poblacion indo-mestiza." In *Acculturation in the Americas: Proceedings and Selected Papers of the XXIXth International Congress of Americanists*, edited by Sol Tax, 267–70. Chicago: University of Chicago Press, 1952.
García, Jacobo. "Estado de México, capital del feminicidio." *El País*, May 18, 2017. http://internacional.elpais.com.
García Hernández, Arturo. "El caso de La Mataviejitas, retrato de la degradación social que vivimos." *La Jornada*, July 16, 2006.
Gaskell, Katja. "Lucha Libre—an Introduction to Mexican Wrestling." *Lonely Planet*, February 2017. www.lonelyplanet.com.

Gaytán, Felipe. "Santa entre los malditos: culto a La Santa Muerte en el México del siglo XXI." *LiminaR. Estudios sociales y humanísticos* 6 (2008): 40–51.

Gilbert, Paula Ruth. "Discourses of Female Violence and Societal Gender Stereotypes." *Violence against Women* 8, no. 11 (2002): 1271–300.

Gittings, Christopher. "*Zero Patience*, Genre, Difference, and Ideology: Singing and Dancing Queer Nation." *Cinema Journal* 41, no. 1 (2001): 28–39.

Gómez, Michel Gerardo, and Jungwon Park. "The Cult of Jesús Malverde: Crime and Sanctity as Elements of a Heterogeneous Modernity." *Latin American Perspectives* 41, no. 2 (2014): 203–14.

Gonzáles, Daniel "¿Es que no sábes que eres un hombre? Star system y masculinidades en cinco autores del cine mexicano." Paper presented at Cineteca Nacional, July 22, 2015.

González, Sergio. "Bajo la protección de la santísima." *Reforma*, October 28, 2001.

———. *Huesos en el desierto*. Editorial Anagrama, 2002.

Grayson, George W. *The Evolution of Los Zetas in Mexico and Central America: Sadism as an Instrument of Cartel Warfare*. Carlisle Barracks, PA: United States Army War College Press, 2014.

Green, David. "Veins of Resemblance: Photography and Eugenics." *Oxford Art Journal* 7, no. 2 (1984): 3–16.

Grindstaff, Laura, and Martha McCaughey. "Re-Membering John Bobbitt: Castration Anxiety, Male Hysteria, and the Phallus." In *No Angels: Women Who Commit Violence*, edited by Alice Myers and Sarah Wight, 142–60. London: Pandora, 1996.

Gutmann, Matthew C. *The Meanings of Macho: Being a Man in Mexico City*. Berkeley: University of California Press, 1996.

Hacking, Ian. "Making Up People." In *The Science Studies Reader*, edited by Mario Biagioli, 161–71. New York: Routledge, 1999.

Haley, Shawn D., and Curt Fukuda. *Day of the Dead: When Two Worlds Meet in Oaxaca*. New York and Oxford: Berghahn Books, 2004.

Hall, Linda. *Mary, Mother and Warrior: The Virgin in the Spain and the Americas*. Austin: University of Texas Press, 2004.

Hall, Stuart, Chas Critcher, Tony Jefferson, John Clarke, and Brian Roberts. *Policing the Crisis: The State, Mugging and Law and Order*. London: Macmillan, 1978.

Ham, Ricardo. *México y sus asesinos seriales*. Mexico City: Ediciones Samsara, 2007.

———. "Historia 'El Sádico' que atemorizó a la comunidad gay." *El Universal*, June 1, 2014.

Ham, Ricardo, and Cutberto Enríquez. *Exposición asesinos seriales*. Mexico City: Centro Cultural Policial, 2007.

Hare, Robert. "This Charming Psychopath." *Psychology Today*, January 1, 1994. www.psychologytoday.com.

———. *Without Conscience: The Disturbing World of the Psychopaths among Us*. New York: Guilford Press, 1999.

Hasel E., Lisa, and Gary L. Wells. "Catching the Bad Guy: Morphing Composite Faces Helps." *Law and Human Behavior* 31, no. 2 (2007): 193–207.

Heredia, Renato Sales. "Seis visiones en busca de un serial." *Proceso*, February 12, 2006, 46–49.

Hernández López, Julio. "Teatritos." *La Jornada*, February 13, 2006.

Herrera, Óscar. "Hampones comunes copian el estilo del mataviejitas." *El Universal*, January 24, 2006.

Herrera, Óscar, Icela Lagunas, and Rubelio Fernández, "Luchadora de 48 años fue detenida luego de estrangular a una mujer. Cae presunta mataviejitas." *El Universal*, January 26, 2006.

Hoechtl, Nina. "Lucha libre: un espacio liminal. Lis Exótiquis 'Juntopuestas' a las categorías clasificadoras, unívocas y fijas." In *La memoria y el deseo. Estudios gay y queer en México*, edited by Parrini Rosas Rodrigo and Alejandro Brito, 223–51. México Centro de Investigaciones y Estudios de Género. Universidad Nacional Autónoma de México, 2014.

Holmes, Ronald M., and James E. De Burger. *Serial Murder*. Newbury Park, CA: Sage Publications, 1988.

Huffschmid, Anne. "Devoción satanizada: la muerte como nuevo culto callejero en la Ciudad de México." *Mex Revista Mexico Interdisciplinario* 2, no. 3 (2012): 105–7.

Jack, Dana Crowley. *Behind the Mask: Destruction and Creativity in Women's Aggression*. Cambridge, MA: Harvard University Press, 2001.

Janowitz, Nathaniel. "Así es como los padrotes de Tlaxcala atraen niñas al mundo de la trata." *Vice News*, July 9, 2015. www.vice.com.

Jarcoreradiotj. "La lucha libre femenil en México, grandes mujeres que forjaron una trayectoria en tiempos difíciles." *Superluchas*, March 26, 2013. https://superluchas.com.

Jarvis, Brian. "Monsters Inc.: Serial Killers and Consumer Culture." *Crime, Media, Culture* 3, no. 3 (2007): 326–44.

Jiménez, Carlos. "Atrapan a La Mataviejitas: es mujer y es luchadora." *Crónica*, January 26, 2006, 1.

———. "Juana Barraza: analfabeta, su madre la regaló a los 12 años, fue violada y le mataron un hijo a batazos." *Crónica*, January 27, 2006.

———. "La Mataviejitas coleccionaba recortes de periódicos con las historias de sus homicidios." *Crónica*, January 30, 2006.

———. "Mataviejitas fue a PGJDF a entregarse y no la atendieron." *Crónica*, February 8, 2006.

Jiménez, Carlos, and R. Sánchez. "Detiene PGJDF a 49, pero ninguno es El Mataviejitas." *Crónica*, October 5, 2005.

Jiménez Hernández, Nora Edith. Introduction to *Familia y Tradición. Herencias tangibles e intangibles en escenarios cambiantes*, edited by Nora Edith Jiménez Hernández, 11–34. Zamora: El Colegio de Michoacán, 2010.

Jones, Ann. *Women Who Kill*. 2nd ed. New York: Feminist Press, 2009.

Jónsdóttir, Kristín Guðrún. "De bandolero a ejemplo moral: los corridos sobre Jesús Malverde, el santo amante de la música." *Studies in Latin American Popular Culture* 25 (2006): 25–48.

Juárez, Blanca. "Marcha de la primavera feminista: 'hartas de la violencia.'" *La Jornada*, April 24, 2016.

Kahn, Carrie. "How Mexico Quietly Legalized Same-Sex Marriage." *Parallels*, NPR, June 16, 2015. www.npr.org.

Knight, Alan. "Racism, Revolution, and Indigenismo: Mexico, 1910–1940." In *The Idea of Race in Latin America, 1870–1940*, edited by Richard Graham, Thomas E. Skidmore, Aline Helg, and Alan Knight, 71–113. Austin: University of Texas Press, 1990.

Lagarde, Marcela. "Del femicidio al feminicidio." *Desde el Jardín de Freud. Revista de Psicoanálisis*, no. 6 (2006): 216–25.

Laguarda, Rodrigo. *Ser gay en la ciudad de México: lucha de representaciones y apropiación de una identidad, 1968–1982*. Mexico City: Instituto Mora, 2009.

———. *La calle de Amberes: Gay Street de la ciudad de México*. Mexico City: Instituto Mora, 2011.

Lamas, Marta. "De trasvestis y asesinos en serie." *Proceso*, November 6, 2005.

Lara, Estela Bravo. "Bajo tu manto nos acogemos: devotos a La Santa Muerte en la Zona Metropolitana de Guadalajara." *Nueva Antropología A.C.* 26, no. 79 (2013): 11–28.

Lara Mireles, María C. "El culto a La Santa Muerte en el entramado simbólico de la sociedad del riesgo." *Anuario CONEICC de Investigación de la Comunicación*, no. 15 (2008): 285–98.

Lemus, Rafael. "La raza cósmica." *Letras Libres*, March 31, 2010.

Levi, Heather. "Lean Mean Fighting Queens: Drag in the World of Mexican Professional Wrestling." *Sexualities* 1, no. 3 (1998): 275–85.

Lewis, Vek. *Crossing Sex and Gender in Latin America*. New York: Palgrave Macmillan, 2010.

"Liberan a el cerillo, inculpado en asesinatos de mujeres en Cd. Juárez." *Proceso*, July 15, 2005.

Limón, José. "La Llorona, the Third Legend of Greater Mexico: Cultural Symbols, Women, and the Political Unconscious." In *Between Borders: Essays on Mexicana/ Chicana History* edited by Adelaida del Castillo, 399–432. Encino, CA: Floricanto Press, 2005.

List Reyes, Mauricio. "Construcción de lugares gay en la Ciudad de México: el Bol Polanco y la cervecería La Lilí." *Iztapalapa* (1999): 309–18.

———. *Jóvenes corazones gay en la Ciudad de México: género, identidad y socialidad en hombres gay*. Puebla: Universidad Benemérita Autónoma de Puebla, 2005.

Logan, Samuel. "Preface: Los Zetas and a New Barbarism." *Small Wars and Insurgencies* 22, no. 5 (2011): 718–27.

Loizidou, Elena. *Judith Butler: Ethics, Law, Politics*. New York: Routledge-Cavendish, 2007.

Lomnitz, Claudio. *Death and the Idea of Mexico*. Brooklyn, NY: Zone Books, 2005.

Lomnitz, Larissa, and Marisol Pérez Lizaur. "Dynastic Growth and Survival Strategies: The Solidarity of Mexican Grand-Families." In *Kinship Ideology and Practice in Latin America*, edited by Raymond T. Smith, 183–95. Chapel Hill: University of North Carolina Press, 1984.

López, Óscar David. "Macho calado: ya probaste y no te gustó, ¿o sí?" *Vice News*, August 10, 2005. www.vice.com.

Marchi, Regina. "Hybridity and Authenticity in US Day of the Dead Celebrations." *Journal of American Folklore* 126, no. 501 (2013): 272–301.

Martín, Desirée A. *Borderlands Saints: Secular Sanctity in Chicano/a and Mexican Culture*. New Brunswick, NJ: Rutgers University Press, 2013.

Martínez Baca, Francisco, and Manuel Vergara. *Estudios de antropología criminal*. Puebla: Benjamin Lara, 1892.

Martínez, Fernando. "Dan 280 de cárcel a asesino de homosexuales." *El Universal*, February 7, 2010.

———. "Detienen a 'El Coqueto'; un feminicida serial." *El Universal*, February 27, 2012.

Martínez-Zalce, Graciela, Laura Carballido, and Victor Manuel Grandos. "Representaciones cinematográficas y cartográficas de la violencia en la Ciudad de México." *El cotidiano: revista de la realidad mexicana actual* 22, no. 145 (2007): 40–56.

"Matanovias destrozó la vida de mi hermana en dos meses." *Milenio Digital*, March 15, 2017.

Maudeleón, Hector. "En el 2003 iniciaron los asesinatos del 'Mataviejitas,'" *El Universal*, November 8, 2005.

McCaskell, Tim. *Queer Progress: From Homophobia to Homonationalism*. Toronto: Between the Lines, 2016.

Medina, Cuauhtémoc. "Alarma! Crime and Publishing." *Poliester* 2, no. 6 (1993): 18–27.

Mejía, Fabrizio. "Mi mente radiante." *Proceso*, December 5, 2004, 40–42.

Mexico City Comisión Nacional de Derechos Humanos. "Recomendación Atenco." 2006.

Mexico City Human Rights Commission. *Special Report on Homophobia and Hate Crimes*. Mexico City, 2007.

Mogrovejo, Norma. *Un amor que se atrevió a decir su nombre: la lucha de las lesbianas y su relación con los movimientos homosexual y feminista en América Latina*. Mexico City: Plaza y Valdés, 2000.

"Los momentos importantes de la lucha libre femenil en México." *Excélsior*, July 19, 2017.

Monárrez Fragoso, Julia Estela. "La cultura del feminicidio en Ciudad Juárez." *Frontera Norte* 12, no. 23 (2000): 87–117.

———. "Feminicidio sexual serial en Ciudad Juárez: 1993–2001." *Debate Feminista* 25, no. 13 (2002): 279–305.

———. *Trama de una injusticia: feminicidio sexual sistémico en Ciudad Juárez*. Chihuahua: El Colegio de la Frontera Norte, 2012.

Monárrez Fragoso, Julia, and César Fuentes. "Feminicidio y marginalidad urbana en Ciudad Juárez en la década de los noventa." In *Violencia contra las mujeres en contextos urbanos y rurales*, edited by Marta Torres Falcón, 58–66. Mexico City: Colegio de México, 2004.

Moneda, Comandante Victor Hugo. Interview by the author, August 13, 2007.

Monsiváis, Carlos. "¿Tantos millones de hombres no hablaremos inglés? (La cultura Norteamericana y México)." In *Simbiosis de culturas*, edited by Guillermo Bonfil

Batalla, 455–516. México, D.F.: Fondo de Cultura Económica. Consejo Nacional para la Cultura y las Artes, 1993.

———. *Mexican Postcards*. Translated by John Kraniauskas. Edited by James Dunkerly and King John. Critical Studies in Latin American and Iberian Cultures. London: Verso, 1997.

———. "Un mal día en la vida de Daniel Arizmendi." *Proceso*, August 28, 1998.

———. *Lourdes Grobet: Lucha Libre, Masked Superstars of Mexican Wrestling*, edited by Alfonso Morales. Mexico City: DAP/Trilce, 2008.

———. *Pedro Infante: Las leyes del querer*. Mexico City: Ediciones raya en el agua, S.A. de C.V, 2008.

———. "¡Esa no es mi hija!, ¡Ésa es una perdida! El melodrama y la invención de la familia." In *Familia y tradición. herencias tangibles e intangibles en escenarios cambiantes*, edited by Nora Edith Jímenez Hernández, 605–10. Zamora: El Colegio de Michoacán, 2010.

———. *Los mil y un velorios: crónica de la nota roja en México*. Mexico City: Debate/Fondo de Cultura Económica, 2010 (original edition, 1994).

Moreno Figueroa, Mónica G. "Historically Rooted Transnationalism: Slightedness and the Experience of Racism in Mexican Families." *Journal of Intercultural Studies* 29, no. 3 (2008): 283–97.

———. "Looking Emotionally: Photography, Racism and Intimacy in Research." *History of the Human Sciences* 21, no. 4 (2008): 68–85.

———. "Distributed Intensities: Whiteness, Mestizaje and the Logics of Mexican Racism." *Ethnicities* 10, no. 3 (2010): 387–401.

Moreno Figueroa, Mónica G., and Emiko Saldívar Tanaka. "'We Are Not Racists, We Are Mexicans': Privilege, Nationalism and Post-Race Ideology in Mexico." *Critical Sociology* 42, nos. 4–5 (2015): 1–9.

Mulhare, Hielen. "Respetar y confiar: ideología de género versus comportamiento en una sociedad nahua." In *Familia y parentesco en México y Mesoamérica: unas miradas antropológicas*, edited by David Robichaux, 267–91. Mexico City: Universidad Iberoamericana, 2003.

Mulholland, Mary-Lee. "Mariachi, Myths and Mestizaje: Popular Culture and Mexican National Identity." *National Identities* 9, no. 3 (2007): 247–64.

"La Múltiple Lucha. Mesa de diálogo y proyección de cine." Museo Universitario de Arte Contemporáneo, October 21, 2017.

Muñoz, Alma. "Mueren siete mujeres al dia en promedio presuntamente víctimas de homicidio." *La Jornada*, November 13, 2014.

Muñoz, Fernando. *Sara García*. Mexico City: Editorial Clío, libros y video, S.A. de C.V., 1998.

Nabhan-Warren, Kristy. *The Virgin of El Barrio: Marian Apparitions, Catholic Evangelizing, and Mexican American Activism*. New York: New York University Press, 2005.

Nájar, Alberto. "La cacería de El Mataviejitas, el costo de negar al asesino." *La Jornada*, October 9, 2005.

Nesving, Martin. "The Complicated Terrain of Latin American Homosexuality." In *Hispanic American Historical Review* 81, nos. 3–4 (2001): 689–729.
Nila, Miguel. "Ningún trasvesti resultó ser El Mataviejitas: Bátiz." *Noticieros Televisa*, October 24, 2005.
Nuñez, Lucía. "Contribución a la crítica de feminismo punitivo." In *La bifurcación del caos: reflexiones interdisciplinarias sobre violencia falocetrica*, edited by María Guadalupe Huacuz Elias, 173–95. Mexico City: ITACA-UAM Xochimilco, 2012.
Núñez Cetina, Saydi Cecilia. "Delito, género y transgresiones: los discursos sobre la criminalidad femenina en la Ciudad de México, 1877–1910." MA thesis, Colegio de México, 2005.
Nuñez Noriega, Guillermo. *Sexo entre varones. Poder y resistencia en el campo sexual.* México, El Colegio de Sonora. PUEG: Universidad Nacional Autónoma de México 1999.
———. *Just between Us: An Ethnography of Male Identity and Intimacy in Rural Communities of Northern Mexico.* Tucson: University of Arizona Press, 2014.
ONU Mujeres México. "Eliminación de la violencia contra mujeres y niñas." Accessed May 2017. http://mexico.unwomen.org.
Ostrosky, Feggy. *Mentes asesinas: la violencia en tu cerebro.* Mexico City: Hachette Filipacchi Expansión de R.L. de C.V., 2008.
Otero, Silvia. "Presenta AFI a asesino serial de homosexuales." *El Universal*, January 26, 2006.
———. "Reconoce crímenes contra gays 'sin remordimientos.'" *El Universal*, January 27, 2006.
Padgett, Humberto, and Eduardo Loza. *Las muertas del estado: feminicidios durante la administración mexiquense de Enrique Peña Nieto.* Mexico City: Grijalbo, 2014. E-book.
Padilla, Jesús. "Es 'serial' prioridad para Bátiz." *Reforma*, September 1, 2005.
Padilla, Jesús, and Jorge Pérez. "Tarda hasta 20 años captura de asesinos." *Reforma*, November 12, 2005.
Palacios, Agustín. "El problema de La Malintzin como expresión concreta del encuentro." In *El mexicano: educación, historia y personalidad*, 47–63. Mexico City: Secretaría de Educación Pública, Insituto Federal de Capacitación del Magisterio, and Ediciones Oasis, S.A., 1966.
Pantoja, Sara. "México, segundo lugar mundial en crímenes por homofobia." *Proceso*, May 11, 2015.
Parrini Rosas, Rodrigo. *Panópticos y laberintos: subjetivación, deseo, y corporalidad en una cárcel de hombres.* Mexico City: El Colegio de México, 2007.
Parrini Rosas, Rodrigo, and Alejandro Brito Lemus. *Crímenes de odio por homofobia: un concepto en construcción.* Mexico City: Letra S and Sida, Cultura, y Vida Cotidiana, A.C., 2012.
Paz, Octavio. *El laberinto de la soledad.* 2nd ed. Mexico City: Fondo de Cultura Económica, 1998.

"Pediran panistas destituir a Bátiz por no atrapar al 'mataviejitas,'" Agencia Mexicana de Noticias, December 8, 2005.

Perdigón Castañeda, Katia. *La Santa Muerte, protectora de los hombres*. Mexico City: Instituto Nacional de Antropología e Historia, 2008.

Pérez, Jorge. "Desoye Bátiz a ALDF." *Reforma*, September 15, 2005.

Pérez Jiménez, Marco Antonio. "Nación deseada, nación heredada: la población negra y el imaginario de las élites dirigentes en México: el caso de Guanajuato (1808–1830)." PhD diss., Universidad Nacional Autónoma de México, 2011.

Phillips, Sandra S. "Identifying the Criminal." In *Police Pictures: The Photograph as Evidence*, 11–31. San Francisco: San Francisco Museum of Modern Art/Chronicle Books, 1997.

Picart, Caroline. "Crime and the Gothic: Sexualizing Serial Killers." *Journal of Criminal Justice and Popular Culture* 13, no. 1 (2006): 1–18.

Picart, Caroline, and Cecil Greek. "The Compulsion of Real/Reel Serial Killers and Vampires: Toward a Gothic Criminology." *Journal of Criminal Justice and Popular Culture* 10, no. 1 (2003): 39–68.

Piccato, Pablo. *City of Suspects: Crime in Mexico City, 1900–1931*. Durham, NC, and London: Duke University Press, 2001.

———. "'El Chalequero' or the Mexican Jack the Ripper: The Meanings of Sexual Violence in Turn-of-the-Century Mexico City." *Hispanic American Historical Review* 81, no. 3 (2001): 623–51.

———. *A History of Infamy: Crime, Truth, and Justice in Mexico*. Violence in Latin American History. Oakland: University of California Press, 2017.

Poniatowska, Elena. "'El Santo' a dos de tres caídas." In *Todo México*, 255–84. Mexico City: Editoriales Diana, 1990.

Price, Patricia. "Of Bandits and Saints: Jesús Malverde and the Struggle for Place in Sinaloa, Mexico." *Cultural Geographies* 12, no. 2 (2005): 175–97.

Prieur, Annick. *Mema's House, Mexico City: On Transvestites, Queens, and Machos*. Chicago: University of Chicago Press, 1998.

Procuraduría General de Justicia del Distrito Federal. "El sistema de retrato hablado más avanzado del país en la PGJDF." News release, June 20, 2004.

Puar, Jasbir K. *Terrorist Assemblages: Homonationalism in Queer Times*. Tenth-anniversary expanded edition. Next Wave. Durham, NC: Duke University Press, 2017.

"¿Qué dice el frente nacional por la familia?" *Excélsior*, August 23, 2016.

"¿Qué pasó con? . . . 'El Coqueto,' el feminicida que violaba en un microbus." *El Universal*, June 12, 2017.

Quinney, Richard. "Who Is the Victim?" *Criminology* 10, no. 3 (1972): 314–23.

Quiroz Cuarón, Alfonso. *Un estrangulador de mujeres*. Mexico City, S.E., 1952.

Radford, Jill, and Diana Russell. *Femicide: The Politics of Woman Killing*. New York: Twayne, 1992.

Rafter, Nicole Hahn, and Frances Heidensohn. *International Feminist Perspectives in Criminology: Engendering a Discipline*. Buckingham: Open University Press, 1995.

Raine, Adrian, "Psychopathy, Violence and Brain Imaging." In *Violence and Psychopathy*, edited by Adrian Raine and José Sanmartín, 35–55. New York: Kluwer Academic/Plenum Centro Reina Sofia, 2001.

Ramón, Rene. "Sospechan de asesino serial en Edomex." *La Jornada*, April 24, 2006.

Ramos-Araizaga, Michael, dir. *Los Exóticos: Luchadores completos, pero con diversidad arriba del cuadrilátero*, 83 min. Erika Magaña Euroza/Ñaña Films, 2013.

Rapisardi, Flavio. "Regulaciones políticas: identidad, diferencia y desigualdad. Una crítica al debate contemporáneo." In *Sexualidades migrantes: género y transgénero*, edited by Diana Maffía, 97–116. Buenos Aires: Librería de Mujeres Editoras, 2009.

Reina, Elena. "Ecaptec despierta los demonios de Ciudad Juárez." *El País*, April 22, 2016. https://internacional.elpais.com.

Reisinger, Deborah S. "Murder and Banality in the Contemporary *fait divers*." *South Central Review* 17, no. 4 (2000): 84–99.

Reséndiz, Francisco. "La detención por suerte y no por investigación." *Crónica*, January 26, 2006.

Ressler, Robert, with Tom Shachtman. *Whoever Fights Monsters: My Twenty Years Tracking Serial Killers for the FBI*. New York: St. Martin's Press, 1992.

Reyes, Adrián. "Seguridad-México: ancianas en la mira de la misoginia." *Inter Press Service*, December 16, 2005.

Rincón, Fernando del. "La verdad de Juan Gabriel." *Primer Impacto*, December 17, 2002.

Rivas, Carlos Coria. "Sentencian en Juárez a asesinos de 15 mujeres." *El Universal*, January 7, 2005.

Robichaux, David. "Familia, grupo doméstico y grupos localizados de parentesco en el área cultural mesoamericana." In *Familia y tradición: herencias tangibles e intangibles en escenarios cambiantes*, edited by Nora Edith Jímenez Hernández, 83–108. Zamora: El Colegio de Michoacán, 2010.

Ronquillo, Víctor. *Ruda de corazón: el blues de La Mataviejitas*. Mexico City: Ediciones B, S.A. de C.V., 2006.

Roush, Laura. "Santa Muerte, Protection, and Desamparo: A View from a Mexico City Altar." *Latin America Research Review* 49 (2014): 129–48.

Rubin, Gayle. "The Traffic in Women: Notes on the 'Political Economy' of Sex." In *Toward an Anthropology of Women*, edited by Rayna Reiter, 157–210. New York: Monthly Review Press, 1975.

Ruiz, Claudia. "Historia y actualidad del culto a La Santa Muerte." *El Cotidiano. Revista de la Realidad Mexina*, no. 169 (2011): 51–57.

Rushton, Richard. "What Can a Face Do? On Deleuze and Faces." *Cultural Critique*, no. 51 (2002): 219–37.

Sada, Daniel. "Cada Piedra es un Deseo." *Letras Libres*, March 2000.

Salgado, Agustín. "Del mataviejitas, 24 de 32 asesinatos: Renato Sales." *La Jornada*, November 17, 2005.

Salgado, Agustín, Angel Bolaños, and Rene Ramón. "Tras las rejas, *La Mataviejitas*; el lunes se define su situación legal." *La Jornada*, January 28, 2006.

Salgado, Agustín, and Mirna Servín. "A Juana Barraza Zamperio le gusta el rojo y prefería los martes y miércoles para matar." *La Jornada*, January 26, 2006.

———. "Cae mataviejitas tras consumar otro de sus crímenes; es mujer." *La Jornada*, January 26, 2006.

Sánchez, Raymundo. "No era compló, sí existía, ya confesó." *Crónica*, January 27, 2006.

Sanders, Nichole. "Mothering Mexico: The Historiography of Mothers and Motherhood in 20th-Century Mexico." *HIC3 History Compass* 7, no. 6 (2009): 1542–53.

Schaefer, Claudia. *Danger Zones: Homosexuality, National Identity, and Mexican Culture*. Tucson: University of Arizona Press, 1996.

Schell, Patience A. *Church and State Education in Revolutionary Mexico City*. Tucson: University of Arizona Press, 2003.

Schram, Pamela J., and Barbara Koons-Witt. *Gendered (in)Justice: Theory and Practice in Feminist Criminology*. Long Grove, IL: Waveland Press, 2004.

Sedgwick, Eve Kosofsky. *Epistemology of the Closet*. Berkeley and Los Angeles: University of California Press, 1990.

———. "Queer Performativity: Henry James's *The Art of the Novel*." *GLQ: A Journal of Lesbian and Gay Studies* 1, no. 1 (1993): 1–16.

Segato, Rita. "¿Qué es un feminicidio? Notas para un debate emergente." In *Fronteras, violencia, justicia: Nuevos discursos*, edited by Marisa Belausteguigoitia and Lucía Melgar, 37–43. Mexico, D.F.: UNAM, 2007.

"SEGOB emite alerta de género para el Estado de México." *Excélsior*, July 31, 2015.

Sekula, Allan. "The Body and the Archive." *October* 39 (1986): 3–64.

Seltzer, Mark. *Serial Killers: Death and Life in America's Wound Culture*. New York: Routledge, 1998.

Serrano Sánchez, Carlos. Interview by the author, April 27, 2017.

———. "Un sistema automatizado de identificación de rasgos faciales (retrato hablado) para la población mexicana." In *La bibliotecología y la documentación en el contexto de la internacionalización y el acceso abierto*, 1–12. Mexico City: Universidad Nacional Autónoma de México, 2013.

Serrano Sánchez, Carlos, María Villanueva Sagrado, Jesús Luy, and Karl F. Link. "Los rasgos faciales del mexicano y los retratos hablados por computadora." *Revista Universidad de México*, no. 575 (1998): 61–63.

Servín, Mirna. "Asesiné por las 'malas compañías': La Mataviejitas." *La Jornada*, January 27, 2006.

———. "La Dama del Silencio." *Reforma*, March 23, 2008.

———. "Dan 759 años de prisión a *La Mataviejitas*." *La Jornada*, April 1, 2008.

Servín, Mirna, and Agustín Salgado. "De 1998 a la fecha, 49 asesinatos de ancianos." *La Jornada*, January 26, 2006.

Shuessler, K. Michael, and Miguel Capistrán, eds. *México se escribe con J*. Mexico City: Editorial Planeta Mexico, S.A. de C.V., 2010.

Sierra, Arturo. "Analizan a seriales de Europa." *Reforma*, October 24, 2005.

———. "Usan estilo francés con asesinos seriales." *Reforma*, January 10, 2006.

———. "Ligan a luchadores con 'Mataviejitas.'" *Reforma*, January 31, 2006.

---. "Intenta PGJDF encuandrar perfil de asesina serial." *Reforma*, February 16, 2006.

---. "Es 'poeta caníbal' tercer serial en D.F." *Reforma*, October 15, 2007.

Sierra, Arturo, and Antonio Baranda. "Toman huellas de 46." *Reforma*, October 5, 2005.

Sierra, Arturo, and Leticia Fernández. "Tienen 64 rostros del 'Mataviejitas.'" *Reforma*, November 29, 2005.

Sierra, Arturo, Luis Ocampo, Luis Brito, Leticia Fernández, and Jorge Pérez. "Asesina Juana por coraje." *Reforma*, January 26, 2006.

Sierra, Arturo, Ricardo Zamora, and Antonio Baranda. "Abusan en infancia de asesino en serie." *Reforma*, August 31, 2005.

Sifuentes Jauregui, Ben. "Gender without Limits: Transvestism and Subjectivity in *El Lugar Sin Limites*." In *Sex and Sexuality in Latin America*, edited by Daniel Balderston and Donna J. Guy, 44–61. New York: New York University Press, 1997.

Simmons, William Paul. "Remedies for Women of Ciudad Juárez through the Inter-American Court of Human Rights." *Northwestern Journal of International Human Rights* 4, no. 3 (2006): 492–517.

Simpson, Phillip L. "Serial Killing and Representation." In *Oxford Research Encyclopedia of Criminology*, edited by Henry N. Pontell. Oxford: Oxford University Press, 2017. doi: 10.1093/acrefore/9780190264079.013.117.

Skrapec, Candice. "The Female Serial Killer." In *Moving Targets: Women, Murder and Representation*, edited by Helen Birch, 241–68. Berkeley: University of California Press, 1994.

Spade, Dean. *Normal Life: Administrative Violence, Critical Trans Politics and the Limits of Law*. Revised and expanded edition. Durham, NC: Duke University Press, 2015.

Speckman Guerra, Elisa. *¿Quién es criminal? Un recorrido por el delito, la ley, la justicia y el castigo en México (Desde El Virreinato Hasta El Siglo XX)*. Mexico City: Ediciones Castillo, 2006.

---. "La bella criminal que mató por amor. Justicia, honor femenino y adulterio (Ciudad de México, década de 1930)." *Historia. Questões & Debates. Curitiba. Universidad Federal de Paraná. Brasil* 64, no. 1 (2016): 19–48.

Speckman Guerra, Elisa, and Salvador Cárdenas, eds. *Crimen y justicia en la historia de México: nuevas miradas*. Mexico, D.F.: Suprema Corte de Justicia de la Nación, 2011.

Speckman Guerra, Elisa, and Fabiola Bailón Vásquez. *Vicio, prostitución y delito: mujeres transgresoras en los siglos XIX y XX*. Mexico, D.F.: Universidad Nacional Autónoma de México, 2016.

Straw, William. "Nota Roja and Journaux Jaunes: Popular Crime Periodicals in Quebec and Mexico." In *Aprehendiendo al delincuente: crimen y medios en América del Norte*, edited by Graciela Martínez-Zalce, William Straw, and Susana Vargas Cervantes, 53–67. Mexico City: Universidad Nacional Autónoma de México, Centro Estudios sobre América del Norte, and Media@McGill, 2011.

Tabuenca, María del Socorro. "Baile de fantasmas en la Ciudad Juárez al final/principio del mileno." In *Más alla de la ciudad letrada: crónicas y espacios urbanos*, edited by Boris Muñoz and Silvia Spitta, 411–37. Pittsburgh: Biblioteca de América, 2003.

"Tiene Bátiz 10 días para atrapar al 'Mataviejitas': diputadas del Pan." *Agencia de Noticias Notimex*. November 30, 2005.

Tuckman, Jo. "Computer Files Link TV Dirty Tricks to Favourite for Mexico Presidency." *Guardian*, June 7, 2012. www.theguardian.com.

———. "Pressure on Mexican Presidential Candidate in Televisa Media Row." *Guardian*, June 8, 2012. www.theguardian.com.

Tuñon, Julia. *Las mujeres en México. Una historia olvidada*. Mexico City: Grupo Editorial Planeta, 1987.

UN Commission on Human Rights, Civil and Political Rights, Including the Question of Disappearances and Summary Executions / Report of the Special Rapporteur on Extrajudicial, Summary or Arbitrary Executions, submitted pursuant to Commission on Human Rights resolution 1999/35, Addendum, Visit to Mexico, 2000.

Van den Berghe, Pierre L. *Race and Racism: A Comparative Perspective*. New York: Wiley, 1967.

Vargas, Angel. "Sara Aldrete escribe 'para convertir las remembranzas en historia.'" *La Jornada*, October 11, 2003.

Vasconcelos, José. *La raza cósmica: misión de la raza iboeroamericana*. Madrid: Agencia Mundial de la librería, 1925.

Vázquez, Juan de Dios. "La fábrica del asesino: El Goyo Cárdenas y las transformaciones identitarias de un asesino serial." *Estudios de historia moderna y contemporánea de México*, no. 42 (July–December 2011): 109–40.

Villafranco, Gerardo. "Ecatepec y naucalpan, los peores lugares para vivir en México." *Forbes México*, February 16, 2017. www.forbes.com.mx.

Villanueva Sagrado, María, Jesús Luy, and Karl F. Link. *Se Buscan: sistema de retrato hablado asistido por computadora*. 2nd ed. Mexico City: Instituto de Investigaciones Antropológicas and Procuraduría General de Justicia del D.F., 2002.

Villarreal, Andrés. "Stratification by Skin Colour in Contemporary Mexico." *American Sociological Review* 75, no. 5 (2010): 652–78.

Vivas, María Luisa. "Es Tenancingo, Tlaxcala la capital de la trata de personas." *Proceso*, May 6, 2013.

Wade, Peter. *Blackness and Race Mixture: The Dynamics of Racial Identity in Colombia*. Baltimore: Johns Hopkins University Press, 1993.

———. "Rethinking 'Mestizaje': Ideology and Lived Experience." *Journal of Latin American Studies* 37, no. 2 (2005): 239–57.

Walkowitz, Judith R. *City of Dreadful Delight: Narratives of Sexual Danger in Late-Victorian London*. Chicago: University of Chicago Press, 1992.

Washington Valdez, Diana. *The Killing Fields: Harvest of Women—The Truth about Mexico's Bloody Border Legacy*. Burbank, CA: Peace at the Border, 2006.

Whaley, Jaime. "En aumento, la adoración a la Santísima Muerte." *La Jornada*, November 2, 2003.

Yañez, Israel. "Encuentran ahorcado a el caníbal en su celda." *Crónica*, December 11, 2007.

Yañez, Israel, and Hilda Escalona. "El caníbal de la guerrero quería ser madre." *Crónica*, October 13, 2007.

Zires, Margarita. "Los mitos de la Virgen de Guadalupe: su proceso de construcción y reinterpretación en el México pasado y contemporaneo." *Mexican Studies/Estudios Mexicanos* 10, no. 2 (1994): 281–313.

Zuñiga, Alejandra. "Ecatepec es el lugar con peor calidad de vida en México." *Vice News*, October 6, 2016. www.vice.com.

INDEX

absent presence, in serial killing, 58
Adios Lecumberri (Cárdenas), 51
aggression, 96–98
Aguayo, Perro, 123
Alarma!, 53
Alderete, Sara. *See* narcosatánicos
Alert of Gender Violence against Women (Alerta de Violencia de Género contra las Mujeres) (AVGM), 162
Alfaro, Ana María Reyes, 1, 14, 91–92, 116–17
Almazán, Alejandro, 179
Álvarez Ledesma, Mario, 153
Amandititita, 117, 138–40, 142, 144
Amnesty International, 152, 155, 161
Amores perros, 44
Anaya, Ricardo, 89
The Anvil (El Yunque), 89
Arias Córdoba, Miguel, 50
Aridjis, Homero, 173
Arizmendi, David (El Mochaorejas) (The Ear Chopper), 178
Ascencio, Renato, 158
El Asesino del Bordo de Xochiaca (The Killer of Xochiaca). *See* Galván, Francisco
Ávalos, Graciela Arias, 50–51
AVGM. *See* Alert of Gender Violence against Women
Ávila, Eruviel, 160
Aztec Empire, 30

Bailón, Fabiola, 53
Balsamo, Anne, 134
Barraza Samperio, Juana, 1, 23, 54–55, *112*; altar at house of, 145, *146*, 174; appearance of, 5; arrest of, 14, 39, 63, 92–93, 111; Barrón photographing, 66; bust of, 65–66, 93, *94*, 95; childhood and upbringing of, 105–6, 185–86; children of, 6–7, 196; comparison of predicted and real busts of, *103*; constructions of criminality linked to, 185; criminalization of, 198; as La Dama del Silencio, *3*; declared serial killer, 95; as depicted in media, 134; diagnosis for, 118; disguises of, 136; emphasis on motherhood, 200; facial expressions of, 104–8; house of, 182–83; identification of, 14; inability to feel emotions, 109–10, 120; letter from, *197*, *199*; living in poverty, 188; lucha libre and, 113–15, 119; media representations of, 97–98; nicknames for, 131; Ostrosky interviewing and testing, *101*; photographs of eyes of, *107*; profile of, 83–86; psychological tests on, 99; rape of, 185–86; resemblance to sketches, 92; as scrutinized, 148; search for, 58–61; sentence of, 10, 96–97; sketches of, 66, *67*; strength of, 135; superimposition of photographs of, *102*
Barrio, Francisco, 160
Barrón, Martin, 5, 15, 54, 104–6, 183–84; Barraza photographed by, 66; on basis of criminality, 121; biological attributes used by, 100–101; *The knot of silence* (book), 66, 117–18, 182; objectivity of, 120; psychopathy and, 119; on serial killers, 59. See also *El nudo del silencio*
Bartra, Roger, 16, 30–31, 116
Báthory, Elizabeth, 142

259

Bátiz, Bernardo, 11, 27, 59, 79–80, 207n20; on CaraMex software, 68; fingerprint inconsistency from, 198; profile presented by, 87; women described by, 32–33
Berkowitz, David, 25
Bertillon, Alphonse, 76, 78
betrayal, 16, 186, 188
Birch, Helen, 96
blackmail, 44
Bliss, Katherine, 39
born criminal theory, 72
Borrego, Genaro, 158
Botsch, Robert J., 181
bravery, 60
brutality, 9; by police, 150, 162–63; of serial killing, 48, 59
Bueno, Isabel, 104
Buffington, Robert, 72
Bundy, Ted, 25, 58–59
Buscaglia, Edgardo, 161, 234n86
Butler, Judith, 116

Cabrera, Miguel, 69
calavera (skull), 145, 176
Calderón, Felipe, 11, 207n17
Calva Zepeda, José Luis (El Poeta Canibal) (The Cannibal Poet), 55–56, 132
Cameron, Deborah, 152
Campbell, Anne, 98
cannibalism, 55, 91
The Cannibal Poet (El Poeta Canibal). *See* Calva Zepeda, José Luis
Caputi, Jane, 152
CaraMex software, 65, 77, 79, 191–92; development of, 68–70; final archive of, 78; mestizaje and, 75; objective of, 76
Cárdenas, Gregorio ("Goyo") (El Estrangulador de Tacuba), 8, 15, 46, 133; hospitalization of, 51; in popular culture, 51–52; serial killing by, 50
Carillo, Héctor, 126
Carrier, Joseph, 124

Catholicism, 17, 89, 90, 125, 164; practices of, 173; virginity in, 209n38
La Catrina, 148, 174–78
Cazals, Felipe, 53
Celda 16 (Cárdenas), 51
censorship, 45
El Chalequero. *See* Guerrero, Francisco
chastity, purity, virtue and, 31
Chávez, Esther, 150–51, 231n23
La Chingada. *See* La Malinche
Ciudades oscuras, 43
Ciudad Juárez, feminicides in, 8–9, 37–38, 150–65, 191
Clarke, James, 109
class, 15, 19, 27, 61; differentiation of, 29; gender, nationality and, 6; gender transgression defined by, 89; race and, 20, 35, 72–73, 149
classism, 192; criminality and, 104–5; in sketches, 83
Clemente Orozco, José, 73–74
Collier, Richard, 58
colonial caste system (*sistema colonial de castas*), 69–70, 171
colonialism, 73
colonization, 19, 69–70, 90, 129–30, 170, 187
Columbine High School, massacre at, 36
Comisión de Derechos Humanos del Distrito Federal (Human Rights Commission of Mexico City), 88
commercialization, 140, 175
"Como México no hay dos," 17
Constanzo, Adolfo de Jesús (El Padrino). *See* narcosatánicos
coordinator of nongovernmental organizations in favor of women (Coordinadora de Organismos no Gubernamentales en Pro de la Mujer), 151
El Coqueto (The Flirt). *See* Librado Legorreta, César Armando
Corona, Juan, 54
Corral Jurado, Javier, 160

corruption, 44; of government, 43; involving drug trade, 47
Cortés, Hernán, 16, 30, 186–89
crime, 8; distinguishing types of, 47; due to economic circumstances, 44; globalization of violence and, 39; Heredia distinguishing, 59; increase in, 11; marginalization, poverty and, 43–44; reasons for committing, 47; red note reporting, 46–47; as senseless, 38; sexual, 50
Los criminales en México (Criminals in Mexico) (Roumagnac), 73
criminality, 4; anxiety surrounding, 71; Barraza Samperio linked to constructions of, 185; Barrón on basis of, 121; classism and, 104–5; contemporary discourses around, 58; femininity, Mexicanness and, 133; gendered construction of, 90; history of, in Mexico, 53; The Holy Death and, 145–50, 178–79; increase in, 47; interpretation of, 104–5; masculinization of, 64; measuring, 73; Ostrosky on basis of, 121; personal beliefs and, 147; photography and, 108; predisposition to, 120; presumptions about, 77; resources used as evidence of, 110; as result of environmental circumstance, 79, 103
criminal justice systems, 19
criminology, 10; feminist approaches to, 96; in Mexico, 71; objective language of, 19; popular culture and, 18; shift in, 103
cultural anxiety, 16
cultural beliefs, 18–19; about elderly women, 28; of Mexicanness, 62; surrounding serial killing, 26–27; surrounding victimization, 192
cultural bias, 110
cultural movements, 16
cumbia music, 15

La Dama del Silencio. *See* Barraza Samperio, Juana
Darwin, Charles, 97
decomposition: serial killers representing societal, 48; society in, 37
dehumanization, 28
De la calle, 43
Derba, Mimi, 31
desire: to kill, 91; negotiating, 18
Dexter Morgan, 25
Día de Muertos (Day of the Dead), 148, 175–78, 236n124
Díaz, Porfirio, 29, 180
Díaz Ramírez, Pablo, 46
Dicen que soy mujeriego, 32
diezmo payment (a tenth), 173
domesticity, 29
double life narrative, 158
drug dealers, 39, 41
drug trade: corruption involving, 47; Malverde and, 181–82
Duggan, Lisa, 18–19, 20, 217n1
Dussaix, Philippe, 85

The Ear Chopper (El Mochaorejas). *See* Arizmendi, David
Ed Gein, 42
education: family formation, protection and, 39; race and, 75
Edwards, Susan, 96–97
electroencephalograms (EEGs), 15, 99
electroshock therapy, 51
emotions, Barraza Samperio inability to feel, 109–10, 120
Estado de México, feminicides in, 150–65, 191
Estrada González, Pedro, 27
El Estrangulador de Tacuba (The Strangler of Tacuba). *See* Cárdenas, Gregorio
Estudios de antropología criminal (Studies of criminal anthropology) (Martínez Baca and Vergara), 71–73

ethnicity, 19
eugenics, 72
evangelization, 170–72
exotic wrestlers (exóticos), 122–29
exploitation, by media, 22
extortion, 141

family formation, 29, 39, 213n42
family values, 21, 26–27; culture of, 44; devotion to, 48; lack of, 158; Mexicanness promoting, 39, 46; strength of, 36
FEIHM. *See* Special Government Department for the Investigation of Homicides against Women
feminicides (feminicidio), 23, 147, 205n6, 214n56, 232n52; analyzing, 149; in Ciudad Juárez, 8–9, 37–38, 150–65, 191; in Estado de Mexico, 150–65, 191; lack of media attention for, 163; term of, entered into penal law, 157
femininity, 10, 194; art and, 127; ideologies surrounding masculinity and, 19; Mexicanness, criminality and, 133; normative, 18, 113, 129, 185; La Virgen de Guadalupe representing, 172
fetishism, 58, 183
films, serial killing in, 42–43, 47
Fiscalía Especial para la Investigación de Homicidios contra la Mujer (Special Government Department for the Investigation of Homicides against Women) (FEIHM), 150
The Flirt (El Coqueto). *See* Librado Legorreta
Flores Domínguez, Moisés, 141
Foucault, Michel, 18, 117, 121
Fox, Alan, 59
Fox Quesada, Vicente, 161, 206n12
fragmented family, 158
Fragoso, Julia Monárrez, 152, 154, 156, 158, 160, 214n54, 231nn22–23

Fragoso, Perla, 165, 168, 177–78
Frazer, Elizabeth, 152
French, William, 29
Frente Nacional por la Familia (National Front for the Family), 89

Gabriel, Juan, 126–27
Galton, Francis, 72–73
Galván, Francisco (El Asesino del Bordo de Xochiaca) (The Killer of Xochiaca), 154
Garavito, Alejandra Galeana, 55
García, Elizabeth Castro, 156
García, Sara, 31–35, 193
García Mena, Gilberto (El June), 179
García Uribe, Víctor Javier, 155
Gayón, Berlanga, 151–52
gender, 15, 19, 61; class, nationality and, 6; class defining transgression of, 89; criminality construction based on, 90; negotiating, 18; performativity, 116, 224n14; roles of sex and, for women, 135; women deviating from norms of, 96
gender identity, 86
gender/sex system, 20
gentrification, 4
Gifford, Barry, 40
Gilbert, Paula Ruth, 96
The Girlfriend Killer (El Matanovias). *See* Martínez Cortés, Jorge Humberto
globalization, of violence and crime, 39
Gómez, Mariana, 207n20
González, Delfina. *See* Las Poquianchis
González, Lola "Dinamita," 128
González, María de Jesús. *See* Las Poquianchis
González, María de Los Ángeles, 50
González, María Luisa. *See* Las Poquianchis
González, Sergio, 153, 178
González Meza, Gustavo, 155
González Rascón, Arturo, 159–60

grandmothers, 31; absence of, 36; role of, 34; stereotype of, 36
gran familia (great family) concept, 37
Greek, Cecil, 42, 91
Green, David, 108
Guerra, Margarita, 198
Guerrero, Francisco (El Chalequero), 8, 215n84; history of, 48–49; Jack the Ripper compared to, 49–50; serial killing by, 45
guilt, 5
Guzmán Huerta, Rodolfo, 130
Guzmán López, Oliver, 224n6

Ham, Ricardo, 52, 53–54, 215n84, 224n1
Hannibal, 42
Hannibal Lecter, 25
Hare, Robert D., 109, 119–20
Hare Psychopathy Checklist–Revised (PCL-R), 119–20
Hartmann, Borda, 27–28
Henry: Portrait of a Serial Killer, 41–42
Heredia, Renato Sales, 8–9, 36, 37, 205n2; crimes distinguished by, 59; fingerprints inconsistency from, 198; on serial killers, 58; on serial killing in film, 43
Hernández, Juan Carlos, 57
Hernández, Luis Miguel, 155
Herrera, Oscar, 2
Hidalgo y Costilla, Miguel, 170–71
Hinojosa, Luis José, 197
hogares blancos (white homes), 29, 39
The Holy Death (La Santa Muerte), 7–8, 99, *166*; criminality and, 145–50, 178–79; cult of, 147, 165–69, 173; Jesús Malverde and, 178–84; as La Llorona, 192; media stigmatizing, 183–84; rituals related to, 148, 165–68; three main features of, 168; La Virgen de Guadalupe and, 164–74
homoeroticism, 125
homonationalism, 88

homophobia, 10, 55, 57; as dominant, 90; ignorance, discrimination and, 86
homosexuality, 55, 85, 124, 193; acceptance of, 87–88; equated with sexual failure, 61, 91; hybridity and, 126
Huffschmid, Anne, 165–66
Human Rights Commission of Mexico City (Comisión de Derechos Humanos del Distrito Federal), 88
humiliation, 151
hybridity, 70, 126, 134

Ibargüengoitia, Jorge, 47
de la Iglesia, Álex, 40
independence, Mexico achieving, 16
indigenous (*indígena*), 20
indigenous communities (*republicas indias*), 19
individualism, 36
Infante, Pedro, 194, 212n39
information pamphlets, distribution of, 13
injury, spine, 7
Institutional Revolutionary Party (PRI), 162
Inter-American Commission of Human Rights, 152, 155

Jack, Dana Crowley, 97
Jack the Ripper, 8, 25, 46, 49–50, 58, 142
Jahangir, Asma, 159
Jenkins, Philip, 121
Jesus Christ, 31
Jiménez, Nora, 36
El June. *See* García Mena, Gilberto

Kahlo, Frida, 177
kidnapping, 41, 55, 178
The Killer of Gays (El Matagays). *See* Marroquín Reyes, Raúl Osiel
The Killer of Xochiaca (El Asesino del Bordo de Xochiaca). *See* Galván, Francisco

Kilroy, Mark, 40, 41, 54
Knight, Alan, 69

labor, 89–90
The Labyrinth of Solitude (Paz), 29–30
Lagarde, Marcela, 149–50
Last Rampage (Clarke), 109
Leatherface, 25
Letra S gay rights group, 88
Levi, Heather, 123–24
Levin, Jack, 59
Librado Legorreta, César Armando (El Coqueto) (The Flirt), 56, 216n123
Link, Karl F., 76
Livia, Olga, 55
La Llorona (The Weeping Woman), 16, 23, 189–92
Lolo, 43
Lombroso, Cesare, 72–73
Lomnitz, Claudio, 175–76
Lomnitz, Larissa, 37
loneliness, 38–39
López Molinar, Jorge, 157
López Obrador, Andrés Manuel, 11–12, 206n12
Loza, Eduardo, 150, 154, 161, 230n9
lucha libre, 2, 93, 111–31, 136–37, 225n46, 226n51
Lugo, Benitez, 35–36
Lugo, José, 105, 185–86, 237n1
Luy, Jesús, 76

Macedo de la Concha, Rafael, 161
machismo, 16–17, 23, 98, 123–25; constitution of, 127–28; Monsiváis on, 140; as reinscribed and resisted, 128
macho figure, 15, 23, 115, 195, 208n34
macho probado (proven macho), 17, 195, 208n35
Madrazo Cuellar, Jorge, 161
Madrid Manuel, Juan Enrique, 55, 132
La Malinche, 16, 29–30, 186–87, 237n2
Malverde, Jesús, 99, 145–47, 178–84

Mancera, Miguel Ángel, 87
"March of Silence," 206n12
marginalization, 8; crime, poverty and, 43–44; as tradition, 64; of women, 37, 60; Wournos history of, 105
marriage, 61; acceptance of gay, 87–89; virginity until, 18
Marroquín Reyes, Raúl Osiel (El Matagays), 14, 54–55, 131–32
Martin, Desirée, 178
Martínez, Benjamín A., 79
Martínez, Patricia, 57
Martínez, Patricio, 158–59
Martínez Baca, Francisco, 71–73, 104
Martínez Cortés, Jorge Humberto (El Matanovias) (The Girlfriend Killer), 56
máscara contra cabellera (mask against hair), 129
máscaras (masks), 137
masculinity, 17, 194–95; demonstrating, 124; ideologies surrounding femininity and, 19; Mexicanness and, 125; of violence, 97; women embodying, 129
El Matagays (The Killer of Gays). See Marroquín Reyes, Raúl Osiel
El Matanovias (The Girlfriend Killer). See Martínez Cortés, Jorge Humberto
"La Mataviejitas," 15, 138–40
maternity, mythical figures of, 16
Maynez, Oscar, 155
Máyrez Grijalva, Óscar, 153
Mecánica nacional, 35
media, 17, 20; depictions of Barraza Samperio in, 134; exploitation by, 22; The Holy Death stigmatized in, 183–84; lack of attention to feminicides by, 163; narrativization by, 64; persuasion by, 95; reports by, 5, 82; representations of Barraza Samperio by, 97–98; sensationalizing by, 21
media events, 131
Me dicen La Narcosatánica (They call me the Narcosatanic) (Aldrete), 40

INDEX | 265

menstrual cycles, aggression associated with, 98
mental illness, 51
Mentes asesinas: la violencia en tu cerebro (Killer minds: violence on your brain) (Ostrosky), 117
Mesoamerican Mexico, 19
mestizaje (racial mixture), 19, 68–69, 170, 210n47; CaraMex software and, 75; mythohistory of, 74; La Virgen de Guadalupe signifying, 171
mexicanidad. *See* Mexicanness
Mexican imaginary, 16, 115
Mexicanness (mexicanidad), 10, 15–18; cultural beliefs of, 62; double life narrative and, 158; family values promoted by, 39, 46; femininity, criminality and, 133; films contributing to, 43; hegemonic constructions of, 187–88; Jesús Malverde and, 99; logic of, 48; masculinity and, 125; myths in construction of, 147, 164; norms of, 137; parameters of, 22, 115; performance of, 122, 130; performativity of, 225n46; in relation to womanhood, 164; shift in conception of, 193–94; symbols of, 148
México y sus asesinos seriales (Ham), 53–54
El Mochaorejas (The Ear Chopper). *See* Arizmendi, Davidé
Moctezuma, Matos, 176
modernization, 71
Molina, Francisco, 153
Moneda, Victor Hugo, 20, 63–65, 80
Monsiváis, Carlos, 16, 31, 46, 115–16, 140, 193
Monster, 105
de Montúfar, Alonso, 170
Moors (moriscos), 30, 212n25
Mora, Valeria, 190
moral reformation, 29
moral values: intertwined with religious discourse, 159; lack of, 36

the morbidly curious (morbosos), 8
Moreno Figueroa, Mónica, 74–75
moriscos (Moors), 30, 212n25
motherhood: archetypes of, 29–30; Barraza Samperio emphasis on, 200; constructions of, 31; as institution, 34; notion of, 28
Las Muertas de Juárez, 37–38
Las muertas del estado (The [female] deaths of the state), (Padgett and Loza), 150
Mulholland, Mary-Lee, 122, 226n48
Mujeres asesinas (Women killers), 15
Mundo de juguete, 35
Un mundo raro, 44
muralism, Mexican, 16
muralist movement, 73–74
musicians, 8
mythohistory, 74

nahua indegenous group, 30
Náhuatl language, 30
narcosatánicos, 8, 40, 205n3; sentence for, 96; victims of, 54; violence committed by, 41
narrativization, 64, 217n1
National Front for the Family (Frente Nacional por la Familia), 89
National Human Rights Commission, 37, 152, 162–63
national identity, 15; Mexicanness influence on, 191; negotiating, 18; questioning, 48; strengthening, 175
National Institute for the Elderly, 27
nationalism, 16–17, 177; Bartra on, 30–31; creation of Mexican, 171
National Public University of Mexico, 65, 74
nation-building period (1820–1825), 19
Norris, Joel, 182
North American Free Trade Agreement, 150
Northern Preventative Male Prison (Reclusorio Preventivo Varonil Norte), 125

nota roja. *See* red note
El nudo del silencio: tras la pista de una asesina en serie, La Mataviejitas (The knot of silence: Following the tracks of a female serial killer, Las Mataviejitas) (Barrón), 66, 117–18, 182
Nuñez, Lucía, 4–5, 232n52

objectivity, of sketches, 82
Osorio, Lesby Berlin, 192
Ostrosky, Feggy, 15, 99–105, 116; on basis of criminality, 121; *Killer minds: violence on your brain* by, 117; neuropsychological tests performed by, 118

Pabellón de locos (Cárdenas), 51
Padgett, Humberto, 150, 154, 161, 230n9, 234n86
Palacio de Lecuberri prison, 51
Palou, Matilde, 31
PAN. *See* Partido de Acción Nacional
Parra, Antonio, 158
Parrini, Rodrigo, 125–26
Partido de Acción Nacional (PAN), 11, 89, 160
Partido de la Revolución Democrática (PRD), 11
Payán, Patricia, 93, 98, 142
Paz, Octavio, 16, 17, 29–30, 115, 137, 175, 211n21
PCL-R. *See* Hare Psychopathy Checklist–Revised
Peña Nieto, Enrique, 161–63
Perdita Durango, 40
Pérez Lizaur, Marisol, 37
performativity: gender, 116, 224n14; of Mexicanness, 122, 130, 225n46; of serial killing, 136, 139
Perfume de violetas, nadie te oye, 43
photography: body as readable through, 83; criminality and, 108; of criminals, 72; as delimiting terrain of other, 90; digital, 77; as forensic aid, 66–68; as scientific truth, 79; typology developed through, 73
phrenology, 68
physiognomy, 68, 78, 101, 109
Picart, Caroline, 42, 91, 97
Piccato, Pablo, 49–50
pigmentocracy, 19–20, 149
pigmentocratic system, 20, 67, 75, 78
pleasure: killing for, 8–9, 41, 42, 48, 61, 91; sexual, 153
El Poeta Canibal (The Cannibal Poet). *See* Calva Zepeda, José Luis
Police Cultural Center exhibition (Mexico City), 53, 65, 93–94, 116, 142–44
Poniatowska, Elena, 207n17
popular culture: Cárdenas in, 51–52; criminology and, 18; serial killers in, 25, 41
Las Poquianchis, 53–54, 224n1
Posada, José Guadalupe, 17, 148, 174–76
poverty: Barraza Samperio living in, 188; crime, marginalization and, 43–44; of peasant families, 54
PRD. *See* Partido de la Revolución Democrática
PRI. *See* Institutional Revolutionary Party
Prieur, Annick, 127–28
prostitutes. *See* sex workers
prostitution, abolition of, 53–54
protection: for drug dealers, 41; family formation, education and, 39
protests, against gay marriage, 89
proven macho (macho probado), 17, 195, 208n35
psychopathy, 26, 99, 119
public aid, 11
public transportation, 11
pureza de sangre (purity of blood), 171
purity, chastity, virtue and, 31
purity of blood (pureza de sangre), 171

Quinney, Richard, 28, 38
Quiroz, Rosa Reyes, 50

race, 19, 61; class and, 20, 35, 72–73, 149; classification of, 69; education and, 75
racial mixture. *See* mestizaje
racial privilege, 75, 90
racism, 70, 73, 192; as persistent, 115–16; within sketches, 83
Raine, Adrian, 100
Ramírez, Santiago, 17
Ramos, Samuel, 17
rape, 30, 37, 56, 163; of Barraza Samperio, 185–86; of sex workers, 49
La raza cósmica (The cosmic race) (Vasconcelos), 74
Los Rebeldes, 155
Reclusorio Preventivo Varonil Norte (Northern Preventative Male Prison), 125
red note (nota roja), 17, 44; characterization of, 45; crimes reported by, 46–47
republicas indias (indigenous communities), 19
Reséndiz, Rafael, 54
resentment, 59
resistance, 18
Ressler, Robert K., 142–43, 231n32
Revolution, Mexico, 16
Revueltas, José, 47
Ripstein, Arturo, 47
Rivera, Angélica, 162
Rivera, Diego, 17, 73–74, 175; *Sueño de una tarde dominical en la Alameda*, 177
Robichaux, David, 34
Romano, Arturo, 76
Romero, Enriqueta, 167
Ronquillo, Victor, 15, 117, 140–41, 144
rosaries, 164
Rossy Moreno, 128
Rougmanac, Carlos, 49, 73, 103–5, 108
Rubin, Gayle, 20
Ruda de corazón: el blues de La Mataviejitas (Rude at heart: The blues of the old lady killer (Ronquillo), 15, 117, 140–41

rude wrestlers (luchadores rudos), 93, 111, 130
Ruiz Mares, Trinidad, 46

sacrifice: for family, 31; during satanic rituals, 40–41
The Sadist (El Sádico), 14
sadomasochism, 58
Sagrado, María Villanueva, 76–77
de Sahagún, Bernardino, 169–70
Salamerón Solano, Salvador, 51
Sánchez, Ana Luisa, 4–5, 7
Sanders, Nichole, 28
Santa Martha Acatitla, 4
La Santa Muerte. *See* The Holy Death
santería religion, 40, 165
satanic rituals, 9, 39, 40–41
Schaefer, Claudia, 87
Sedgwick, Eve, 193, 238n19
Sekula, Allan, 76, 78, 90
Seltzer, Mark, 38, 41–42, 58–59; on profiling, 60–61; on serial killer identity, 91, 143
serial killers, 4; Barraza Samperio declared, 95; Barrón on, 59; capture, sentencing and imprisonment of, 57; conceptualizing, 6, 21, 27; confessions by, 51; defining, 210n4, 224n1; exhibition about, 53; as female, 60, 87; Heredia on, 58; identification of, 42; look of, 106–9; in popular culture, 25, 41; presence of, 39–40; prototypes of, 64, 84; psychological phases of, 182–84; qualifications for, 54; searching for, 38; Seltzer on identity of, 91, 143; set of traits applied to, 58; shift in narrative of, 95–96; societal decomposition represented by, 48; stereotyping of, 83; trust used by, 36; vampires compared to, 91
serial killing, 6; absent presence in, 58; acknowledgment of, 26; brutality of, 48, 59; by Cárdenas, 50;

serial killing (*cont.*)
 by El Chalequero, 45; courses on, 12; cultural beliefs surrounding, 26–27; definitions of, 106; fact, fiction and, 25; in film, 42–43, 47; impulse for, 15; as isolated phenomenon, 57; as normalized, 160; performance of, 136, 139; for pleasure, 8–9, 41, 42, 48, 61, 91; as repetitive, 143; representations of, 41–42; as sexual, 152; sexual failure correlated with, 91; stereotypical narratives of, 52; as US phenomenon, 43
Serrano Sánchez, Carlos, 65, 68, 76–77, 79
sex reassignment surgery (SRS), 86
sexual aggressors, 4
sexual failure, correlated with serial killing, 91
sexuality, 15, 19, 27, 39, 87, 192
sex workers, 8, 38; detention of, 86; hazards faced by, 45; killing of, 25, 46, 55, 57; rape of, 49; as representing degeneracy, 39; stigmatization of, 52
Sharif Latif, Omar, 155
The Silence of the Lambs, 42, 91
Siqueiros, Alfaro, 73–74
sistema colonial de castas (colonial caste system), 69–70, 171
Sí Vale government program, 12, 35–36, 66
sketches, 22; Barraza Samperio resemblance to, 92; as based on assumptions, 80; based on witness accounts, 85; body as readable through, 83; composite, *81*, *82*; of El/La Mataviejitas, 66, *67*; objectivity of, 82; prototypes depicted in, 90–91; racism and classism within, 83; release of, 79–80; of suspect, *84*; as tool, 63–65
Skrapec, Candice, 60
skull (calavera), 145, 176
slavery, abolition of, 70
slaves, 69
soap operas (telenovelas), 17, 162
Sobre ella, 43

social change, 6
social isolation, 36
social maladaptation, 42
social readaptation, 4
social security program, 12
social values, 28
social vulnerability, 10, 86
solidarity, 37
solitude, 28, 36
Spade, Dean, 88
Special Government Department for the Investigation of Homicides against Women (Fiscalía Especial para la Investigación de Homicidios contra la Mujer) (FEIHM), 150
SRS. *See* sex reassignment surgery
stereotypes, 5, 15; of domestic violence, 47; of grandmothers, 36; of serial killing, 52; used for serial killers, 83
The Strangler of Tacuba (El Estrangulador de Tacuba). *See* Cárdenas
Sueño de una tarde dominical en la Alameda (Rivera mural), 177
syncretism, 164, 172

Tablas Silva, Jorge Mario, 14, 113
Tabuenca, María Socorro, 151, 159
technical wrestlers (luchadores técnicos), 118, 130
telenovelas (soap operas), 17, 162
a tenth payment (diezmo payment), 173
Tepeyac Hill (Mexico City), 169
theatricality, 116
Theron, Charlize, 105
Thierry, Paulin, 80, 84–86
Tison, Gary, 109
Tonantzin goddess, 169–70
torture, 9, 37, 205n3
Totonatzin, 31
tourism, 177–78
transphobia, 10, 90
transvestites (travestis), 10, 27, 86–90, 193–95

Los tres García, 32–33, 35
trust: used by serial killers, 36; from victims, 85
Tuñón, Julia, 31

United Nations, 159

Valdez, Diana Washington, 152–53
vampires, serial killers compared to, 91
Van den Berghe, Pierre L., 74–75
Vargas, Octavio, 190
Vasconcelos, José, 74, 171. See also *La raza cósmica*
Vázquez García, Araceli, 14, 111–13
Vergara, Manuel, 71–73, 104
victimization, 141, 192
victims, 9; classifying, 21–23, 28, 38, 57, 62, 147–48, 188–89; criminals and, 7; defining, 194; elderly women as, 38, 106; of feminicides, 205n6; identifying, 155–56; of narcosatánicos, 54; photographs of, 45; Quinney on, 38; searching for, 54; selecting of, 12; trust from, 85
Villalobos, Martha, 129
Villarreal, Andrés, 74
Villicaña, Abel, 154–55
violence, 8, 17; addiction to, 41, 143; committed by narcosatánicos, 41; gender, 37–38, 52, 57, 150; globalization of crime and, 39; increase in, 47, 206n12; intradomestic, 153; as masculine, 97; predisposition to, 100; protesting against, 208n33; stereotype of domestic, 47; waves of, 9–10; woman-on-woman, 54; women capacity for, 96
La Virgen de Guadalupe, 16, 23, 122–23; appearance of, 30–31; as archetype, 147; devotion to, 179–80; femininity represented by, 172; The Holy Death and, 164–74; mestizaje signified by, 171
virginity: in Catholicism, 209n38; until marriage, 18
virtue, purity, chastity and, 31
Vuelvan los García, 32

Walkowitz, Judith, 18–19
War of Independence, 170–71
The Weeping Woman (La Llorona), 16, 23, 189–92
white homes (*hogares blancos*), 29, 39
whiteness, 58, 75, 78, 90, 134
womanhood: determining ideas of, 158; Mexicanness in relation to, 164
women, 9; capacity for violence, 96; deviating from gender norm, 96; gender and sex roles for, 135; governmental sympathy for, 212n29; ideal, 174; marginalization of, 37, 60; masculinity embodied by, 129; sexuality and sexualization of, 39, 158, 188–89, 191–92; vulnerability of, 155
women, elderly, 139–40, 191; cultural beliefs around, 28; killing of, 37, 79–80; loneliness of, 38–39; as victims, 38, 106; vulnerability of, 158–59
Women killers (*Mujeres asesinas*), 15
World Women's Wrestling Championship, 2, 134
wound culture, 41, 43, 44, 47–48
Wournos, Aileen, 105–6

El Yunque (The Anvil), 89

Zapata, Luis, 87
Los Zetas, 8, 42, 205n3
Zodiac Killer, 25
de Zumárraga, Juan, 169

ABOUT THE AUTHOR

Susana Vargas Cervantes is a writer, researcher, and teacher. Her research mines the connections between gender, sexuality, class, and skin color to reconceptualize pigmentocracy. She is the author of the book *Mujercitos*. She coordinates Mesas de Diálogo: Subjectification South-North, a project that creates a space of dialogue between North American Anglo theorists and their Latin American counterparts; participants have included Judith Butler, Leticia Sabsay, Ma. Amelia Viteri, Ameilia Jones, Eli Vásquez, and Dean Spade. She is currently pursuing a Fulbright Fellowship at Columbia University.